MORE PRAISE FOR *THE TOGETHER TEACHER*

"We know from Teach For America's research that organizational ability is a vital differentiating factor among the most successful urban and rural teachers. No one has contributed more to the organization skills of our teaching and alumni force than Maia Heyck-Merlin—her workshop ratings are off the charts!—and I am thrilled for the sake of the broader movement for educational excellence and equity that she has written this book to share her breakthrough insights and tools with all who are aspiring to increase their classroom impact."—Wendy Kopp, chief executive officer and founder, Teach For America

"Great teachers have to master the art of juggling and prioritizing—first there's working with kids and parents. Then there is student data to be analyzed, papers to grade, instructional materials to be prepared, papers to return, staff meetings to attend, and reading all those professional development materials buried in the closet! Oh yeah, let's not forget trying to make time for a personal life. *The Together Teacher* has practical answers to all of the above so that we're maximizing our instructional time and personal time, too. I use Maia's techniques on a daily basis and I think every teacher will find tons of wisdom within."—Dave Levin, co-founder of KIPP (Knowledge Is Power Program)

"If you're trying to be a rock-star teacher, you're probably overwhelmed. So. Much. To. Do. *The Together Teacher* is the only book that deals with your uber-busy workplace reality. Maia Heyck-Merlin's strategies aren't just good, they're *grrreat*. Our teachers adore Maia and her methods."—Mike Goldstein, founder, MATCH Teacher Residency

"In a job that's constantly pulling you in all directions, this book provides a blueprint for keeping it together…teacher. Maia's time-saving techniques have allowed me to focus on what's really important—teaching. You might not be able to work any harder as a teacher, but I guarantee these strategies will help you work smarter."—Josh Lee, high school teacher, New York City Public Schools, South Bronx, New York

"Maia Heyck-Merlin knows that teaching can be an overwhelming experience, and over the years she has collected a toolkit full of personal organization practices that put teachers in control of the daily details in their lives. This book will help teachers become more organized, more effective, and less stressed by the multiple demands of the job."—Jay Altman, co-founder and chief executive officer, FirstLine Schools, New Orleans, Louisiana

THE TOGETHER TEACHER

Plan Ahead, Get Organized,
and Save Time!

Maia Heyck-Merlin

Foreword by Norman Atkins

JOSSEY-BASS
A Wiley Imprint
www.josseybass.com

Author photo by Carla Licavoli
Cover images by
Russell Tate/@iStockphoto RF,
Bill Noll/@iStockphoto RF,
Bam Bam Images/@iStockphoto RF,
Gaffera/@iStockphoto RF

Published by Jossey-Bass
A Wiley Imprint
One Montgomery Street, Suite 1200, San Francisco, CA 94104-4594—www.josseybass.com

Jossey-Bass books and products are available through most bookstores. To contact Jossey-Bass directly call our Customer Care Department within the U.S. at 800-956-7739, outside the U.S. at 317-572-3986, or fax 317-572-4002.

Wiley publishes in a variety of print and electronic formats and by print-on-demand. Some material included with standard print versions of this book may not be included in e-books or in print-on-demand. If this book refers to media such as a CD or DVD that is not included in the version you purchased, you may download this material at http://booksupport.wiley .com. For more information about Wiley products, visit www.wiley.com.

Library of Congress Cataloging-in-Publication Data
Heyck-Merlin, Maia, 1977–
    The together teacher : plan ahead, get organized, and save time! / Maia Heyck-Merlin ; foreword by Norman Atkins. – First edition.
        1 online resource.
      Includes index.
      Description based on print version record and CIP data provided by publisher; resource not viewed.
      ISBN 978-1-118-22539-4 (adobe pdf) – ISBN 978-1-118-23888-2 (epub) – ISBN 978-1-118-26348-8 (mobipocket) – ISBN 978-1-118-13821-2 (pbk.) (print)
    1. Teachers–Time management.   2. Lesson planning.   I. Title.
    LB2838.8
    371.102–dc23

                                        2012005715

Printed in the United States of America

FIRST EDITION

PB Printing   10 9

CONTENTS

PART ONE: GET CLEAR ON WHAT MATTERS 1

Introduction   3

Planning, Organization, and Efficiency Matter Even *More* for Teachers • What Do I Mean by *Together*? • Why This Matters to Me • How the Book Is Arranged • How to Use This Book

Chapter 1: Rules Over Tools: Create Your Ideal Week   13

It *Can* Get Easier—A Step-by-Step Approach • I'm Not a Dictator, but There Are *Some* Rules • The Tools • Components of a Great Organization System • Let's Get Started

PART TWO: TAKE THE LONG VIEW 29

Chapter 2: No More Missed Deadlines: Make a Comprehensive Calendar   31

The Multiple-Calendar Dilemma • The Comprehensive Calendar: What Is It? • Together Teachers' Comprehensive Calendars • Pick Your Tool: Where Will You Keep Your Comprehensive Calendar? • The Up-Front Investment: Create Your Comprehensive Calendar • Keep Your Comprehensive Calendar Alive • Why Is This Important, Again? • Get Started: Next Steps

 Nilda: A Day in the Life   57

CONTENTS OF THE CD

PROFESSIONAL DEVELOPMENT IDEAS FOR SCHOOL LEADERS AND PROFESSORS

THE TOGETHER TEACHER'S READER'S GUIDE

SAMPLES

Chapter 7: Automate

Alice's Weekly Preparation Plan

Chapter 9: Tame the E-Mail Beast

Anna's Outlook In-Box with Simple Folders

Chapter 10: Create Stations

Classroom Set-Up Examples

Chapter 11: Subdue the Backpack Explosion

Kevin's Expectations for How Students in K–4 Organize Their Desks

Expectations for Elementary Homework Folders from AF Brownsville

Seat Sacks at AF Brownsville

Elementary School Bulletin Board Highlighting High-Quality Student Work

Middle School Display of Exemplary Student Work

Student Files for Martin's High School Math Classroom

Chapter 12: Deal with *Your* Paper and Stuff

Kate's Project Materials and Wire File Rack 1

Kate's Project Materials and Wire File Rack 2

A Teacher's Suitcase to Transport Papers Between Work and Home

First Level: Joe's Unit Plans

Second Level: Joe's Sub-unit Plans

Third Level: Joe's Lesson Plans

Appendix 3

Kate's Project Plan

CD Only

Example of Classroom Expectations

TEMPLATES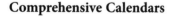

Comprehensive Calendars

Comprehensive Calendar 2012-13

Comprehensive Calendar 2011-12

Daily Worksheet

Daily Worksheet

Meeting PD Notes

Group Meeting Notes

Professional Development Session Notes

Meeting Notes

Planning Routines

Planning Routines

Project Plans

Project Plan – MS Word

Project Plan – MS Excel

Thought Catchers

Thought Catchers

Time Trackers

Time Tracker – Daily Time

Time Tracker – Ideal Week

Together Teacher Binder Label

Together Teacher Binder Label

Upcoming To Do Lists

Upcoming To Do List – MS Word Version 1

Upcoming To Do List – MS Word Version 2

Upcoming To Do List – MS Excel

Weekly Worksheets

Weekly Worksheet – Version 1

Weekly Worksheet – Version 2

Weekly Worksheet – Version 3

Weekly Worksheet – Version 4

To my husband, Jack, for your eternal kindness. You have taught me most of all.

FOREWORD

One sweaty August morning, underneath an ExxonMobil plant in East Baton Rouge, Louisiana, a passel of 9-year-olds, all eligible for free lunch, filled a trailer-cum-classroom in one of the poorest performing schools in the parish. It was the first day, and their rookie teacher greeted them at the threshold, offering three choices: handshake, high-five, or hug. "Hello, my name is Ms. H-M," said Maia Heyck-Merlin, a freshly-minted 22-year-old Tufts University developmental psych major—a hip, vivacious transplant from rural Maine who'd come to East Baton Rouge in response to Teach For America's trumpet blast for educational equity.

If the students regarded Maia with a modicum of skepticism, that's largely because they'd seen passionate, well-intentioned, idealistic teachers come and go, unhinged in the face of such complex work. Low-income students are disproportionately the victims of teacher failure, losing thousands of hours of learning time each year, falling further behind their more affluent peers.

Maia already understood that the risks of premature burn-out were high and the consequences of failure ran deep. From the very start, she embraced the complexity of teaching, breaking the task down into its component parts. An inveterate organizer, she crafted minute-by-minute plans for each day, orchestrated routines to keep students on-task, and carefully assigned desks. She distributed elaborate writing assignments with step-by-step instructions. She constantly circulated among her students, clipboard in hand. She asked for "exit tickets" at the end of class to track student progress. She handed out "differentiated homework" so that students' nightly assignments were customized to reflect precisely where they needed to review or to stretch toward more challenging material. Maia's relentless consistency made her students feel safe, productive, and self-sufficient. That, in turn, resulted in a joyful classroom culture and a happy, flourishing teacher.

Maia thrived her first season and was voted "Teacher of the Year" at the end of her second, not because of her abundant charisma, warmth, and energy. Rather, she became the consummate *together* teacher by determined planning and by her commitment to mastering all the organizational details of running an A+ classroom.

Three years later, recognizing her great success, Teach For America (TFA) implored her to *lead* 120 incoming novice teachers in Louisiana. She agonized over the decision, ultimately concluding that her impact could be larger in that capacity. And so she left the classroom. She went on to run new teacher summer training institutes, and then to operational work for TFA. For the past five years, she's played key roles at Achievement First, one of the nation's strongest charter school operators in Connecticut and New York.

Through her work at these leading education reform organizations, Maia honed planning systems, time management routines, and classroom organization details, training hundreds of leaders and teachers in her techniques. Maia's training itself, modeling the very skills that made her a champion teacher, has cultivated a folk following, as thousands around the country have learned what she's called "brass tacks" lessons in organizing their classrooms and lives. A longtime fan, after I witnessed her training at our new Relay Graduate School of Education in New York, I—along with so many other friends and fans—encouraged her to be systematic about capturing this training in book form.

The Together Teacher arrives now, full of low-hanging fruit for those who understand that a disciplined approach to planning is necessary for all great teachers. This book is not only for novice teachers or for teachers serving disadvantaged students. In fact, this can be game-changing for *all* teachers who have a deep sense of urgency and excitement about—and responsibility for—making every moment count for all their students.

If you take this book seriously, soon you will be asking the question Maia puts to herself each Sunday: "I have 168 hours per week: how can I best spend them?" Far from sapping energy and getting lost in arcane time management worksheets, Maia's process engenders an "abundance" mindset. "I know when my work is going to get done," says Maia, "because I've made a plan for it so that I can enjoy life more." To see Maia in action is to recognize a transformational, *together* teacher and person, one who gets it all done with joy and exuberance. May this book help you become together, too.

NORMAN ATKINS IS CO-FOUNDER AND PRESIDENT
OF RELAY GRADUATE SCHOOL OF EDUCATION AND FOUNDER, BOARD CHAIR,
AND FORMER CHIEF EXECUTIVE OFFICER OF UNCOMMON SCHOOLS.

THE
TOGETHER
TEACHER

PART 1

Get Clear on What Matters

Introduction

et's first picture the *not*-together teacher. This may be you on some days; I know it was certainly me. You race into the school parking lot, mug of coffee in hand (but lunch forgotten in the refrigerator at home), your backpack stuffed full of the papers you intended to grade last night but were simply too exhausted to do so. As you sign in at the front office, stammer "hello" to the office staff, and walk quickly to your classroom (wait—why are there *children* in the building already?!), you realize you don't have copies of the unit test you are giving that morning and the copier is jammed. It's only 7:15 AM and you already feel overwhelmed. If you can relate to this scene, then this book will help you plan ahead and work smarter so you are more prepared and less discombobulated.

The Together Teacher™ is the teacher who makes it *look* easy. You know, that person in your building who never scrambles to make copies at the last minute, has lessons planned a week or more in advance, gets her progress reports in early, makes time for positive parent phone calls, conducts remedial tutoring after school, *and* packs healthy homemade lunches. Don't stress—this teacher was not born that way. Countless routines, systems, and tools go into pulling off that level of togetherness, and they cannot be discovered overnight. Throughout this book you will meet teachers with varying years of classroom experience, in multiple subjects and grade levels, who work in unique school environments. Some of them began their teaching career highly organized, others learned organization skills on the job in order to deal with the demands of teaching. For some readers this book will affirm things you are already doing and give you ideas for how you might refine your systems and coach newer teachers. For others it will serve as a "how-to" guide on getting organized (enough) to be a great classroom teacher.

The Together Teachers I have met execute their work with an incredible degree of intentionality. They rely on simple yet sophisticated systems that hold up under the complexity and fast pace of teaching. These systems require tremendous discipline, a little bit of time, and a firm belief that planning and organization will actually free you up to focus on bigger, more fun, and interesting things. To be clear, this is *not* a book that is going to tell you how to color-code folders and make picture-perfect charts. (Nor will it help you organize your closets at home!) It will not tell you precisely which planner or electronic application to use. **This book is about cultivating habits that let you become organized *enough* to get results for your students and to make your life more fun and less stressful.**

PLANNING, ORGANIZATION, AND EFFICIENCY MATTER EVEN *MORE* FOR TEACHERS

As teachers, we face a unique set of challenges compared to the average professional. We have little to no discretionary time, stand on our feet most of the day, incur large amounts of take-home work, deal with mandated technology systems as well as old-fashioned paperwork, and manage constantly shifting schedules that allow for virtually no moments of concentration or focus. To-dos come at us from a million different directions—e-mail inboxes, phone messages, text messages, paper memos, and staff meetings. Although the bulk of our role as teachers is to design and deliver outstanding instruction on a daily basis, there is a lot of other work that needs to be done in the background to ensure that those lessons are the best they can be. Given all of these demands, it is easy to understand how we may scramble to plan lessons, miss progress report deadlines, and hand back student essays two months after students turn them in!

Add to this complex set of responsibilities the additional duties involved in providing strong instruction—deeply analyzing our student data, ensuring that our lesson plans have high-quality rigorous questions built in, and making time for one-on-one tutoring with struggling students, all of which takes extreme focus and planning—and pile on the emotional toll of breaking up a fight in the hallway, calming the upset parent of a perpetually tardy student, and comforting a kid who is trying to comprehend a death in the family—and you have a recipe for stressed and undoubtedly less effective teachers.

Many resources are available for setting ambitious goals and getting your students invested in school. There are a ton of tools that will help you with unit planning, lesson planning, and making the right assessments to determine content mastery. However, there are few accounts of how outstanding teachers actually spend their limited free time, plan ahead, and organize their work and classrooms to arrive at strong outcomes. As someone who has been a teacher, recruited teachers, hired teachers, trained and evaluated teachers, and worked like heck to retain great teachers (and is married to a teacher!), I believe that being organized is an invaluable skill to possess in *the* most demanding and important profession there is. Paul Bambrick-Santoyo describes the importance of time management in his most recent book about how leaders spent their time, "Exceptional school leaders succeed because of how they use their time: what they do, and how/when they do it." There is no doubt that teachers must rely on solid organization and planning skills to meet the needs of their students. This book aims to be that resource.

WHAT DO I MEAN BY *TOGETHER*?

Together can take on a whole host of meanings. To some teachers it means having neat filing systems that allow them to find the exact overhead transparency required for a social studies lesson. To others it means always meeting deadlines for lesson plans or using time efficiently to get more done in fewer minutes. To yet another group it means having the perfect plan for a field trip. Regardless of how they define it, Together Teachers all demonstrate five essential skills.

1. **Prioritization.** This means you are focusing on the *right* things and not speeding through your day mindlessly checking things off a list just to get them done. You have determined what matters most at school and at home and have aligned your schedule to fit those priorities. The bulk of your time goes to what is most important. A teacher who does not prioritize well may focus too heavily on the aesthetics of his or her classroom at the expense of effective lesson design.

2. **Planning.** Planning well means you consistently look ahead to what is coming next and determine the steps to get there, often pausing to write them down. A teacher who plans well looks ahead on his calendar, notices that progress reports are due in three weeks, and diligently writes three per evening. Conversely, a teacher who doesn't plan well is often up until 2 AM finishing progress reports because the deadline crept up on her.

3. **Organization.** Organized teachers have a clear process and clear systems for all important classroom functions. For example, they have systems for collecting and handing back student work, and likely have designated folders for this. Organized teachers are the people who can respond in ten minutes when you ask to borrow a visual anchor from a poetry lesson she conducted a few weeks ago. Disorganized teachers often have desks buried in papers—and maybe a car trunk full of still more papers they meant to return to students. Laugh, but trust me, it happens.

4. **Execution.** The ability to *do* your work with intentionality is a clear sign of a Together Teacher. Sometimes teachers make a lot of lists yet fail to accomplish their stated tasks. Teachers who execute well are aware of their energy levels, can accurately estimate how

long things will take to complete, and know what steps to take to check items off their lists. They enjoy getting things done!

5. **Efficiency.** Given the limited amount of discretionary time in a teacher's day, efficiency matters a ton. You can save a lot of time by making all of your copies for the week at once instead of running to the copier a few times per day. Efficient teachers take little bits of time and maximize them to the fullest. They leave positive voice-mail messages for parents while walking to the car, thereby freeing up their evenings for personal priorities.

As teachers, we need to develop habits in all of these areas in order to be "together." Here's why. If you are a person who loves organizing and making lists but never plan to refer to the lists, you will accomplish little. If you spend all of your time fiddling with perfect color-coded file folders that have every lesson categorized by day but do not efficiently use them, you will not move forward. Together Teachers take a balanced approach and hone each of the five skills in order to become their maximally together selves.

WHY THIS MATTERS TO ME

When I started teaching more than a decade ago, I consistently worked eighty or ninety hours per week. In a last-ditch attempt at self-preservation, I read a ton about how professionals with insane amounts of volume and lots of people to answer to managed their jobs. Although I found some strong resources to help me "get things done," "put in the big rocks first," and "not check e-mail in the morning," (David Allen, Steven Covey, and Julie Morgenstern, to name a few of my favorite resources), nothing *totally* fit into my daily teaching life—the one during which I was consistently on my feet, had my precious planning time eaten up by student issues, was rarely in front of a computer, struggled to understand the announcements made over the garbled intercom, and dealt with more pieces of paper than I knew what to do with. There are some amazing resources out there in the vast field of productivity and time management, and more tools are made available each and every day in the blogosphere. The challenge, however, is that none of them truly addresses teaching, a unique profession that varies so greatly depending on how our schools function, what technology we are issued, and what expectations are set for our roles.

And very honestly, none of the existing materials addressed jobs as *complex* as mine was. I was responsible for sixty students (three sections of writing), the parents of all of those students, and a fourth-grade teaching team. I received feedback from a literacy coach and work from graduate classes; handled papers to collect, papers to grade, papers to return, papers to be filed, and professional development resources to be used now and later; and I needed an inordinate amount of *stuff* in my classroom. I spent a lot of money at office supply stores trying to find the perfect planner for teachers but was annoyed when I couldn't customize the templates that accompanied them. I put together a huge binder with tabs for every aspect of teaching, but it got too heavy to lug around school all day. I bought a PalmPilot with a nifty stylus pen (remember those?!) when they first came out and started keeping an electronic calendar, but I couldn't find a way to enter stuff fast enough during the teaching day. I tried black-and-white composition books, graph paper, and Action Pads. Nothing could keep up with the pace and volume of my job teaching fourth grade.

In the meantime, I was slowly learning to teach, taking graduate classes, and picking up more responsibilities, such as tutoring my students on Saturdays. I quickly realized that fumbling for the right overhead transparency or flipping through stacks of papers to locate copies for that day's lesson resulted in lost instructional time for my students and was an open invitation for them to misbehave. If I wasn't sure when my progress reports were due or when an important assembly was scheduled, I would enter the day unprepared and then become incredibly stressed when someone would remind me. When I told a student, "That is a two-point deduction for talking out in class" or "Great work on your spelling test! I am going to make a positive phone call to your parents tonight," and promptly forgot, I lost credibility in the eyes of my fourth graders. And when I spent too much time hanging out in Mrs. Russell's classroom chatting during a prep period, it meant I had yet another hour of work to take home. The only way I could survive was to be incredibly organized and super efficient, and to plan as far ahead as possible in order to deal with the unexpected stuff (both the good and the bad) that inevitably comes up in school environments.

During my time teaching at Delmont and Children's Charter School, my fellow teachers and I experimented with purely paper-based organization systems and then attempted to upgrade to the recently released Palm Pilot. After experiencing the deluge of responsibility in my first year of teaching, I became determined to make my second year more manageable. At the time, I outlined my to-do lists using the same Day Runner planner (a popular commercial brand) that I had in college. Unfortunately, it contained too small a space to capture the millions of things I had to do today, tomorrow, or next year. Additionally, the planner itself became too heavy to lug around while teaching, had no room for my lesson plans, and zero space for the notes from my professional development workshops. The Palm Pilot was even less help as I couldn't enter data during class and parents found it off-putting. Life got a little easier when I began implementing great ideas from experts such as David Allen, Steven Covey, and Julie Morgenstern, but none of their approaches truly aligned with my teaching lifestyle—unpredictable, on your feet, and bursting at the seams with paper and supplies. Organization was a critical skill for success and survival, yet no one was explicitly teaching it to teachers.

After I stopped teaching, I was fortunate to spend a decade working in two other high-performing, disciplined environments—Teach For America and Achievement First. At TFA, many of us used a "Weekly Action Plan" to stay organized for the week, but we often found it was too short-term a view of our work and duplicative of our electronic systems. At Achievement First, many teachers tried to use the Outlook tools, but found it hard to organize their work in an exclusively electronic way while teaching. There had to be some way to take practices experts recommended, what I had observed my talented colleagues try, and what I had experimented with myself, and make it work for *teachers*!

I was fortunate that Achievement First, and then Relay Graduate School of Education, provided me with an informal research lab to take what I learned from other organizations, external experts, and my own experimentation to try and create approaches that would meet the demands and needs of teachers. Slowly, and with much trial and error, I eventually landed on the set of tools you find in the first half of this book. Over time I learned there was no single system that all teachers could rely on to become magically more organized. What's more, individual teachers (and all people) have different work habits, particular affinities for paper versus electronic systems, varied teaching loads, and different personal obligations and dreams. So, although there is no silver bullet, there is a practical set of tools, habits, and skills that can make teachers increasingly effective—and help them eradicate the perpetual feeling of being underwater and behind. And so was born the concept of The Together Teacher.

This book aims not only to teach you those critical organization skills but also to provide you with tools, samples, and templates to support them. Throughout this book I feature many teachers at different stages in their careers, from the first-year elementary teacher to an English teacher with fifteen-plus years of experience. Some of the teachers I met once or twice in workshops or came to know through single thought-provoking conversations. Others I have had long-standing relationships with and know every detail of their lives. No matter how long you've taught, this book will enable you to become better organized and to plan better by learning from these Together Teachers.

HOW THE BOOK IS ARRANGED

This book is designed to help you deliver better results for your students and to make your important work more sustainable. In each chapter I provide multiple tools that will enable you to enforce the rules discussed. I also share tips on how to adapt the tools to meet your particular work style and preferences. The book's order is designed to help you build your Together Teacher System as you read, starting with how you manage your time, to-dos, thoughts, and notes—and moving into how you juggle e-mail, organize your space, and deal with your papers. Most teachers actually assemble a small binder for their Together Teacher System as they read, printing materials from the CD after customization, and creating tabs in their binders that mirror each chapter. For example, after reading Chapter Two on the Comprehensive Calendar, you would select your calendar tool, print it out, and insert it as a section in your Together Teacher System. To show that there are many different ways to stay organized and manage time, we will also meet various Together Teachers and learn more about what a day in their lives looks like—from the moment the teachers wake up to when heads hit the pillow. (For the sake of privacy I have often used pseudonyms when referring to the colleagues, students, and parents of featured teachers.) It is important to point out that none of these Together Teachers is perfect in every aspect of organization. Each teacher has chosen to focus on those particular aspects of being "together" that help him or her to be a better teacher—and have a life!

The book is organized into the following five parts:

Part One: Get Clear on What Matters. Time is a finite resource and often our ideas, ambitions, and deadlines come into conflict with the limited amount of time we have. In the chapters in this initial section, I help you focus on creating your Ideal Week Template, tracking your time, and figuring out how best to use the hours we all have in any given week. I also outline the rules I believe we all must follow in order to be more organized. Without a clear point of view on what matters most to each of us, it doesn't matter a lick how efficient we are or how well we plan.

Part Two: Take the Long View. The chapters in this section focus on four practical tools. I discuss how to manage your time, track your to-dos, capture your thoughts and brainstorms, and deal with meeting/professional development notes. In each chapter I first illustrate the *not*-together way. (Warning: graphic descriptions ahead.) I then describe the tool or concept along with the rationale behind it. After that I share multiple ways in which Together Teachers have implemented personal systems using these tools, habits, and skills. Finally, I help you select which tool might work for you, discuss the up-front investment, and coach you on how to keep it alive.

Part Three: Narrow Your View. Next we discuss how to put together all of the tools previously discussed to create your very own to-do list for one week at a time. We walk through a day in the life of a teacher and review the many things that come our way. We make sure that every single thought, deadline, and to-do clearly has a place to go in your organization system. We close this section by discussing the routines you need to follow to keep your tools current, the ways you can slip back into your "untogether" habits, the reasons this happens, and what to do to maintain your Together Teacher status.

Part Four: All That Other Stuff! Now we turn to the external environment. E-mails, papers, classroom supplies, and student backpacks can bring either calm or chaos into our classrooms. In these chapters I share ways in which teachers have set expectations and handled some of the additional elements that are thrown at them on a daily basis. These chapters are organized around a set of reflection questions, examples, and photographs.

Part Five: Become a Together Teacher. In the book's final section we test how your organization system will hold up under the stresses of daily teaching life, and discuss ways to slowly implement the tools and habits introduced throughout the book. Additionally, there are resources that list some of my favorite organization tools, a glossary of terms, and notes on interesting books on the topic of organization.

Oh, yes: now is often when people wonder if I subscribe to a particular system, tool, or school of thought. Although I certainly have opinions about everything (just ask my husband!), in this case I care whether your system is effective for *you*, and I'm indifferent about the exact tools you use. If you are worried that I'm going to force you to part with your paper planner and make you switch to an entirely electronic system, or if you're concerned that I might snatch your trusty smartphone out of your hands, have no fear! I aim to meet your specific needs. I will work with you throughout the book to create and customize your own personal organization system.

The Paper Versus Electronic Debate

The great debate: paper versus electronic. I have not yet met a teacher who can be entirely electronic, because most schools are not technologically equipped to accommodate that preference. Too much data is still kept in dusty file cabinets, there are still too many students who turn in five-paragraph handwritten essays, and in most family meetings it would still not be culturally acceptable to position your laptop between you and your students' parents. Increasingly, however, teachers are relying on iPads, notebook computers, Androids, and other gadgets to stay organized. Additionally, lots of effective free or low-cost applications are available for smartphones (such as Remember The Milk and Toodledo). Throughout the book I recommend various electronic or online tools that I have seen teachers find helpful.

HOW TO USE THIS BOOK

To use this book to create your own complete personal organization system, here are the steps I suggest you follow:

- Open the accompanying CD or visit http://www.thetogetherteacher.com and download the free *Together Teacher Reader's Guide,* which contains all of the learning objectives, reflection questions, key summaries, and next steps for each chapter.

- As you read, keep the Reader's Guide by your side and make notes for each chapter. You can answer the reflection questions, make notes about your own habits, and select the tools that best match your needs and preferences. The Reader's Guide also allows you to put dates beside each next step so you pace the work over a few months to allow yourself time to build the habits, customize the tools, and create the space to become a Together Teacher.

- Explore the accompanying CD. It is full of Together Teacher sample templates for you to personalize, and other great resources. This process is really about customizing your own personal organization system, so I encourage you to start testing the templates and adapting them to meet your own specific needs.
- Purchase a thin (less than one-inch) binder and at least five divider tabs so you can create your Together Teacher System as you read the book and explore the CD. It feels wonderful to finish the book with your system already assembled!

Like trying to live a more healthy lifestyle (and isn't that on *everyone's* New Year's resolution list?!), getting organized is a process. No one *arrives* after just reading one book. You will find that some habits are easier to adopt than others and that some days we slip and rely on our old Post-it® Note habits and on others we go on strict efficiency frenzies. Being organized is a learned skill and, as with any other skill, takes time to become a habit. Steven Brill's book *Class Warfare* points out that "effective teaching is a marathon, not a sprint" (something I also heard Wendy Kopp say when I worked at Teach For America). Throughout this book you will hear from teachers who have balanced their lives while remaining effective; they have paced their work to be sustainable for the long term.

I look forward to joining you on our journey. Let's dive in to define the ten Together Teacher rules and work together to create your Ideal Week Template!

CHAPTER 1

Rules Over Tools:
Create Your Ideal Week

■ As dedicated teachers we will always work long hours, but it *can* get easier. If you're intentional about how you use your time each week, more minutes will materialize. It may sound crazy but as someone who taught and who has worked with hundreds of teachers—from the most novice to the most experienced—I know it is possible to balance the professional with the personal. There are teachers who plan and execute awesome lessons and find time to train for a marathon. It requires discipline and diligence—and may not feel natural at first—but it will increase your effectiveness and make your life easier. I promise.

IT *CAN* GET EASIER—A STEP-BY-STEP APPROACH

Often we teachers are not as intentional as we should be because we fall back on easily available excuses: "My day is just planned for me by someone else" and "I have no free moments for the entire day." This is true: for the most part our days *are* dictated by others' demands. That said, there are large chunks of time (before and after school, during preparation periods and hallway transitions) when all of the other work outside of executing excellent lessons can get done. As Nilda, a middle school English teacher, says, "There are a lot of distractions to the main 90 percent of my job—which is to design and execute excellent instruction every day. The massive amount of information that comes my way can easily take my eye off the main goal, and anything that can streamline [my work] can only help kids." People assume that professionals know how to plan ahead, get organized, and sort through the daily deluge. And we assume that some people are born magically organized and that for others it is a lost cause. I'm here to tell you that organization is a learned skill that can fundamentally help you focus on the main 90 percent of your job that Nilda mentions.

Reflection Questions:

What tools or habits do you currently employ to stay organized?

What already works well?

Where do you need to improve?

I'M NOT A DICTATOR, BUT THERE ARE *SOME* RULES

Remember I said we are creating a personalized organization system to meet *your* specific needs? Well, we are, *except* for a few critical commandments that must be followed— no matter whether your personal organization system is an index card in your shirt pocket (yes, this was done by someone I used to date, and proved highly effective for prioritization), an incredibly detailed paper-based Franklin Covey planner (Franklin Covey is a popular brand of planners sold in most office supply stores), or a carefully synchronized iCal (iCal is a personal calendar application made by Apple). Before we dive in, let's review the *Rules*.

The Rules

1. Get everything in one place.

2. Take it with you.

3. Write everything down.

4. Make it bite-size.

5. Keep like items with like items.

6. Create a trigger for what you put away.

7. Mind your energy levels.

8. No tool is forever.

9. Own your schedule.

10. Pause to plan.

Reflection Exercise

Take out your personal organizational tools and habits and rate them against the following rules:

> **Rule 1: Get everything in one place.** People tend to keep the things they need to do in disparate places: we have one notebook for meetings, one for ideas, an online mechanism for tracking tasks, as well as one or two electronic calendars. We have an abundance of systems—too many tools telling us what we need to do. As much as you possibly can, keep your tools in as few locations as possible. This means everything should sync to your smartphone or everything should be in one folder. You don't want to carry around a phone, laptop, two folders, one clipboard, and two legal pads to deal with all of your to-dos.

Reflection Question:

In how many places do your to-dos currently live?

> **Rule 2: Take It with You.** You are on your feet in your classroom and moving through the hallways of your school all day. Whatever tools you use to stay organized, you must have them on you at all times. Whether in a staff meeting, parent conference, or your classroom, you want to have a copy of your calendar and to-do list with you so you can record any to-dos that fly your way in the moment. For most teachers I recommend carrying no more than two tools around with you at all times. For some this may be a smartphone and a clipboard. For others it may be a binder and a notebook.

Reflection Question:

When another teacher asks you to do something as you walk down the hall, do you have a place to record your next step?

Rule 3: Write everything down. I want you to write everything down so you can empty your brain and focus on the hard work of teaching your students, and so you don't waste energy and time trying to remember and re-remember what you need to do. This concept is nothing revolutionary but it was made popular by David Allen, author of *Getting Things Done*. I don't want you to experience that dreaded feeling in the middle of teaching when you think, "Holy *&%, I forgot to [insert your own missing deadline story here]." I don't want you to have an idea of how to improve a lesson for the coming year and have nowhere to write it down. I don't want you to lose credibility with your students because you said you would give an extra-credit assignment but failed to follow through because you forgot.

Reflection Questions:

Do any of your to-dos live in your head?
When you have an idea for a colleague, what do you do with it?

Rule 4: Make it bite-size. Many to-dos get stuck because it is not explicitly clear what needs to be done. To avoid a to-do traffic jam, break tasks down as much as possible. Instead of writing "field trip" on your list, write "Call bus company to make field trip reservations." It may make your to-do list feel longer, but ultimately it will articulate an aim for those five extra minutes you squeeze out of your prep period. David Allen calls this making to-dos "actionable." This will help you avoid procrastination and make strides toward bigger, more important projects.

Reflection Question:

When do your to-dos get stuck? Think of one to-do currently on your list (or in your head!) and consider how you would break it down into steps.

Rule 5: Keep like items with like items. A lot of old-fashioned to-do lists fail because people keep big to-dos, small to-dos, short-term to-dos, long-term to-dos, and personal and professional to-dos tied together in one place. This approach is wonderful because everything is written down (see Rule 3), but it is far from the ideal because the jumbled nature of your to-dos makes it hard to scan your list and pick out the right thing to do at the right time. Eventually those long-term to-dos stop getting recopied each day and it becomes impossible to pick out what to do when. Assembly lines are efficient for a reason. It doesn't make sense to make your lunch for work every single morning as you are racing out the door. It doesn't make sense to run to the copy machine three times per day. When I was teaching I would make five peanut butter and jelly sandwiches on Sunday evening and stick them in the freezer.

Reflection Questions:

Does your organization system distinguish between short-term (today!) and long-term (in a few months . . .) to-dos?

Is there anything you can batch process, like my peanut butter and jelly sandwich example?

Rule 6: Create a trigger for what you put away. Although it is easy to innocently set down a stack of papers on your desk or file an e-mail carefully in a folder, you should remember—anything you "put away" has a way of never coming back to you. If you want to file papers, e-mails, or other items that truly require action, jot yourself a note within one of the organization tools we discuss in later chapters about where you put those papers or e-mails and when you plan to return to them. Then you won't find yourself scrambling through the pile of mail at home looking for the wedding RSVP card or using the search feature of your e-mail in-box in creative ways for that article you *had* to read!

Reflection Question:

What papers, e-mails, or other items do you have buried on your desk or in a file cabinet that you wish you had time to return to?

Rule 7: Mind your energy levels. Have you ever tried to write a unit plan when you were incredibly tired? Or found yourself grading relatively simple student work when you were most alert? This book encourages you to mind your energy levels and perform your hardest work when you are most alert and focused. Tony Schwartz, author of *The Power of Full Engagement,* thoughtfully describes how professionals need to manage their energy like Olympic athletes. Save the smaller, mindless to-dos, such as making charts and posters, for when your brain is fried. If you know you cannot get anything done right after lunch duty, reserve that time for making copies so that your low-energy time is not entirely wasted. Do the big stuff, such as lesson planning, unit planning, or data analysis, when you are most awake and energetic.

Reflection Questions:

When do you do your hardest work that isn't teaching, such as writing lesson plans or grading those end-of-term essays?

Are there times when it takes you longer to get something done?

Rule 8: No tool is forever. Your job will change constantly. The organization system that worked in your last nonteaching job or in college is unlikely to hold up under the demands of being a teacher. If you are just starting out in this profession, you may have graduate school or certification responsibilities to juggle. If you are further along in your career, you may have to balance department-head duties with your teacher-coaching obligations. Regardless of the responsibilities on your plate, you must consistently adjust your system to meet your ever-evolving roles and responsibilities.

Reflection Questions:

What organization systems have you already tried? What has worked about them? Not worked?

Rule 9: Own your schedule. There are certain things you have to do every day, week, and month. They should not routinely take you by surprise and force you to stay up until 2 AM to complete them (let's save that scary situation for *real* emergencies, which hopefully will become few and far between). Grading, planning, and progress reports are known events. Why not reserve the time for them now? This step will ensure that the known work doesn't creep up on you, and it will help you pace the work to meet looming deadlines, such as progress report completion or unit plan writing. Let's make sure your calendar holds not only important deadlines but also your priorities.

Reflection Questions:

How do you plan time for those big projects you *know* are coming, like progress reports or the next field trip?

How do you nicely turn away colleagues who always want to chat during your prep period?

> **Rule 10: Pause to plan.** To maintain a high-functioning organization system you will need to take a little time each week and each month to define what needs to be done in the weeks ahead. This may feel unnecessary at first, but it will ensure that you know what deadlines, personal activities, and meetings you have coming up. Most important, it will allow you to feel in control of your time instead of at the mercy of it.

Reflection Questions:

Do you pause and figure out what you have to do before you start doing it?

What might be a good time to do this during your day or week?

It is important to remember that these rules rather than the concrete tools we are about to review are the keys to your becoming a Together Teacher. In fact, overreliance on a tool may give you a false sense of security. Sometimes teachers will come to me and say, "Maia, I tried everything you told me and bought what you said at Staples, but it just isn't working!" Once the person's problem is diagnosed, I often conclude that it is not the *tool* that is weak. Instead, it is our habits that are out of whack.

THE TOOLS

Although I am fairly neutral about *which* tools you use—whether index cards, paper planners, laptops, tablets, or clipboards—I do care that each of your chosen tools is utilized to its fullest. Each of the following chapters goes into great detail about various tools and skills to stay organized, but it will help you to become familiar with where we are headed on our personal organization journey. At the end of the day, your goal is to have created an hour-by-hour schedule for the upcoming week as the product of a weekly meeting with yourself, called *Weekly Round-Up.*

Where most of us fail is in ensuring that our to-do list is created with intentionality and accounts for the short-term and long-term as well as the proactive and reactive. Therefore, before we create your to-do list for the week, let me introduce you to the four tools that will lead you there and the key habits you will need to create a complete list. You can also see them listed in the center of Figure 1.1.

- The left-hand portion of the figure depicts all the places where to-dos can pop up—your e-mail, paper memos, text messages, meeting notes, phone calls, and more.

- The middle portion displays the main tools on which you will force all of your time, to-dos, thoughts, and notes to land.

  ○ **The Comprehensive Calendar** lays out all of your time meetings and deadlines in one easy-to-reference location. It is most often a monthly view of your calendar.

- **The Upcoming To-Do List** is a list of your long-term to-dos organized by the month in which you want to begin the task. This list is a combination of deadlines, interim steps, and rainy-day items.

- **Thought Catchers** provide you with a place to track nonurgent ideas related to specific people or areas of responsibility. You can then refer to your Thought Catchers whenever you have sufficient time to actually talk them through with someone else. Most teachers have Thought Catchers for people with whom they regularly interact, such as a co-teacher, a coach, or a department head, or for communications they write, such as a monthly parent update or a motivational letter to students.

- **Meeting/Professional Development (PD) Notes** enable you to organize your professional learnings so that you can reference and implement them more easily in the future.

• The right portion of Figure 1.1 represents the short list of what you intend to accomplish in the coming week—the *Weekly* or *Daily Worksheet.*

- The Daily or Weekly Worksheet is a very intentional and narrow view of your work for either a particular day or week. But how exactly do you actually get to that detailed to-do list? The answer lies in the Weekly Round-Up, described in great detail in Chapter Seven.

- The Weekly Round-Up is a weekly routine that involves reviewing the work of the previous week, then planning your time and identifying the to-dos for the week ahead. Kerri K., a middle school special educator, describes the positive impact of being highly organized: "Taking the time to preplan your week and month is definitely worth the peace of mind and clarity of responsibilities that come later!"

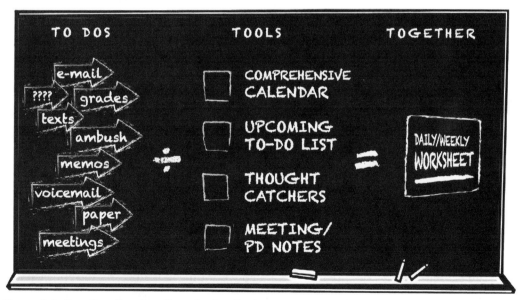

Figure 1.1 Together Teacher Organization Tools

Imagine Your Ideal Week

It is important that you establish how you would *ideally* spend your time in any given week, and you can do this using a combination of the rules and tools introduced in this chapter. The reason I want you to imagine your ideal week is that when I have worked with teachers who are struggling to keep their heads above water, the first questions I ask them are, "What work do you have to do?" "Where is your time going?" and "Where would you ideally like it to go?" Many of them are not able to answer that last question clearly. The following exercise will force you to consider how you would like to spend your time each week.

Let's consider what your ideal week would look like. The idea here is that you want to have a philosophical, big-picture view of your time so you can manage your calendar—before your calendar manages *you*! Doing so helps you to accomplish Rule 9—Own your schedule! This book is *not* a life-coaching-get-Zen guide. Julie Morgenstern, author of *Time Management from the Inside Out* (who started her career organizing *stuff*!) says it well: "The time you have in a day, week, or month is like the space in the top of your closet: only a certain amount of things can fit in it. Before you start dashing from one thing to the next, deliberately decide on how you want to fill the limited space of your day by creating a time map. A time map is a simple chart of your waking hours which displays how much time per day you devote to different areas of your life."

As you consider your ideal week, think about the following questions.

Reflection Questions:

When would you ideally go to sleep and wake up?

When are you teaching and when are your preparation periods?

What things must you do each week at a certain time, for example, student attendance submissions?

What meetings or events occur regularly, for example, staff meetings and coach meetings?

What things must you do each week at a time of your choosing, such as grading or planning?

When do you deal with answering communication, such as parent e-mails or student text messages?

What are some personal priorities that would enhance your week, such as exercise, church, and friends?

When are you ideally *not* working, for example, Saturdays or after 6 PM on weeknights?

What is something you *wish* you were better at planning?

When is your energy the highest? Lowest?

When, if at all, do you find yourself procrastinating?

What are some personal things you wish you had more time for?

What do you find yourself never, ever getting done?

Now that you have considered these questions, let's get more specific. We are going to block out how Kate, a new teacher, would ideally spend her time. As you review Kate's Ideal Week Template (see Figure 1.2), consider the following questions:

- When does she plan?
- When does she grade?
- When does she do personal routine activities, such as cooking, cleaning, and commuting?
- When is she not working?

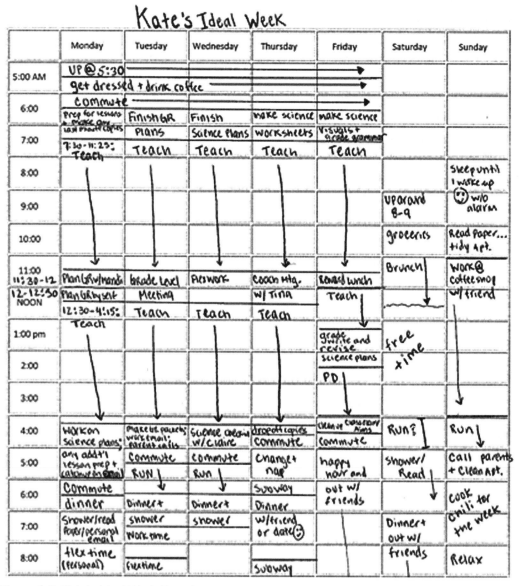

Figure 1.2 Kate's Ideal Week Template

As you can see, Kate's Ideal Week Template is very, very full. Here is what she did to build it:

- She put in the times her alarm goes off in the morning and her lights go out at night. These boundaries ensure that she is operating with the maximum amount of sleep she needs to teach well. Have you ever tried teaching while tired? I have and it is not a pretty picture.
- She inserted her work—teaching, grade-level meetings, schoolwide professional development, and so on—along with each meeting's time commitments.
- She added buffer times and other necessary items, such as commuting and showering.
- She added when she would do her lesson planning, grading, and classroom materials preparation. This scheduling allows her to not feel like she is *always* grading, planning, and copying—and to maximize her limited prep time.
- She left some time unscheduled for simply not working or for doing whatever she felt like doing.
- She built in time for such things as happy hour on Fridays, cooking chili, running, brunch, and calling her family.

To be clear, this plan is not meant to be followed to the letter each week. It is simply to give you insight into when, ideally, you would accomplish all the work on your plate for a given week. Although you may feel that mapping out your time restricts you, I believe that this high degree of planning actually allows you to be *more* flexible. For example, one night a friend offered Kate tickets to a comedy show on a Wednesday evening. Although Kate had planned to go to bed early that evening and to go out on Thursday evening, she did a switcheroo and planned to go out that Wednesday evening instead of on Thursday. By knowing roughly what she would accomplish (or not accomplish) each evening, Kate could take advantage of opportunities that came her way. The same can be true for you! By becoming extremely aware of how you use your time, you actually gain a great degree of flexibility and relief. You can relax because you know you have time set aside later in the week to unit-plan. You have become more agile and spontaneous because you are aware of the work on your plate and how much time it will take to complete it.

Build Your Ideal Week Template

Now build your own Ideal Week Template using the following checklist. Do not worry about being very specific right now. Concern yourself only with including these essential components on your calendar:

- *Physical needs:* sleep, exercise, eating
- *Scheduled time:* teaching, lunch duty, staff meetings
- *Discretionary work time:* preparation periods, before and after school
- *Big work:* lesson planning, grading papers, writing a weekly parent update (This work usually requires a high-level of focus and brainpower.)
- *Little work:* entering attendance data, answering short e-mails (This work can most likely be done during lower-energy times.)
- *Discretionary personal time:* relaxing at home, reading, visiting a museum, writing letters
- *Emergency buffer:* It's unavoidable—emergencies happen in schools. This would be when you would make urgent phone calls.

Now complete the Ideal Week Template. (See the example in Figure 1.3.)

Inevitably conflicts will arise between what you hope to accomplish and what you absolutely must get done. Conflicts will also arise between how you ideally would like to spend your time—watching *The Office* with your partner and friends—and the work you are required to do to meet the deadlines you have for the week.

All of this is to be expected. What is important in creating your Ideal Week Template is not that everything fit within the seven-day parameter with which you're forced to reckon but that you provide yourself with a clear picture of your ideal schedule before you enter the weekly shuffle. You may not be able to make it to the gym three times this week because of meetings you must attend before and after school, but at least you'll be aware of the various sacrifices and compromises you're making as you chug along.

Rule 7: Mind Your Energy Levels

I am a morning person. To an annoying extreme. To the point where in college I used to call my girlfriends at 6 AM on Sunday mornings and ask if they were ready for brunch. Unsurprisingly, my inquiry was always met with a dial tone. (My husband finds my morning cheeriness annoying enough that when we used to commute together via train, he begged to put on his iPod to block out my jabbering as we crossed the East River.) I am beyond useless, however, after 8 PM. I have been known to sleep through Eric Clapton concerts at Madison Square Garden, to snooze through Al Pacino's Shylock soliloquies in *The Merchant of Venice*, and to take "disco naps" well before the ball drops on New Year's Eve. Thankfully I know when I am on my game and when I'll be too tired to lift a finger. I try not to do much work in the evenings beyond answering short e-mails, preparing invoices, processing receipts, and so on, and I save work that requires focused thinking for those early morning hours.

As you build your Ideal Week Template, be mindful of your energy levels. Corey, a middle school math teacher in her fourth year of teaching, hit a point where she felt overwhelmed

	Monday	Tuesday	Wednesday	Thursday	Friday	Saturday	Sunday
5:00 AM							
6:00 AM							
7:00 AM							
8:00 AM							
9:00 AM							
10:00 AM							
11:00 AM							
NOON							
1:00 PM							
2:00 PM							
3:00 PM							
4:00 PM							
5:00 PM							
6:00 PM							
7:00 PM							
8:00 PM							
9:00 PM							
10:00 PM							
11:00 PM							

Figure 1.3 Example of Your Ideal Week Template

at the amount of work she had to deal with on a daily basis. She worked with her principal to track and analyze her time, and soon realized that after daily lunch duty she could not focus sharply on lesson planning. Knowing that her energy level wanes after monitoring a cafeteria full of middle school students, Corey no longer plans lessons after lunch. Instead she uses that time to return parent phone calls and make photocopies. Although these tasks are small, they must still be completed and are now tackled at a strategic time that Corey has reserved for lower-energy, easy-to-accomplish tasks.

Reflection Questions:

When are your energy levels highest? Lowest?

What times of day are you most productive? Least productive?

Some teachers have found that after creating their Ideal Week Template it is helpful to track their actual use of time against the ideal to see how they match up. Does grading take longer than they anticipated? What emergencies, if any, could they have prepared for? Did the unplanned visits to the teacher's lounge mean they had to make five parent phone calls at night instead of during the day? If you are interested in tracking your time, a template is provided on the accompanying CD.

COMPONENTS OF A GREAT ORGANIZATION SYSTEM

Now that you have a clear view of where you would ideally like your time to go, let's consider *how* you will get there. Remember the Trapper Keeper you had in third grade? The one covered in Lisa Frank and Tonka Truck stickers? There was a *reason* you loved that thing so much. All of your spelling lists, homework assignments, field trip permission slip, pens and pencils, and class work were in *one* neat place. No more racing to your locker to find that scrap of paper for your math teacher.

The problem is that most of us have not built an "adult" version of the Trapper Keeper. Instead we have allowed our organization system to spread out across pieces of paper, electronic notebooks, real notebooks, e-mail in-boxes, and real and electronic Post-it Notes. As you read each chapter of this book I want you to keep the concept of the Trapper Keeper front and center in your mind. Although I'm not asking you to keep an *actual* Trapper Keeper, I am asking you to work toward articulating clearly each component of your organization system. For some of you that system may be a one-inch binder containing all of your materials in hard copy; for others it may be a clipboard and a paper to-do list; and for others it may be simply an iPhone. Throughout the rest of this book I refer to the total system as your *Together Teacher System*.

What Your Together Teacher System Has to Do for You

As you go through the remainder of the book and I ask you to select the tools that work best for you, keep in mind that I don't have a preference for what you select. However, to be an effective system, your set of tools has to do *all* of the following things for you (consider this a way to ensure that you have an airtight system—and yes, there is a quiz at the end!):

- **Be portable.** Many of your to-dos come flying in when you are on an innocent walk to the restroom. Whatever you use to stay organized, be sure it can be on you at all times as you move through your day. This means if you carry an iPhone you either have to wear clothing with pockets, carry a purse or satchel, or wear an apron with big pockets. This also means that a fat two-inch binder will likely not work.

- **Be readily accessible.** If you get stopped by one of your colleagues in the teacher's lounge who asks you to share a particular resource, I want you to have a place handy to write it down immediately so you can follow up. For many people, paper entry is faster, but for others, entering it into their smartphone works equally well. Whatever it is, it should be swift and simple.

- **Be forward looking.** Because you have only 168 hours in any given week and much of that time is spoken for by teaching and planning, I want your Together Teacher System to allow you to plan how you will use the discretionary time you have. For example, a single notebook wouldn't allow you to plan ahead because it is just lines of empty space with no scheduling format overlaying it.

- **Efficiently group.** I want your Together Teacher System to allow you to do the less important work incredibly quickly (I call this the "not run to the photocopier three times per day" syndrome) and to have time to do the more important work when you have larger chunks of time. An example of a nonefficient system is one in which your big to-dos are mixed with your small to-dos and your long-term ideas are mixed with what you have to get done right this minute.

- **Quickly capture papers and stuff.** Your Together Teacher System needs literal space in which you can grab the incoming work and immediately put it where it needs to go rather than recording everything in an e-mail draft, jumbling it in a notebook, or shoving it into a pocket. For many teachers, this place is a pouch or folder they constantly carry as part of their system.

- **Store stuff.** Most teachers will want to carry some "stuff," such as a pen or pencil, *plus* have a place to store stuff you collect throughout the day, whether a thoughtful thank-you note from a student whom you let re-take a test, a confiscated student cell phone, or a tardy slip handed to you as you are teaching.

As you go along the journey of creating and customizing your personal and classroom organization system, we will check your selection of tools against the components just listed.

LET'S GET STARTED

Let's get started on your journey to becoming a more Together Teacher. Remember, the purpose here is *not* to become an overscheduled robot who can never relax and who focuses only on your to-do list all day. The goal is to have a clear view of all of your work—both big and small items—and a system that allows you to juggle everything as it comes in.

As Gilbert, a pre-K teacher, notes, "When you start to look at your day a little differently, through the 'I have this amount of time, I could get something done' lens, it makes you more productive and more relaxed at the same time. I set deadlines for myself, and I know I will end my workday at 7:30 PM because I know the last two to three hours per day are with my girlfriend. I have literally blocked time for not working, and I force my school work into the allotted time." As you will see in the multiple examples throughout this book, careful planning of your time, organization of your to-dos and stuff, and figuring out what simply can be done faster or at different times of the day can make you noticeably better at your job—and a lot less overwhelmed and stressed.

Let's get started with our first tool—the *Comprehensive Calendar*—which will provide you with a practical way to record your appointments, deadlines, and *Time Blocks*.

PART 2

Take the Long View

CHAPTER 2

No More Missed Deadlines: Make a Comprehensive Calendar

Learning Objectives

■ Consolidate multiple calendars into one comprehensive view of your time.

■ Identify important Time Blocks to hold in your calendar.

■ Ensure that all deadlines, events, and meetings are recorded in one easy-to-see place.

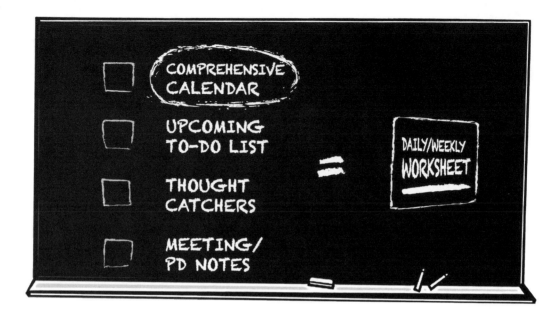

First things first: the calendar. The mainstay of our day-to-day, month-to-month, and year-to-year life. In this chapter you'll find tools to help you determine what sort of calendar to keep, how to put the calendar together using the Ideal Week Template you created in the previous chapter, and finally how to maintain your calendar so that it can sufficiently guide you from month to week to day. What follows may push you a bit out of your comfort zone because it will require some up-front time, but I promise the payoff is tremendous. Plus you'll uncover a terrific batch of calendars of Together Teachers that will help you determine what may work best for you.

THE MULTIPLE-CALENDAR DILEMMA

Multiple calendars—whether a hard-copy testing calendar placed in your mailbox by your principal, an e-mailed syllabus outlining graduate coursework, or a special services calendar listing days for speech therapy—can lead to collisions (a field trip scheduled on picture day, report cards due the same day your graduate school thesis is due) when they are not synchronized and put in one place. No one has time to review multiple calendars to identify overlaps and competing deadlines. Nonetheless, we often find ourselves juggling or toggling between multiple calendars, dreading the moment when we realize that our students' basketball playoff is the same night as Grandma's ninetieth birthday party. Most of us have not taken the time to put all of our time commitments and deadlines into one place.

Reflection Questions:

How do you keep track of deadlines?

How effective is your method? 5 = I never miss a deadline, 1 = My nickname is I-Need-A-Reminder Heyck-Merlin.

The best way to deal with this issue is to keep one master calendar—the Comprehensive Calendar—on which you record dates from all of the sources (work, family, graduate school) that generate deadlines and events. This is the only way you can tell if a late night of coaching basketball might collide with the deadline for your progress reports. Combining multiple calendars takes an up-front investment of time, particularly at the beginning of the school year, but it pays off hugely when you can save time by just looking in one place.

 Comprehensive Calendar: A calendar that lays out all of your time commitments and deadlines in one easy-to-access location.

We do not intend to miss deadlines or forget things. It just *happens,* because there is a *lot* coming at us from many directions every minute of the day. On some level it can become easier to stop tracking the deadlines and just go with the flow and hope (pray!) someone reminds us if we miss something. However, at some point this habit takes a toll on us personally and professionally. You miss the memo from your principal telling you when to start reading testing and end up having to test twenty first graders in two days. You don't realize that Mother's Day is early this year and spend a stressful hour calling your sister and begging her to tack your name onto the gift she purchased. We seek to be Together Teachers so we can eliminate the frenzy that accompanies forgetting a deadline.

THE COMPREHENSIVE CALENDAR: WHAT IS IT?

To solve the challenge of juggling multiple calendars and deadlines we will go deeper into Rule 1: Get everything in one place. The goal is to consolidate all of your important deadlines and time commitments into *one* calendar so that you can record deadlines clearly, know where you need to be and when, and regularly check for scheduling smashups. The Comprehensive Calendar is exactly what it sounds like—a calendar that presents a comprehensive view of your time. Most of us already keep some form of calendar, but most of us have not made it truly comprehensive. Your Comprehensive Calendar may be electronic, such as iCal; it may be Web based, such as Google Calendar; it may be a straightforward paper calendar; or it may be a hybrid—a printed version of your electronic or Web-based calendar. Your choice of paper, electronic, or Web based will determine the level of detail you can put on

September

SUNDAY	MONDAY	TUESDAY	WEDNESDAY	THURSDAY	FRIDAY	SATURDAY
				1	2	3
4	5 Labor Day	6	7	8	9	10
11	12	13	14	15	16	17
18	19	20	21	22	23	24
25	26	27	28	29	30	

Figure 2.1 Example of a Paper-Based Monthly Calendar Template

your Comprehensive Calendar, because each option allows a different amount of room to write and edit. Let's look at a few examples of what I mean by Comprehensive Calendar. The first example (Figure 2.1) is on paper, the second (Figure 2.2) is Web based.

At the minimum your Comprehensive Calendar should contain a monthly view of the following items:

- Deadlines, one-time and recurring, such as turning in attendance records and when progress reports are due
- School holidays and special events, such as assemblies and field trips
- Standing meetings, such as grade-level and staff professional development meetings
- Personal events, such as dentist appointments and birthdays

If you stopped there, you would have the *basic* components of a Comprehensive Calendar. However, many teachers take it a step further and plug in elements from their Ideal Week Template to ensure they are scheduling time for other priorities. For example, you may want to insert Time Blocks for the following items:

- Sacred nonwork activities, such as exercise, family time, relaxing
- Lesson planning at a particular time of the week when your energy is high
- Routine data entry when your energy is lower

Figure 2.2 Example of a Web-Based Monthly Calendar

Time Block: An appointment with yourself at a time specified on your Comprehensive Calendar or Weekly or Daily Worksheet (see Chapter Six for details about these worksheets). It is meant to preserve professional or personal time for working on what matters most, rather than just trying to squeeze it in around the edges of your teaching duties.

Some teachers initially view calendar consolidation as extra work, but the reduced stress and increased effectiveness it yields will make the time you devote to it well worth the effort. Imagine how good it will feel to see a snapshot of your life laid out month-by-month. Imagine pushing aside the constant worry that you're forgetting stuff because you know you have captured all of your important milestones in your Comprehensive Calendar! Unfortunately, getting the important dates *onto* a Comprehensive Calendar is not enough. Once you have set up your calendar, you must review it regularly (such as in the Weekly Round-Up introduced in Chapter One and examined more closely in Chapter Seven). Ideally you will set up this calendar at least an entire academic year ahead of time in order to see what events or deadlines lay ahead on which you must make early progress.

TOGETHER TEACHERS' COMPREHENSIVE CALENDARS

Let's look at a few examples of Together Teachers' calendars. I recommend you first glance at the sample calendar, then make your own observations, and finally read the description following the calendar—keeping the following questions in mind:

- How much detail is on the sample calendar? What do you see included? What is not included?

- What is your preferred way to enter items onto a calendar? By keyboard or by hand?

- What appeals to you about the calendar? Some teachers find themselves drawn to color-coding, others like neat places where they can check off the boxes for completed to-dos.

The examples start with paper calendars and move into electronic versions.

Anna's Comprehensive Calendar

Anna is an elementary school teacher with five years of teaching experience. She currently teaches half of the day and has responsibilities related to attendance, student behavior, and teacher coaching for the remainder of the day. Anna is also a marathoner and very devoted to her family.

As you can see in Figure 2.3, Anna used her paper Comprehensive Calendar to keep a high-level overview of her personal and professional responsibilities. (The template for her

November

SUNDAY	MONDAY	TUESDAY	WEDNESDAY	THURSDAY	FRIDAY	SATURDAY
⑦ 1 5 miles TLM PD Practice —	2 Coach GLM	3 Coach 5 miles SG	4 3 miles	5 5:30 Victors ⑧ Dad comes! → 8:00 MM	6 1 mile 5:30 Malatesta
7 ☆☆ ☆ MARATHON ☆ ☆☆	8 Leadership Stvy TLM PD Practice —	9 Coach → Snacks to GLM	10 Coach → SG	11 Air Hockey ½ Day 'till 6:00 Report Card Night →	12 AF PD Day	13 ④ 9:00 Leadership Fellows
14 12:00 Rock Climb ⑤ LP FD	15 Send Andreas present TLM	16 Coach PGP Meeting ③ GLM	17 Coach SG	18 Attendance ① Dinner w/ Nibelle 7:00	19 - Call families meetings ⑥	20 Prepare sistas gift
21 LP FD - Thanksgiving Dinner!	22 TLM ② Analyze math Hadiyah's Party GLM	23 Coach Vet: 11:00 am GLM	24 Coach SG ½ Day	25 Andreas B-day Thanksgiving Break EAT!!	26 Thanksgiving Break Nayeem's parents	27
28 LP FD	29 Attendance Awards → Prepare TLM	30 GLM				

Figure 2.3 Anna's Paper Comprehensive Calendar: A "Big Stuff" Overview of the Professional and the Personal

calendar was created in Microsoft PowerPoint and is included on the CD that accompanies this book.) Anna notes the "big stuff" on her calendar (where the circled numbers correspond to the numbered items in the following list):

1. Dinner plans with friends

2. Veterinarian appointments for her pets

3. Grade-level meetings (GLMs)

4. Special group membership meetings, such as the Leadership Fellows event

5. Weekend lesson planning (LP)

6. Calling families

7. Marathon training

8. Visits with her dad

At first glance, this looks like a very full month. Notice, however, that Anna has carefully looked ahead at the entire month (and beyond!) to ensure that she can fulfill the obligations that make her a great instructor *without sacrificing her personal goals.* Anna carefully plotted her work so she could hang out with her dad *and* run the marathon the first weekend of the month, by moving her lesson planning to earlier that week. Without a thoughtful plan in place, Anna could easily have gone into the teaching week after the marathon unprepared because her family and marathon commitments ate all of her weekend work time. Instead she thought ahead and reserved time to complete this work during the week before the marathon so she could preserve her time with her dad and for running.

It is important to note here that the Comprehensive Calendar is not an hour-by-hour list of everything Anna does each day. She limits it to the big stuff. Her daily play-by-play will be discussed in more detail later. The Comprehensive Calendar is meant to give an overview of deadlines, events, and commitments—both personal and professional. Anna keeps an entire academic year of monthly calendars and initially lists big events for the school year and then writes in additional appointments as they come up.

Brendan's Comprehensive Calendar

Now let's look at another Together Teacher, one who admits that organization was a real challenge in his first year as a special educator. Brendan is a middle school teacher who juggles a massive amount of deadlines and papers related to being a special educator. He keeps a slightly more electronic Comprehensive Calendar than Anna (see Figure 2.4). Each kind is equally effective.

Brendan spent initial time consolidating all of his calendars into a template on his computer; you can see he typed in the "big predictable stuff," such as:

1. Teach For America (TFA) events on weekends (from his Teach For America calendar e-mailed to him at the beginning of the year)

2. School holidays such as Presidents' Day (from his school district's calendar)

3. State discipline monitoring (from a calendar circulated by his principal)

(Here, too, the circled numbers on the calendar correspond to the numbered items in the list.)

After capturing those key dates, Brendan printed out a copy of his Comprehensive Calendar and inserted it into his Together Teacher System (a small, flexible binder). Throughout the busy teaching day, as new calendar items, such as church service on the 20th and the Prescott middle school's basketball tournament on the 9th, come up, Brendan handwrites them into his Comprehensive Calendar. Then, during his Weekly Round-Up, he updates his electronic calendar and reprints it for his Together Teacher System.

Because Brendan first updates his calendar by hand and later types the updates into his computer template, his Comprehensive Calendar is slightly more electronic than Anna's and counts as a hybrid. Now let's move to looking at some Web-based calendars.

February

SUNDAY	MONDAY	TUESDAY	WEDNESDAY	THURSDAY	FRIDAY	SATURDAY
		1	**2**	**3** *Dinner w/ Amy*	**4** **February Roll to Dottie**	**5**
6	**7**	**8**	**9** *Preset Ball tkme* **NOLA Dinner**	**10**	**11** **TFA Summit- DC**	**12** TFA Summit- DC
13 TFA Summit- DC	**14** *LOS Appt 7:30* **State Discipline Monitoring** ③	**15** **IV/IGG @ 1:30**	**16** **Open** **IEP** **Learning Team (5:30)** *Preset Ball Game*	**17** **Open** **IEP**	**18**	**19** ① TFA All-Corps
20 *Church Service 3 pm*	**21** **President's Day** ②	**22** *TFA Brunette* **Open** *office* **IEP**	**23**	**24**	**25** *FE9Re-Ev @ 12:30 pm*	㉖
27	**28**					

Figure 2.4 Brendan's Hybrid Comprehensive Calendar: The Big Stuff Typed in, with Additions Captured by Hand

Gilbert's Comprehensive Calendar

Gilbert is a pre-K teacher with three years of teaching experience. He has a lot of hobbies and interests outside his classroom and prioritizes spending time with his friends and girlfriend.

Gilbert's Comprehensive Calendar (see Figure 2.5) has the same idea as Brendan's but uses a different format. Gilbert records everything *outside* his routine teaching schedule on his calendar. It contains a combination of events, deadlines, and meetings. Similar to Anna and Brendan, he does *not* put his exact teaching schedule and prep periods onto this calendar. Unlike Anna and Brendan, Gilbert uses color-coding to separate his various responsibilities. You can view a full-color version of Gilbert's calendar on the accompanying CD. Gilbert has noted the following items (again, the circled numbers on the calendar correspond to the numbered items in the list):

1. Hard deadlines, such as when his lesson plans are due (November 19) are listed at the top of each day.

2. Specific time commitments, such as when he needs to drive someone to the airport (November 26 at 5 PM), are listed as specific times.

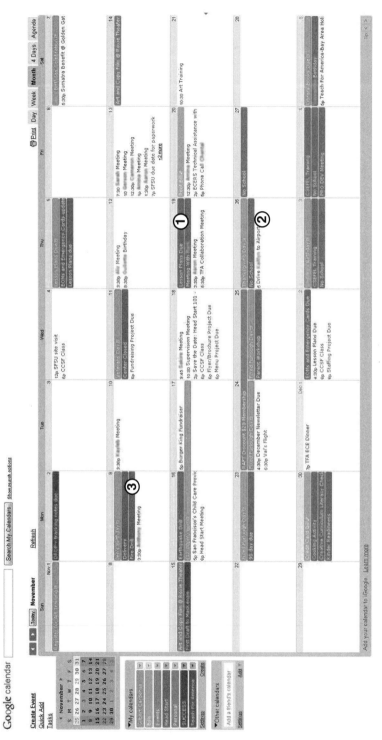

Figure 2.5 Gilbert's Comprehensive Calendar: An Electronic Snapshot Using Google

3. Events that are happening in his school that he needs to be aware of, such as a fire drill on November 9, are also listed.

How does Gilbert actually make this happen? When he gets a memo outlining when lesson plans are due, he inserts the deadline into his online Comprehensive Calendar as soon as possible.

Option A: If he is in front of his computer and online, he enters the information directly into his Google calendar.

Option B: If he is not in front of his computer, he enters the information into his Google calendar using his smartphone.

Option C: If he is not in front of his computer or his smartphone, he records the deadline on a printed-out version of his Google calendar that he keeps in his Together Teacher System (a small binder).

This method prevents him from having to find his deadlines in multiple locations. This principle applied when his colleague asked for a ride to the airport. Let's talk about that example in detail:

Step 1: Gilbert had a phone conversation with his colleague, who asked him to drive her to the airport on Thanksgiving Day.

Step 2: He checked his Comprehensive Calendar in Google, which was open on his computer, and said, "Sure thing, I'm free. What time do you need to be picked up?"

Step 3: She replied, "5 PM," and Gilbert entered the time directly into his Comprehensive Calendar. Gilbert will now be sure not to accept a dinner invitation for this time!

Technology Tip: If you choose to use an electronic calendar and have a smartphone—such as a BlackBerry, Android, or iPhone—it helps to ensure that they are synchronized so you can view your calendar on the fly. If you do not carry a smartphone but keep a Web-based or electronic calendar, I recommend that you print out your calendar up to six months in advance and put it in your Together Teacher System.

Some school systems rely on Microsoft Outlook for e-mail, and teachers take advantage of other helpful Outlook applications, such as the calendar feature. Let's look now at how a teacher uses Outlook for her Comprehensive Calendar.

Emily's Comprehensive Calendar

Emily is a high school history teacher, grade-level chair, and in graduate school. She has been teaching for four years. Before we go any further, I want to warn you not to freak out when you see Emily's Comprehensive Calendar (see Figure 2.6). At first glance it will appear to be very, very full. This is because Emily takes the additional step of Time Blocking everything up front. Many teachers take this step week-by-week (discussed in Chapter Six), but Emily completes it further in advance because of the flexibility of her Web-based calendar.

Emily color-codes her calendar in Outlook and records a greater level of detail than the teachers in the previous three examples. For example, all of the work related to AP U.S. History II is in the same color. Color-coding allows her to easily see if her time is aligned to what is most important. You can check out a full-color version of her calendar on the accompanying CD.

Emily's Comprehensive Calendar almost mirrors her Ideal Week Template, on which she recorded her class schedule, lunch duty, and grade-level team meetings.

You will note that Emily does the following (again, the circled numbers on the calendar correspond to the numbered items in the list):

1. Records one-time events, such as the dentist appointment she scheduled for after school, and the manicure on Wednesday

2. Pre-inserts Time Blocks from her Ideal Week Template, such as setup and copying on Fridays

3. Assigns Time Blocks for tasks with deadlines, such as the turning in of attendance each morning

Emily's high school also uses Microsoft Outlook to manage the calendar of the school, so on Emily's calendar you can also see such events as:

4. Whole Staff PD on Fridays, which appears as a meeting invitation sent out by the principal

5. Weekly grade-level meeting at 8:15 AM on Mondays, sent from a grade-level leader

At first this level of detail might seem overwhelming, but it ultimately shows how much (or how little) free time Emily has throughout the week. It also enables her to determine precisely how she will use that time to accomplish everything she needs to do. Emily plots her recurring weekly commitments and then adds in her specific items for each week, such as a coffee run for the grade-level team meeting or creating new seating charts, around those routine responsibilities. Emily's Comprehensive Calendar also shows how she incorporates personal appointments, such as the dentist or a manicure, into her week. For those of you who do not want to include such a detailed schedule in your Comprehensive Calendar, that is fine. We will review how to complete this step weekly in Chapter Six.

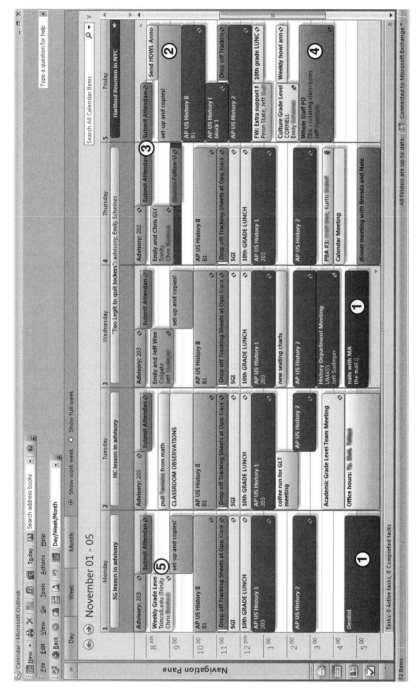

Figure 2.6 Emily's Detailed Comprehensive Calendar: Using Outlook for a View of the Personal and the Professional

Schedule: An hour-by-hour view of how you intend to use your time. Whereas the Comprehensive Calendar is most often just the big picture of deadlines and reminders, the Schedule (discussed in detail in Chapter Six) spells out exactly what you want to do hour-by-hour each week.

Although each teacher includes different levels of information on his or her calendar, all teachers record both personal and professional activities, deadlines, and meetings. As you can see from these samples, the elements shared by all Comprehensive Calendars are as follows:

1. The professional and the personal are in one place.

2. One-time events or deadlines are shown.

3. Meetings and appointments are noted.

4. Regularly repeated deadlines are recorded.

5. Time Blocks are inserted.

Rule 3: Write Everything Down

Often people ask whether it is truly necessary to record *everything*. Isn't that taking "togetherness" a bit too far? I tend to disagree. The reason is that writing everything down on your Comprehensive Calendar enables you to be more productive and efficient during your limited discretionary time each day. The only things that do *not* need to be written down are to-dos that have automatic triggers, such as changing the cat litter. I do not need to write this down because there is a clear "reminder" built in for that one! Jenny, a kindergarten teacher, says, "By my fourth year of teaching it started to hit me that I needed to be more organized. I don't know why it took me so long. At first it wasn't a huge deal, but then I became grade-level chair and it started to get to the point where I could no longer keep it in my head. It just got to be too much, and I never wanted to be the person, particularly as a leader, who had to say, 'I'm sorry I missed this meeting' or 'I missed this deadline.' From this point forward I committed to and continue to write everything down."

PICK YOUR TOOL: WHERE WILL YOU KEEP YOUR COMPREHENSIVE CALENDAR?

As I mentioned before we looked at these examples of teachers' Comprehensive Calendars, there are a few criteria for the selection of your Comprehensive Calendar. Whichever tool you choose, it must be:

• Easy and efficient to add new information, deadlines, and Time Blocks

• Portable so you can take it with you as you move around your school each day

- Readily available in multiple locations, meaning you can see it at both home and school
- Visually pleasing to you, meaning it must allow you to enter the degree of information that you can handle

Let's look further at the options that teachers most commonly prefer. Remember, if you don't love it, you can always change it later.

Paper Calendars

Many teachers keep a paper calendar in their Together Teacher System and write in each important event and deadline by hand.

Benefits of Paper Calendars

- You don't have to deal with a smartphone.
- It is more culturally acceptable to record deadlines on a paper calendar when walking down the hall.
- Many teachers find paper calendars more visually appealing.

If you choose to use a commercial paper planner, try to purchase one that has both a monthly and a weekly view. (We will talk in depth about the usefulness of the weekly view in Chapter Six.)

Common Pitfalls of Paper Calendars

- They can be easy to lose.
- You have to reenter recurring events, such as birthdays and deadlines for paying bills, multiple times each year—and again the following year.

Commonly Used Paper Calendars

- Franklin Covey planners or sheets (found in most major office supply stores)
- Day Runner planners (found in most major office supply stores)
- The UnCalendar (available at http://www.uncalendar.com)
- Moleskine planners (found in many art supply stores and specialty paper shops, and at http://www.moleskineus.com)
- Levenger calendars (available at http://www.levenger.com)
- Customized multitabbed planners (available at http://www.staples.com)
- Self-created versions in Microsoft Word, Excel, or PowerPoint (found on the CD accompanying this book)

Additional commentary on each of these calendars can be found in the Recommended Resources for the Together Classroom section at the back of the book.

Whatever kind of paper planner you use, be sure it includes the following:

- *A monthly view.* Without this you will lose sight of the big picture.
- *A weekly view.* Most paper-based planners also have a daily view. We discuss this more in Chapter Six when we talk about creating a Weekly or Daily Worksheet. For now, do not be concerned with the weekly or daily view.

Web-Based Options

Depending on your school's technology and your personal preferences, several Web-based options are available for maintaining your Comprehensive Calendar (and more are available online every day). It is important to note that if you go this route, you will need to be online a portion of each day. Many teachers who keep a Web-based calendar leave it open and available all day on their school computer. A notable benefit to maintaining a Web-based Comprehensive Calendar is that you can easily insert recurring events, such as birthdays and deadlines for paying your bills, and never have to add them again! For this reason, most teachers who use Web-based calendars keep a more detailed view of their time than those who use other options, often recording prep periods and classes taught, and inserting Time Blocks from their Ideal Week Template. If you choose a Web-based version, you can switch views between day, week, and month more fluidly than with a paper calendar, where you may be forced to copy deadlines into multiple views.

Commonly Used Web-Based Calendars

- Google Calendar is free, available everywhere, and easy to access from a Gmail account.
- Microsoft Outlook's calendar feature is simple and efficient to use, particularly if your school already uses Outlook for e-mail.
- iCal and Microsoft Entourage are often preferred by Mac users.

  Whichever Web-based Comprehensive Calendar you choose, be sure that it is

- Easily synchronized to your smartphone
- Available when you move throughout your school during the day

If you choose to go the Web-based route and it is not culturally acceptable to whip out your smartphone, laptop, or portable notebook during a staff or parent meeting, then I recommend you print out at least three months of your Comprehensive Calendar and keep it in your Together Teacher System, as Brendan does. This will allow you to capture deadlines and appointments that come your way when you do not have your smartphone handy or aren't able to use it. Then each week during your Weekly Round-Up you can transfer the information captured on this hard-copy calendar to your Web-based Comprehensive Calendar so they do not become desynchronized (a scary word, and rightfully so!).

Common Pitfall of Web-Based Calendars: Beware the Pesky Reminder!

A lot of teachers prefer electronic or Web-based calendars because of the reminder feature on their smartphone. I would caution you to use this option very, very carefully. What often happens is we set reminders for everything in our calendar; they accumulate and then we find ourselves "snoozing" or "dismissing" thirty-eight reminders at one time, thus becoming blind to our calendars and following up on nothing!

What if I *love* my wall or desk calendar?

Many teachers prefer a wall or desk calendar. If you need it for the visual appeal, please use it, but you must also maintain another fully portable Comprehensive Calendar like those described in this chapter. If you go this route, you run the risk of having dual calendars neither of which is fully comprehensive.

Each calendar approach has benefits and drawbacks, but all are equally effective as long as you capture all dates, deadlines, and events in one place and ensure that your Comprehensive Calendar remains easily available to you at all times. What no calendar (at least none that I have found) does perfectly is give you a view of both your time *and* your to-dos. You may be wondering where you put your actual tasks. Good question! We will discuss this in Chapter Three.

 Reflection Questions:

What tool will you use as your Comprehensive Calendar?
Why are you choosing this tool?

THE UP-FRONT INVESTMENT: CREATE YOUR COMPREHENSIVE CALENDAR

Now that you have used the information provided in this chapter to select your calendar tool, it is time to actually create your Comprehensive Calendar. The up-front time investment of consolidating your other calendars into one can be annoying, but it is worth it in the end, when you realize you have to look in only *one* place for your deadlines.

Round Up Your Calendars

You must gather up any other calendars or pieces of paper that contain deadlines or appointments. Think of every place you look for deadlines or every piece of paper on your desk. Check for testing schedules, unit plans, ancillary schedules for your students, ongoing due dates, and personal development deadlines such as when your graduate school papers are due.

Reflection Question:

Where do all of your deadlines, appointments, and events currently live?

Now that you have all of your materials in front of you, let's begin creating your Comprehensive Calendar.

Put in the *Hard* Deadlines

Insert each *hard deadline* into your calendar on the appropriate date. By "hard" deadline I mean work that you would stay up until midnight to accomplish. Each deadline should go at the *top* of the due date on your Comprehensive Calendar (as in the examples provided earlier in the chapter) so it is clear that the deadline is on that particular day.

 Hard Deadline: A must-do-at-all-costs-because-other-people-are-counting-on-you deadline.

Hard deadlines include the following:

- Completing your taxes by April 15
- Turning in your lesson plans by Thursday evening
- Getting your attendance to the office each morning

Reorganizing your classroom library and painting your kitchen are *not* hard deadlines. These are tasks you would *like* to accomplish but you are not required to accomplish them by a specific date. They are "soft" deadlines. Do not clutter your calendar with soft deadlines or you will quickly become blind to them. Your brain is very, very astute and knows *exactly* what is a fake, arbitrary, I-would-like-to-do-this deadline. When soft deadlines clutter your calendar, you will often choose to ignore them because you *can,* and then those tasks quickly go to an unvisited calendar graveyard.

 Soft Deadline: A to-do that you would like to accomplish at some point, but it does not have a specific due date.

You are likely wondering how on Earth you will ever accomplish all of the "soft" to-dos if they don't get valuable real estate in your calendar, as well as what to do when you want to turn one of those soft items into a high priority activity. In the next chapter, we will talk about how to take your I-would-like-to-dos and give them space in your schedule. For now let's focus on the hard and fast deadlines.

Reflection Question:

What hard deadlines do you need to add to your calendar?

Insert Events

What types of events should you put on your Comprehensive Calendar? It should include both events, such as report card night and a professional development workshop, and FYIs (for your information), such as fire drills or observation visits.

For example, if you know that your co-teacher will be out attending a literacy conference in two weeks, that event should land at the top of the calendar so you can be sure you are sufficiently prepared for his absence. In this vein, your calendar should capture such events as earthquake drills, family Thanksgiving dinner, and your mom's birthday. If you use a paper calendar, just note such events at the top of the monthly view.

Tech Tip: If you keep a Web-based calendar, use the all-day appointment feature.

Record events with specific times on your schedule in their actual time slots—for example, special field trips or assemblies, book fairs, and career days. If you are using a paper calendar, you can record these events in both the monthly and weekly views (where the layout often includes times of day).

Reflection Question:

What events or FYIs do you need to add to your calendar?

Record Meetings

Many teachers find it helpful to insert unusual events such as professional development workshops, special staff meetings, and parent meetings on their Comprehensive Calendar. Note that these items may conflict with the Ideal Week Template you created in Chapter One. For example, a parent meeting might fall during the period in which you typically plan your lesson objectives for the following week. By identifying this conflict in advance, you will know you need to move your lesson planning time to another Time Block that week.

Reflection Question:

What meetings do you need to record on your calendar?

Should I insert my teaching schedule into my Comprehensive Calendar?

As in the earlier examples, most teachers who use paper Comprehensive Calendars choose not to include every detail of their daily teaching because some things remain the same each day. Given the ease of entering events electronically as recurring events, those teachers who use Web-based calendars often *do* include their detailed teaching schedules. It is truly a matter of preference. What I care about is that you have a system for figuring out the best way to use your nonteaching time. In Chapter Seven we will discuss how to make a plan for your "free" time at school.

Get the Personal Stuff in There

Let's not miss this important step. Personal stuff matters. Some people balk at the thought of putting personal stuff into a calendar because it feels like every part of their life is planned. I think the opposite! For many years my husband and I had a standing Thursday night date with four of our best friends to watch *The Office,* eat good Brooklyn pizza, and share a bottle of wine. I really valued this time with my friends, so it was blocked on my calendar. I worked my tail off during the week so I could have this weekly time with very important people in my life. Did I make it every week? No. Sometimes I had to attend work events or had other personal conflicts, and could join them for only the last half hour. Nonetheless, that time remained blocked so that I knew to schedule around it as best I could each week. As you read the profiles of Together Teachers provided in this book, you will note that many of them have blocked time for family, church, exercise, and favorite television shows. Robby Rutkoff, a third-grade teacher, notes the game times of his favorite football team so he can be sure his lesson plans are done in time for him to enjoy the game!

Jenny, the kindergarten teacher mentioned earlier, describes her approach to personal priorities: "I keep time for exercise blocked in my calendar. For me it's really important to do yoga and get to the gym. Strangely, I have found that morning is best. I know it doesn't work for a lot of people, but I force myself to do it. I get there at 5:30 AM, work out until 6:15, and I have showering down to a science. I'm at school by 6:45 AM. I knew I could pull this off if I packed my bag, my lunch, my clothes, and everything else the night before."

Reflection Question:

What personal events or time do you need to put into your Comprehensive Calendar?

Designate Time for *Not* Working

Many teachers are interested in achieving a strong work–life balance. Me too! During the time I was writing this book I was raising a one-year-old daughter, serving as the chief talent officer for Achievement First, trying to maintain my three-times-per-week swim habit, juggling multiple client requests, and committed to trying to preserve time for my husband and friends. It wasn't easy. For me the key was making sure I was clear about the times I was *not* working, and holding very true to that—except in the case of emergencies. I had Time Blocks in my Ideal Week Template for spending daily morning and evening time with my daughter and special Friday nights with my husband, for having brunch with girlfriends, and for exercising. In particularly heavy weeks, did all of that happen? No, but I had an ideal to which I aspired, and I was aware of the choices I was making. Although it was an insanely busy time, I actually felt a great degree of control because I had gotten very clear about what my priorities were and how much time they deserved.

You probably need time for plain old doing nothing. For many teachers, this is Saturday, or a good portion of it. This is how I did it when I started teaching: I worked like heck all day Sunday, but knowing I had a rejuvenation day built in on Saturday made me feel very energized during particularly long weeks. When I was teaching I planned my down time in a few different ways. There was one year (a few years into my teaching career) when I was *determined* to work very, very little on the weekends, so I arrived at school incredibly early and stayed late, particularly on Thursday nights, to get my lesson plans completed.

Reflection Questions:

When are you *not* working?
What, if anything, are you doing with that time?

As this chapter illustrates, you *can* make time for what matters, but to make it happen you have to define what is important, block time to make sure the big stuff happens, then work like heck to preserve that time! How wonderful would it be to know that Thursday nights are reserved for reading *Vogue* and eating Oreos on your couch (two of my favorite pastimes, which *must* be done simultaneously for full effect!). If you don't put items like church, yoga, or family time onto your Comprehensive Calendar, the daily demands of teaching will easily eat them up. Think about it: Anna could never have successfully trained for a marathon if she hadn't blocked out time in advance for running.

KEEP YOUR COMPREHENSIVE CALENDAR ALIVE

Whew. You *did* it. By now you should have a complete Comprehensive Calendar. It may have taken a few hours, but doesn't that feel great? All of your other calendars can now be thrown away! You have only *one place* to refer to for all your deadlines and events. Now that you have transferred all of your calendars into one, you must keep it alive and update it regularly. Let's talk about what this looks like.

Processing Incoming E-mails and Memos with Deadlines and Events

Most teachers receive some kind of regular communication from their administration, in addition to a lot of one-off deadline communications from various people affiliated with your school. When many of us read a long memo from our principal, we immediately become overwhelmed by the volume of work and the number of deadlines in it. We close the e-mail (or drop the memo on our desk), promising ourselves we will revisit it later. Then we miss the deadlines it contained—and a panic attack ensues. Let's eliminate that feeling!

We will talk about managing paper in Chapter Twelve, but I mention it here because many teachers receive a huge number of deadlines via paper. You may receive something in your school mailbox with district deadlines, a piece of paper with updates to the speech therapy schedule may be dropped off on your desk, or your parent liaison might post a wall calendar with community events. Here is the approach to maintaining your Comprehensive Calendar amid a paper traffic jam:

- Collect all pieces of paper in one place throughout the day in your *Teacher Inbox* (a tool discussed in Chapter Twelve).

- Reserve time once per week, during your Weekly Round-Up, to incorporate these pieces of paper into your Comprehensive Calendar.

Processing Regular or Routine Communication

Figure 2.7 is an example of a weekly memo from a principal, Morgan, that contains deadlines for his teachers. If you receive regular communication such as this, via either e-mail or paper, block recurring time in your schedule to deal with it. If you don't, the deadlines will remain buried within the memo and you will never deal with the important information contained in the memo—and worse, you may miss a deadline request! Let's look at a step-by-step example of how to do this by taking apart a memo and discussing how to approach it.

Morgan, a middle school principal, obviously spends a lot of time thoughtfully communicating what is happening at his school each week. Although it may seem overwhelming at first, this memo actually makes it very easy to deal with all of the deadlines it contains. Let's go piece by piece and see how you should transfer each deadline to your Comprehensive Calendar. (Morgan also used color-coding to help his teachers with the deadlines. A full-color version is available on this book's accompanying CD.)

Morgan has a section in his principal's memo called *Upcoming Weeks*. This is the section where he lists upcoming deadlines and events for the teaching staff. There are two kinds of deadlines that emerge from Morgan's memo.

This Week's Events

Monday 4/4	Tuesday 4/5	Wednesday 4/6	Thursday 4/7	Friday 4/8
Welcome Jamie Baker Running with Megan and Sam Javier's Birthday!!!!	IA#4 K–4 Writing Prompt After School Sports – Gym @ 4:30	IA#4 K–4 Writing Prompt Running with Megan and Sam	IA#4 K–4 math, 2–4 Editing and Revising, 1st grade writing prompt	IA#4 K–4 math, 2–4 Editing and Revising Writing prompt due ③ to scanning room by 8am 1PM Dismissal
Teresa out Morgan & Kevin off-site 10–12 Monday (expulsion hearing)	Morgan off-site at Principal's meeting	Teach For America visitors	Shirley out	Shirley out

Upcoming Weeks:
- Monday 4/11: IA#4 2–4 Reading
- Monday, 4/11: Editing and Revising due to scanning room by 8am
- Monday, 4/11: REACH info due to Monica ①
- Monday, 4/11: Kevin S.'s Birthday! ②
- Tuesday, 4/12: Math due to scanning room by 8am
- Wednesday, 4/13: Reading due to scanning room by 8am

Figure 2.7 Weekly Principal's Memo to Teachers

"Day of" Deadlines

Some activities require no lead-up time to meet the deadline and can be completed in their entirety on the "day of," such as the following to-dos in the Upcoming Weeks section of Morgan's memo (see the items marked 1 and 2 in the figure):

1. REACH (a character program at Achievement First schools) info is due to Monica on Monday, April 11. Record this on your Comprehensive Calendar as a deadline.

2. Monday, April 11, is Kevin's birthday! Record this on your Comprehensive Calendar so you can wish him a happy birthday in the hall.

Deadlines That Require Work *Prior* to the Due Date

Another set of deadlines you receive require advance planning to complete the activity. This is work that cannot all be completed in one day. Let's return to Morgan's memo. In the Upcoming Week section, he notes that on Friday, April 8, your writing prompt is due by 8 AM (see the item marked 3 in the figure). This is a hard deadline and should be recorded in your Comprehensive Calendar. However, now you need to *write* the writing prompt. This is obviously a big deadline that will require lots of work in advance of the deadline. You would approach this by creating a Time Block. For example, you predict it will take an hour, so you put a Time Block for it on April 5 in your Comprehensive Calendar. By taking ten minutes to transfer all of these deadlines into your own calendar, you save yourself the stress of re-reading the e-mail multiple times and carrying the weight of what it contains on your shoulders throughout the week. Instead you simply read it, deal with it, delete it, and never have to think about it again! In Chapter Nine, which is devoted to e-mail management, we will talk about what to do if you receive this e-mail and don't have time to deal with it in the moment.

As you check your e-mail and Teacher Inbox (defined in Chapter Twelve) each day, you should keep your Comprehensive Calendar beside you in your Together Teacher System, or if you keep a Web-based version, then keep it open on your computer. If you make this transfer part of what you do at the end of each day (see the discussion of Closing Routines in Chapter Seven), it becomes automatic and those e-mails and papers full of hidden to-dos get easier to manage.

Reflection Questions:

Do you have any upcoming deadlines that require lead time to accomplish?
What Time Blocks do you need to put in place now?

 Lead Time: The amount of time you need to get something done in advance, often through the use of Time Blocks.

Incoming Deadlines Received on the Phone

The deadlines or events that come through phone conversations are mostly personal, though professional ones emerge as well. You may be on the phone with a parent discussing a student who chronically misses homework deadlines. Let's talk about how to follow up on this conversation step-by-step.

- After a discussion with the mother you determine that you will *each* check in with the student daily to see whether she has copied down the homework assignment. This deadline should go in your Comprehensive Calendar at the top of each day because it is a hard deadline.

- You agree to call the parent in two weeks to discuss progress. Record this deadline in your Comprehensive Calendar. This would be an easy deadline to miss during a busy day of teaching because it is further in the future. Keep your Comprehensive Calendar in front of you as you talk on the phone. While you are talking, at the top of your Comprehensive Calendar record the date to check back with the parent in another two weeks, and then don't think about it until then (except during the daily check-in with that student, of course!).

Even though it could feel overwhelming to record the appointment right this minute, think how much easier it is than trying to keep a date two weeks from now in your head. And think about how good it will feel to that parent to know you are a teacher who consistently follows up on agreed-upon actions.

Deadlines That Come Up in Meetings

Deadlines often emerge verbally in meetings with individuals or in staff meetings. These deadlines are very, very easy to miss in the hustle of a teaching day. For example, you may be in a staff meeting where your school's literacy specialist announces a new assessment that needs to be delivered in a few weeks. Let's talk about what you should do in this case.

- It's September and you are at the weekly staff meeting. You hear the deadline announced about delivering a new assessment in November. Now, it could be easy to ignore this because it appears far away, but these things have a way of creeping up on us and wreaking havoc in our lives.

- Open your Comprehensive Calendar (because of *course* you brought it to the meeting) and record the deadline right at the meeting.

Reflection Question:

Are there any deadlines that have recently emerged from any meetings that you need to record?

WHY IS THIS IMPORTANT, AGAIN?

After both creating and then by faithfully maintaining your Comprehensive Calendar you will feel a great sense of relief and an increase in your effectiveness. Anna, whose calendar we looked at earlier, exclaims, "Holy moly, it is really hard to remember when I didn't write everything down on a calendar. I had a basic calendar, but it was only weekly, nothing long-term. I used a lot of Post-it Notes for deadlines, which was not the best system. It's been so helpful to plan so far ahead and not have to worry about those long-term deadlines until I need to." No longer will you read, re-read, and then frantically search for an e-mail with to-dos buried in it. No longer will you scramble through papers on your desk to unearth the calendar that the speech therapist dropped off. No longer will you pay the overnight shipping fee to get that gift basket for your sister's birthday to arrive in time. You can now confidently review one calendar, see what is coming up, and plan accordingly for those deadlines and events.

GET STARTED: NEXT STEPS

- Research what kind of tools are available to you through existing software at your school, on your personal computer, or on your smartphone.

- Experiment with a few tools to see what works best for you.

- Select your tool (remember, you can always change it later).
  - Paper templates, such as the PowerPoint template on the accompanying CD
  - Commercial planner, such as Levenger products, the UnCalendar, Franklin Covey
  - Google Calendar
  - Outlook Calendar
  - iCal
  - Another Web-based calendar _____

- Gather up your calendars and deadlines.
  - Insert key Time Blocks from your Ideal Week Template.
  - Transfer each hard deadline to the top of the appropriate day on your calendar.
  - Insert personal events and priorities.
  - Select deadlines that need longer lead times and allocate Time Blocks to accomplish the to-dos.

- Keep your Comprehensive Calendar alive by processing incoming information from
  - E-mails
  - Paper memos
  - Staff meetings
  - Professional development
  - Phone calls
  - Grad school

Nilda
A Day in the Life

Name: Nilda Velez

Age: 31

Years teaching: 9

Grades/subject: Middle school language arts

Other school responsibilities: Coaches two teachers and is grade-level chair

Professional goals: Getting scholars' work published in a periodical, becoming a data analysis magician, and continuing on my journey toward teacher mastery.

Personal commitments: Squarely focused on planning our wedding—this is a thrilling time—and making our new place feel like home.

Proudest teaching moment: Fortunately there are many small moments I've been proud of as a teacher. One I'd rank near the top is sharing reading data with a scholar who was several levels below her seventh-grade peers. We were able to talk about it in a way that made sense to her and then she was empowered to track her own growth.

How she is working to become even more together: I think a struggle remains kid organization. There is so much content to do that binder clean-ups don't make it high on the agenda items but, as you know, being organized is not something you do naturally. I would love to teach some organization skills to my scholars, but I just don't know where that would fit in their day. I drop it in here and there, and it's usually a ten-second preach about how not to lose this homework assignment.

A Day in the Life

5:15 AM: Wake up! Breakfast and lunch were prepared the night before so they just need to get bagged. I shower at night to make sure the morning is a quick routine. I leave for school by 6 AM.

6:15 AM: I arrive at school, make coffee, and eat my baked oatmeal while reading that day's lesson plans. Our school plans a week in advance, so I need to refresh myself on the details of my plans daily. I transfer necessary materials to my cart (I move from room to room) and set up my writer's notebook that I use as an anchor or make whatever charts I need. I check e-mail for about fifteen minutes, looking specifically for anything urgent that may change the flow of the day.

7:00 AM: My cart and I zoom to the seventh-grade hall and I prep all boards with my aims, agendas, and homework. This makes transitions into classes a bit easier after breakfast.

7:15 AM: Breakfast duty! I simultaneously finish my own breakfast, review the day's schedule in my Together Teacher System, and check exit tickets from the previous day's last class. This is possible because we have silent breakfast.

7:30 AM: Morning homeroom. Scholars are working silently on morning brain blasts. During this time I take attendance and have any necessary culture talks with scholars.

8:00 AM: Teach writing.

8:45 AM: Between these two classes I have a very short window of just fifteen minutes. This is usually a time to check e-mail, use the restroom, and refill my water bottle.

9:00 AM: Teach small group reading intervention.

10:00 AM: This varies depending on the day, and I have really tried to cluster my work.

- *Monday./Tuesday.* Our school has a Tuesday 6 PM deadline for the next week's lesson plans, so I schedule no meetings on Mondays or Tuesdays because this two-hour window on both days is dedicated solely to lesson plan creation. I sit in the team room, headphones on, and have developed a bit of a reputation for not wanting to be disturbed on these days. This helps me filter out all distractions, and allows me to get all my plans done in school—a great feeling!

- *Wednesday.* I spend my time focusing on the two teachers I coach. I work on their learning plans, create agendas for our meetings, schedule or conduct observations, and review lesson plans.

- *Thursday.* As grade chair I use this time on Thursday for my batch processing. I'll meet with the dean of students to address the grade's culture needs, work on any long-term projects such as end-of-year trips, create the agendas, and tackle any action items.

- *Friday.* I never leave for the week without having all class work, homework, and their photocopies made and stored. I'll look at the following week's lesson plans; create all the materials I need, whether it's my own writing for an anchor text or hunting down the right author for the genre we're studying; and create all copies. Everything is stapled, hole-punched, and put in a plastic drawer behind my desk. They are labeled with the days of the week.

12:00 PM: I usually eat lunch while I'm working. I realize that some people would appreciate having the downtime in the middle of the day, but I prefer to crank it all out. On days I'm finished with tasks early, I eat in the teacher resource room and chat.

12:30 PM: Teach two writing sections and small group interventions.

3:00 PM: My energy level is getting pretty low by this point in the day and I'm usually scouring the school for a chocolaty snack. I save to-dos that don't require much thinking for this time of the day. I check e-mail and call families. I review my Weekly Worksheet and make sure all deadlines for the day have been met. Any unfinished tasks from the morning have to get cranked out here.

4:15 PM: Leave for the day.

5:00 PM: Read, relax, start dinner.

6:00 PM: At least twice during the workweek I'll get in a workout at home. I tried the gym, but leaving the house once I'm there becomes nearly impossible in the cold, dark winter months. Jillian Michaels, on several DVDs, makes every minute of the workouts count.

7:00 PM: My fiancé, who is also an educator, arrives home from work; we eat dinner and pretend we won't talk about work, but we always do!

8:00 PM: My very nice fiancé cleans up from dinner and packs breakfast and leftovers for lunch. We hang out on the couch, watch very important TV like *Top Chef,* and make wedding plans.

10:00 PM: Bedtime!

CHAPTER 3

Corral the To-Dos: Create an Upcoming To-Do List

Learning Objectives

■ Articulate the difference between a hard deadline and a soft deadline.

■ Identify the locations of all of your multiple to-dos.

■ Create an Upcoming To-Do List that tracks to-dos over the long term, organized by start date.

As educators, we are bombarded with a million things to do from multiple directions all day long. As we discussed in the last chapter, some of these things have hard and fast deadlines, some are appointments or meetings: they must be done by or occur at an explicit time so they must be noted on your Comprehensive Calendar. Most items we come across, however, do not have a clear deadline and are things we would *like* to do. What on Earth should we do with examples such as the following:

- Your principal's casual suggestion of a book on teaching autistic students?
- The fleeting thought you had during a read aloud about repainting your kitchen walls?
- The idea you had during a staff meeting for teaching writing?
- The realization that you need to return that birthday gift your great-aunt sent to you?

You may be inclined to jot these thoughts down on a Post-it or in a notebook (or even on your to-do list if you already keep one), but often they get jumbled and forgotten about in the midst of the day-to-day deluge. You want just one place where you can capture your to-dos so you can easily refer to them and complete them in an appropriate time frame.

Reflection Question:

How do you keep track of all your to-dos?

UPCOMING TO-DO LIST: WHAT IS IT?

There will always be more than we can accomplish in any given day or week. Most of you are familiar with the old-fashioned to-do list: that list you write in your notebook, on which you cross off what you can, and then recopy the next day. The challenge with this traditional system is that it fails to hold up as your role grows increasingly complex (and I rank teaching as arguably the most complex job out there). As your job becomes more complicated, your basic list becomes impossible to tackle because the to-dos on it are so disparate, vast, and long-term. Additionally, the list may be long enough that it is not worth your time to continue to recopy the same dratted item over and over each day or each week. You may have "Buy baby shower gift" and "Write *Roll of Thunder, Hear My Cry* unit plan" on the same list. You may also clutter this list with things you would *like* to do but don't have time to get them done. Last, you may have some things that need to be done today mixed up with things that need to be done this week mixed up with things that need to be done this month—you get the picture.

Upcoming To-Do List: A long-term sorted list of your to-dos that will drive the creation of a Weekly or Daily Worksheet (discussed in Chapter Six). The Upcoming To-Do List is a combination of deadlines, interim steps, and would-like-to-dos.

The instinct to keep a written list is the right one, and this chapter focuses on how to make that list more effective by transforming it into an Upcoming To-Do List for all of your deadlines, organized by start date so it is easier to sort through the list items. The Upcoming To-Do List is for work that needs to happen at some point but does not yet have a specific day—or even week—assigned to it. Keeping this list allows you to keep reminders of what must happen in the future, and prevents you from having to recopy long-term projects over and over until the day you're set to activate them arrives.

The item that I have seen come up most frequently in the Upcoming To-Do List is "Reorganize classroom library." Many well-intentioned teachers have this non-urgent but important to-do in their mind. Certainly this task is a noble endeavor, but unless your library is a makeshift pile of ratty books stacked on the floor, this to-do is unlikely to ever escalate to the very top of your to-do list. It may pop up higher on the list, however, when a teacher realizes that, now that independent reading levels have been assigned, the library requires some organization so that students can self-select their reading for the coming week. In this case, it is actually helpful for the teacher to have the trigger "Reorganize classroom library" on his Upcoming To-Do List. Let's look at how this would work.

Upcoming To-Do List

July	August	September
October	**November**	**December**
January	**February**	**March**
		Reorganize classroom library
April	**May**	**June**

Figure 3.1 Upcoming To-Do List Organized by Month in Microsoft Word

As you can see, the template in Figure 3.1 is simply boxes with months of the year in them. As you have thoughts about to-dos or projects that need to be started in particular months, you can simply record them in the appropriate box on your Upcoming To-Do List. Let's play through the "reorganize classroom library" example mentioned in the previous paragraph. Here is how your thought process could work:

You are sitting beside a colleague before a staff meeting starts and you begin talking with him about how to help his struggling readers:

"Boy, oh, boy, my classroom library is a *mess!* Books are mixed up in boxes, some are totally worn out, and some belong to other teachers."

"I really need to reorganize it before we start book clubs. However, my brain is so full right now with updating my classroom management systems, preparing homework packets for February vacation, and report card night."

"I don't want to forget about this though, and I don't know enough about my schedule just to pick any old day in March."

"I'm going to open my Together Teacher System and record this as an Upcoming To-Do for the month of March."

UPCOMING TO-DO LIST

To-Do	Start Date	Category	
Reorganize classroom library	March		

Figure 3.2 Upcoming To-Do List Organized in Excel

"When we approach March during a Weekly Round-Up [discussed later in Chapter Six], I'll consider giving 'Reorganize classroom library' a Time Block in my schedule on a day that I have a lot of time after school."

There, now this teacher has recorded his thought in a place where it does *not* risk getting lost.

Another way to organize your Upcoming To-Do List is to use Microsoft Excel to put it into table form (see Figure 3.2). There are many benefits to maintaining this list electronically. For example, in Excel you can easily enter things neatly within the lines, and sort and rearrange them very quickly.

I discuss the benefits of Excel in more detail at the end of the chapter. Finally, you could choose to organize your Upcoming To-Do List in a Web-based system such as Microsoft Outlook Tasks, Google Tasks, Remember The Milk, Toodledo, or any of what seems like a million other applications out there. We will look at a few examples later in the chapter.

USING YOUR UPCOMING TO-DO LIST

Let's discuss a few examples of to-dos that would land on your Upcoming To-Do List. Remember, these are things you need or want to get done at some point but that do not have a specific due date. However, they do have start dates—when you would ideally like to begin them. In this section we will walk through the different types of to-dos that will end up on your Upcoming To-Do List.

Stuff We Need to Do Eventually That We Don't Have the Mind Space to Deal with Right Now

Let's say your principal asked you in September to present a professional development workshop to your entire staff in December. Most likely you said, "Sure thing!" and hopefully wrote it down to deal with later. Most of us find it easy to agree with a request to do something two or more months in the future because our calendars are not very full that far in advance. However, we are very busy right in the moment and we know we cannot turn any attention to designing that professional development (PD) session until November. Two things would happen in this case:

1. You would enter the hard deadlines associated with delivering this PD session into your Comprehensive Calendar. For example, your principal will want to review the materials on November 20. You would also enter the date of the actual PD session into your calendar.

2. Next you would put this project on your Upcoming To-Do List in the month in which you want to *start* thinking about it. For most people, September is devoted to starting off the school year correctly and your attention won't turn to this PD session until mid-October. Using this method, you would enter "Begin planning PD session for December" into the October box on your Upcoming To-Do List.

What if you are not clear about what an actual deadline is?

Ask! Many times teachers receive to-dos from various directions without a clear understanding of when things may be due, what priority they have, or what is expected. I think it is helpful to really try and understand what is being assigned by asking a few questions, such as the following:

- When is this to-do actually due?

- Would you like to see any examples along the way?

- When will we revisit this project together?

- Do you have any other expectations?

Here are a professional and a personal example:

Professional reading. Let's say my husband's principal recommended that he read *Guiding Readers and Writers* by Irene Fountas and Gay Su Pinnell on English language arts instruction in the middle of the school year. This wasn't an urgent to-do and it didn't make sense to give it a specific date in his Comprehensive Calendar because it would truly be an arbitrary assignment. Instead Jack chose to jot it down on his Upcoming To-Do List for June, when he knows he will have more time to do professional reading.

Planning a vacation. Each summer I rent a beach house at the Delaware shore with some friends and their families. After having a great time playing on the boardwalk each July, I get very fired up about booking a great house for the following summer. However, in July most rental companies do not have their listings posted for the next summer. At the same time, if I do not plan ahead, I lose out on a great house at an affordable price. This is not a to-do with a specific deadline. Sometime in October through December I want to lock down a summer rental. I toss this to-do onto my Upcoming To-Do List for October—thus eliminating the need to think about it again until the beginning of that month. No more recopying the same old to-do over and over.

Reflection Question:

What are some to-dos you want to accomplish a few months down the road—things you don't need to think about for awhile?

Stuff We Need to Do That Needs a Longer Lead Time

By categorizing your to-dos by start date you can give yourself more time to plan to meet upcoming due dates and plan backward to meet deadlines. For example, if you owe promotion in doubt lists to your principal on February 1 (a deadline you will have recorded on your Comprehensive Calendar), you likely will need to do some planning in order to meet that deadline. So how does this work?

- As January, where you've listed this deadline on your Comprehensive Calendar, approaches, you realize you need to allocate time in your schedule to prepare these lists.

- First you have to figure out how you know some of your students are at risk of retention. You might review their mastery of standards, their reading levels, their unit assessments, and other documentation of learning against your school's stated policies.

- You would then realize that completing the lists may take you a few hours during a prep period and one afternoon after school. You would then allocate a Time Block on your Comprehensive Calendar to make that happen.

Reflection Question:

Look ahead on your Comprehensive Calendar. Is there anything coming that you want to start preparing for now?

Stuff You May Want to Do Someday But You Cannot Even Assign It a Month Right Now

As you move about during your busy school day you will often have ideas about things you *want* to do in the future but you cannot even think about a time to start doing them. For most of us, these are a lot of larger personal and professional aspirations that exist in the back of our heads. Let's talk about a few samples of these *rainy-day to-dos*:

- I would like to learn Spanish. I have wanted to learn Spanish for about ten years. It has been sitting on my Upcoming To-Do list with the date February 22, 2022, which is my arbitrary date assignment for "far away." Each week I look at my Upcoming To-Do List and decide if it is time yet for me to learn Spanish. Eventually I might assign a month in the near future to get started—like my boss, who started listening to Spanish language immersion lessons on his commute to work! How's that for being efficient?! But in all likelihood, until I work in a school that has exclusively Spanish-speaking students or until I travel to a country that requires the use of the language, I won't be able to prioritize this.

- Many teachers would like to reorganize their lesson plan files on their computers to be able to recall particular lessons more easily the following year. For most of us, finding the time to do that will not be easy, nor will it ever be the most important thing to do. However, you don't want to lose sight of the thought, and eventually (perhaps on a day during summer vacation when you are preparing for the coming school year) you will want to decide to set aside four hours on your Comprehensive Calendar to watch some good TV and reorganize your lesson plan files.

Reflection Question:

What are some of those rainy-day ideas you have rattling around on Post-its, in your head, or in your journal?

In sum, you need a place to dump and organize *all* of your to-dos that do not require your immediate attention but that you do not want to "lose" or inefficiently copy over day after day.

TOGETHER TEACHERS' UPCOMING TO-DO LISTS

Now let's look at a few examples of how different teachers keep their Upcoming To-Do Lists. The examples are a variety of paper, electronic, and Web-based tools, all of which work equally well. As you look at these examples it will be helpful for you to notice the following:

- How are these to-dos organized?
- What kind of to-dos are captured in this list?
- Do the Upcoming To-Do Lists employ any other levels of categorization?
- Where are examples of backward planning?

July	August	September
Readiness Docs. for Deans New friends - training photos & docs Field Trip Calendar ★ Gifts for Liz & Shannon Spain - traveling to which cities?	AFization Plans GLL gifts ① Arts & Culture Night Plans - ready ★ Dad's Trip - Julia comes - restaurants	★ Plane tickets for Christmas Gift for Kim
October	**November**	**December**
★ Marathon Prep - warm clothes	★ Spring break/Winter break plans? ② Marathon with Dad	★
January	**February**	**March**
★	★ Dr. Lum	★ Dr. Liu
April	**May**	**June**
★ Readiness documents for next year	★	★

Figure 3.3 Anna's Upcoming To-Do List Organized by Starting Month in Box Form

Anna's Upcoming To-Do List

Let's look at a simple yet elegant way of organizing the Upcoming To-Do List of Anna, whom we met in the previous chapter. Anna keeps her Upcoming To-Do List in simple boxes created in Microsoft Word and only records her to-dos by hand (see Figure 3.3).

Anna started keeping her Upcoming To-Do List in May and during the busy end-of-school-year rush there were a lot of things she wanted to be sure she noted for the following academic year. Anna puts her professional items above a star and her personal items below the star. Let's look at a few examples (items 1 and 2 marked on the figure):

1. **Professional example.** Anna is a grade-level leader at her school and while she was sitting in a grade-level training she had an idea about buying gifts for her grade-level team when school started. She didn't want to write this on her Comprehensive Calendar because the deadline was soft and to assign it an exact date right now would be arbitrary. However, she didn't want to lose sight of what she wanted to do in August to welcome her team. She flipped to her Upcoming To-Do List in her Together Teacher System (a small, flexible binder with five sections) and made a small note for the month of August.

2. **Personal example.** Anna loves to travel and knows she can get better deals if she researches locations and prices in advance. However, she also knows if she books too

early there may not be as many options available. To combat this, Anna has noted in November on her Upcoming To-Do List that she wants to *start* thinking about spring break plans.

Kate's Upcoming To-Do List

Let's look at another example. Kate, the teacher we met in Chapter One as she described her ideal week, organizes her Upcoming To-Do List by the month in Microsoft Word (see Figure 3.4). Unlike Anna, Kate keeps her list electronically, but she prints out a copy each week, puts it into her Together Teacher System (a hard, one-inch binder with seven sections), and handwrites additions onto it during the week. During her Weekly Round-Up she types in the to-dos she has added and then prints a copy of the revised list and inserts it into her binder.

Kate organizes her Upcoming To-Do List by start date. As you can see, her list contains nothing that needs immediate attention, but it does include many small things that could constitute missed deadlines if the list is not regularly captured or reviewed. Let's look at a few examples (items 1 and 2 marked on the figure):

1. PD resources she wants to revisit: "Read the 'Framing the Learning' docs from Chi"
2. Errands she needs to run: "Buy two larger binders for Teacher U (graduate school) materials"

These to-dos are not on her Comprehensive Calendar because they do not have to happen at a specific time, nor do they have deadlines. Instead Kate reviews her Upcoming To-Do List each week, focuses on the month at hand and on upcoming months, and looks for the best Time Blocks in which to make the to-dos happen. For example, she might realize that there are other office supplies she needs to purchase and instead of making three separate trips to Staples she makes one trip and gets everything.

Kate eventually shifts her Upcoming To-Do List to Excel, to make her list easier to sort (see Figure 3.5).

Kate sorts her Upcoming To-Do List by starting month. She carefully plots her summer professional reading and personal tasks around the house knowing that she doesn't have time for them as the school year is winding down. She also does an additional layer of organizing by category, such as "Buy," "Read," and "Decide." (David Allen has codified organizing lists by category in his book *Getting Things Done*.)

Kaya's Upcoming To-Do List

Whereas the first example was on paper and the second two were electronic with a paper backup, our last example is Web-based. Let's look at the list of a first-year teacher who chooses to keep her Upcoming To-Do List electronically in an application called Remember

April:

- ✓ April 11 – 15: Edit Video for Teacher U assignment
- ✓ April 11-15: plan science project around earth day for the week after earth day (4/22)
- ✓ April 11-15: do all actions for field trip (see project plan)
- ✓ While in England: Get gift for Laura
- ✓ April 23: Send Dad $53 & invoice mhm
- ✓ Post April 23: Register for 4 more NYRR Races
- ✓ Read the "Framing the Learning" docs from Chi ①
- √ Buy 2 larger binders to TU materials ②

May:

- ✓ ████████████████████████████
- ✓ Register for the rest of the NYRR Races and volunteer NYRR Race
- √ Buy new printer cartridges
- √ reprint MTL w/ more room / month

June:

July:

- ✓ Get some photos from France and prospect park enlarged for bedroom and kitchen
- ✓ Consider painting kitchen

August:

September:

Undated:

- ✓ Read Dad's book

Someday/Maybe:

Figure 3.4 Kate's Upcoming To-Do List Organized by Monthly Start Date in a List in Microsoft Word

Due Date	Category	Task
MAY	Pay	Dr Hansen
MAY	?	Put a dry erase marker on lanyard
MAY	Read	Read the "Framing the Learning" docs by Chi
MAY	Buy	Buy 2 larger binders for Teacher U materials
MAY	Email	FU w/Sarah re: ownership of sustainability
MAY	Decide	Register for the rest of the NYRR Races and volunteer NYRR Race
MAY	Organize	Make project plan for Cyn's baby shower
MAY	Organize	Make Sunday worksheet
MAY	Buy	Buy lilac bush/basil/tomatoes
MAY	Buy	Order: accordion file. Staples racks
MAY		
MAY		
JUNE	Buy	Buy frame for fran
JUNE	Clean	Wash green purse
JUNE	Read	Read common core standards for 2,3, 4
JUNE	Organize	plan baby shower for Cyn

Figure 3.5 Kate's Upcoming To-Do List Organized by Month in Excel

The Milk. The list in Figure 3.6 was created the summer before Kaya's first year of full-time teaching.

As you can see, Kaya had a host of personal and professional to-dos she hoped to accomplish in July and August before she started teaching full time. She gave them all the start date of either July 1 or August 1 so that they would sort together within Remember The Milk. As she adds to-dos for other months, she simply assigns them to dates at the start of the month and as the month approaches she assigns the to-do a more specific time. For example:

1. On the professional front, she wanted to read *Help, I'm Teaching Middle School Science* and a list of books she got from Orin, a professional colleague; and she wanted to make a trip to Staples.

2. Personally, she wanted to do a lot of work in her apartment, such as repaint the kitchen window; she wanted to clean her car; and she wanted to get in touch with a lot of her friends before she started her first year of teaching.

Kaya's Upcoming To-Do List is available to her both on her smartphone and on her laptop, so she can enter her to-dos directly into Remember The Milk as they come to her. If for some reason she is not able to enter a to-do directly into her laptop or smartphone, she keeps a printed copy of her Upcoming To-Do List in her Together Teacher System (a laminated folder with different sections), adds the to-do with a pen, and then inserts it online during her Weekly Round-Up.

As you can see, each of these teachers chose a different tool for her Upcoming To-Do List, but all of them organized that list by the month in which they wanted to begin the to-do.

☐ Try out Remember The Milk	Jul 03
☐ Clean humidifier	Jul 01
☐ Email EEL-podcasts?	Jul 01
☐ Errands - repaint kitchen window ②	Jul 01
☐ Errands - Shades for other room	Jul 01
☐ Errands - Staples list - See note!	Jul 01
☐ Errands - Stock up car for traveling - see note!	Jul 01
☐ Friends - Daria email	Jul 01
☐ Friends - Have Sam over for dinner	Jul 01
☑ Life - learn spanish?	Jul 01
☐ Life - Tapes for dinner	Jul 01
☐ Friends - Call Leah	Jul 02
☐ Friends - Call Lizzie	Jul 03
☐ Organize- Clean Car	Jul 05
☐ Audible.com? Mike ▓▓▓▓	Aug 01
☐ Errands - Change Republic of Wellness email to Kipp	Aug 01
☐ Errands - Kwame and Juana birthdays - cards	Aug 01
☐ Friends - Put all birthdays in next year's calendar	Aug 01
☐ MCAS Questions Chemistry - properties of matter	Aug 01
☐ Organize - figure out car phone	Aug 01
☐ Read - Help I'm Teaching Middle School Science! ①	Aug 01
☐ Talk to apartment about morning car access	Aug 01

Figure 3.6 Kaya's Upcoming To-Do List for July in Remember The Milk, an Electronic Application

Dealing with Being Electronic or Web-Based When It Isn't Easy to Open Your Gadget on the Fly

We have discussed how teachers who use a hybrid organization system keep hard copies with them either because they don't carry a smartphone and cannot access their computer while teaching, or because it is not appropriate to pull out an iPad in a parent meeting. As Kaya prepares to teach full-time, she will want to print out copies of her Upcoming To-Do

List once per week so she can add in her thoughts by hand as she moves around her school each day. This step is critical to capturing everything that comes up. If you can avoid needing to take a paper system with you to capture stuff, by all means skip it. However, I continue to find it easier to write a note quickly on paper than to open a laptop or smartphone when walking down the hall with thirty children. Similarly, putting a screen between you and your students' parents at meetings can be seen as inconsiderate. If you are *very* fast with your thumbs and keyboard, however, *and* you work in an environment where having open laptops or tablets is considered culturally appropriate, by all means enter your to-dos into your gadget on the spot.

Deciding When to "Roll Over" or "Undate" a To-Do

This happens! And it is okay! If you find that you are carrying over a to-do month after month or that you keep giving it a Time Block or a deadline on your Comprehensive Calendar week after week but never achieve it, you might decide to "undate" it. What I mean by *undate* is that you might decide to keep the to-do on your Upcoming To-Do List but assign it to the Rainy Day category. When it becomes important, it will be assigned to a particular month or week.

PICK YOUR TOOL: WHERE WILL YOU KEEP YOUR UPCOMING TO-DO LIST?

There are a number of tools that can house your Upcoming To-Do List. This is one of those times that habit matters so much more than the actual tool, so there are multiple ways in which you can construct your list. Here are a few options.

For teachers who deeply love paper: Simply take one of the Microsoft Word templates on the accompanying CD, print it out, put it in your Together Teacher System, and write to-dos on it as they occur to you.

For teachers who want to keep their Upcoming To-Do Lists electronically but need a paper capture point (this is most of you!): Keep your Upcoming To-Do List in box or list form in Microsoft Word, as in Kate's first example; or keep it in an Excel spreadsheet so it can be sorted easily by month, such as in Kate's second example. Then print out a copy each week and capture other upcoming to-dos with a pen as they come your way. Once per week take the sheet out of your Together Teacher System, type the additional upcoming to-dos you captured as you were moving around your school into the electronic copy, and print out a new version. The benefit here is that you do not need to be online to work on your Upcoming To-Do List, but you are able to keep it neatly organized due to the flexibility of word processing tools. Additionally, you can easily categorize, sort, and filter your upcoming to-dos. You are also less likely to lose your list.

For teachers who prefer completely Web-based tools: If you select this option, you likely already have a smartphone that is synchronized to your Comprehensive Calendar and you find yourself online frequently. Your choice depends on your appetite for fiddling with technology. I have found, for example, that the ability to sort is a very helpful feature, but not essential.

A few teachers like to use the tools that connect to the school's e-mail system, such as Outlook Tasks or Google Tasks. These are both useful. Google Tasks has slightly less functionality than Outlook Tasks but it usually synchronizes neatly with a smartphone and is easily viewed on a regular computer monitor.

Whichever application you choose—please make sure it is designed not *only* for your smartphone. You will enter many items into this list and you want the option of viewing it on a regular computer monitor.

Reflection Question:

Consider how often you are online, whether you carry a smartphone, and whether you prefer paper or electronic tools. What tool will you use for your Upcoming To-Do List?

GET STARTED SLOGGING THROUGH THE POST-ITS

Setting up your Upcoming To-Do List may take a while, but it will prove to be completely worth the initial investment of time. I assure you: the sense of relief you will feel once you get all of these items in one place will be worth the hours you spend getting them out of your brain and off scraps of paper.

Reflection Question:

Where do all of your to-dos currently live?

Get Everything Out of Your Head and Out of Your Stuff

The first step is to get every piece of relevant information out of your head, out of your e-mail in-box, off of any scrap pieces of paper, off the back of your hand, and onto one Upcoming To-Do List. Wait! You may be thinking, that will be *so* many things. You're right—this exercise will force you to encounter a lot of notices and reminders. This list should be so thorough that it should include items you may need in a week, a month, or perhaps never. Regardless of the exact timing of a task, it should be captured so that it doesn't rattle around in your head!

I usually advise you get situated comfortably on your couch over a weekend or in the evening, with all of your papers, your laptop with access to your e-mail accounts, your school bag, your school in-box, your voice mail, your notes from parents, your lesson plans, memos from your principal, and anything else where your to-dos may be lurking—including your brain. Then, step by step, dump all of the relevant items into your chosen Upcoming To-Do List.

Organize Your List

Whichever tool you use, your Upcoming To-Do List should have a few key columns to help you make choices about which to-dos to tackle when.

When to Start the To-Do

This is the beginning of the range of time in which you want to accomplish the upcoming to-do. For some to-dos, this may be a specific week. For others it may be a certain month. Still others may get the categorization *Rainy Day,* meaning you know you want to do it at *some* point but you don't want to assign it a date yet.

The Actual To-Dos

This is the column in which you list the items you want to accomplish. The key here is to be specific and clear. For example, if you want to schedule a doctor appointment for next September but it has to be scheduled in May, this to-do would land in your May list.

Other Possible Columns

Category. This is the category of work into which the to-do falls, such as Grading, Home, Planning, and so on. Organization of lists by categories is the concept (as mentioned earlier) that David Allen codified in *Getting Things Done.* For example, you may generate a bunch of to-dos for your classroom and a few for home. This distinction is useful if one week you have an extra few hours without students in your classroom and want to do more "Classroom" to-dos.

Length of time something will take. Many of us struggle with figuring out how *long* things may take to accomplish. Although some of that ability comes with time, I find it helpful to at least provide an estimate in this list so that I can be aware of when it should be tackled. Even if you have a jam-packed week, a call to the doctor's office will take only ten minutes and could be slotted between your other commitments.

Table 3.1 provides a sample of an Upcoming To-Do List.

This list will get very big very fast. In fact, the longer it gets, the better it is, because this means you are really emptying everything out of your head and putting all of your to-dos in one place where they belong. Having to look in only *one* place for what you have to do or would like to do will save you a ton of time.

Table 3.1 Sample Upcoming To-Do List

Start Date	Category	To-Do	Length
April	Parent relationships	Call Elise's mom to praise Elise's progress	15 minutes
May	Home	Get concert poster framed for bedroom	30 minutes
May	Classroom	Copy shapes to create Gallon Guy	10 minutes
Rainy day	Classroom	Reorganize classroom library	2 hours

Do I include personal and professional items in the same place?

I don't know about you but I do not have time to keep and maintain two to-do lists. Therefore, I keep only one Upcoming To-Do List with *everything* on it, including a ton of personal stuff—everything from "book summer beach house" to "take cats to veterinarian" to "order daughter new sippy cups." Hey, it all has to get done too, right? And I have found it is a mental relief to have it all in one place.

KEEP IT ALIVE: ENTER IT IMMEDIATELY!

Now, once you have invested the time to create your Upcoming To-Do List, you need to keep it alive, to keep feeding it to-dos so it can help you regulate your work. Let's discuss how to do this.

Regular Review

This list will be too big to review every day. It is too scary, and it will inevitably clutter your focus and execution. I recommend reviewing it only once per week in your Weekly Round-Up and scooping out what you *must* get done that week only. Similar to how you would not stand in front of the freezer eating your Ben and Jerry's ice cream straight from the container (right?!), you don't want to eat up all the to-dos all at once. You need to scoop out a reasonable amount at a time for one week only. Everything else can be tucked neatly away for the future. When you review your Upcoming To-Do List each week, you have a few choices about what you can do with them.

Choice 1: Make the To-Dos Happen This Week

First look for items you need to or would like to make happen this month, either because (1) they are *due* this month, (2) you need to start because the due date is fast approaching on your calendar, or (3) you are feeling some energy or interest and want to get started. Once you identify those to-dos that need to happen this week, head directly to your Comprehensive Calendar or to your Weekly or Daily Worksheet and create a Time Block to make them happen. For example, if this is the week you want to make a Gallon Guy for your classroom, determine the day you are going to do so after school and write it into your Comprehensive Calendar. You should feel a sense of relief once you know you have allocated time to make it happen.

Choice 2: Defer the To-Dos

Sometimes when you write something down that you want to do next month, it has a lot of energy. While I was writing this book I was on a tirade about the state of my bedroom in our small Brooklyn apartment. The rest of our place was so nice, but the bedroom was a disaster, a dumping ground for all of my online shopping returns, birthday presents to mail, and clothes never unpacked from travel. Each month I found myself moving this project to my Comprehensive Calendar with every intention of getting it done, but then not making time, putting it back on my Upcoming To-Do List, and then carrying it over to the next month. Finally I just decided there was just not the time or energy for this project yet and it was moved to the Rainy Day list.

Choice 3: Let the To-Dos Die

There will be some things that live on your Upcoming To-Do List for so long that you may eventually decide to kill them off. This is also completely okay. Sometimes you get energy around a particular idea and it *must* be done next month. For example, during October many teachers decide that they may need to revamp their grading, attendance, or behavior systems and they write down that they should accomplish this in December. As time goes by, however, they do a better job of enforcing behavior expectations, and by the time December rolls around they can see a notable improvement in their students' behavior. The original to-do is no longer relevant to their work and can fall off the list.

Ensuring That You Can Capture Incoming To-Dos

You're familiar with this theme already. You guessed it: I recommend printing your Upcoming To-Do List each week and putting a copy in your Together Teacher System. Although it is stressful and unnecessary to review it daily, it is helpful to have your Upcoming To-Do List on hand in order to capture updated or future actions that pop into your mind. If you choose to keep your Upcoming To-Do List completely electronic, make sure you have your smartphone or notebook computer with you at all times and poised for you to enter your to-dos. You also need to ensure that it is consistent with your school's culture to type in a thought in the middle of attending a staff meeting or teaching students. Schools vary on this, so just be sure to observe and ask. The last thing you want is for your colleagues to think you are playing Angry Birds all day!

Rule 2: Take It with You!

As you have seen, I recommend printing out your tools—even if you have a bias toward the electronic—so that you have a single place to catch everything that comes your way, even when your laptop is not open or your gadget is not in front of you—which most often it will not be during the teaching day. You will want to always have your Together Teacher System on you because you never know when a fellow teacher might ask you to send her a resource as you walk to lunch, or when the school office staff will find you in the hallway and give you a quick reminder about an upcoming parent night. Always have your Together Teacher System with you—even when you go to the restroom. I promise: you will thank me later. Walking down the hall empty-handed will guarantee that certain to-dos will fall through the cracks.

WHY IS THIS IMPORTANT, AGAIN?

Sometimes you may come to the end of a month and find things that have not moved off the list. Don't beat yourself up for not accomplishing everything in a given month. The point of this tool is to enable you to make conscious choices about what to do and what not to do. You may have had every intention of reading the book *Yardsticks* in April to learn more about where your kids should be at each grade, but that month may have become busy with preparation for the upcoming state test. *This is okay* because you made the choice to prioritize the state test over *Yardsticks.* You can always move this item to May on your Upcoming To-Do List. As Kate describes, "The Upcoming To-Do List allows me to empty my mind of all the things that I would love to accomplish but just can't take on at the current moment. For example, it allows me to know that I *will* paint my kitchen and frame my photos in July so I don't have to feel guilty about not doing it all winter. It also allows me to ensure that I don't forget about all the things I *can't* do yet—for example, my doctor doesn't make appointments more than four weeks in advance, so if I want an October appointment I put it in my September list so that making the appointment doesn't get lost in the shuffle of my life."

GET STARTED: NEXT STEPS

- Set aside time to corral all of your to-dos for both the short and long terms.
- Determine where you want all of your to-dos to live (whatever you choose, you should be able to view it both on your computer and on your smartphone) and customize it to meet your preferences.
  - Microsoft Excel list (found on the accompanying CD)
  - Microsoft Word list or boxes (found on the accompanying CD)

- Microsoft Outlook Tasks

- Google Tasks

- Various other applications, such as Remember The Milk, Things, TuexDeux, or Toodledo

- Make the initial investment:

  - Go through your e-mail in-box(es).

  - Review any scraps of paper you have collected.

  - Go through all of the papers on your school desk.

  - Review any memos.

  - Empty your brain.

- Determine the month in which each to-do needs to start.

- Take the to-dos for *this* month and create Time Blocks for them in your Comprehensive Calendar.

- If needed, print out your Upcoming To-Do List and put it into your Together Teacher System.

CHAPTER 4

Never Forget!
Capture Your Thoughts

Learning Objectives

■ Identify the various Thought Catchers you may need in your current role.

■ Determine how to utilize your Thought Catchers in the middle of a busy day.

■ Ensure that you return to your Thought Catchers to help create meeting agendas or written communications.

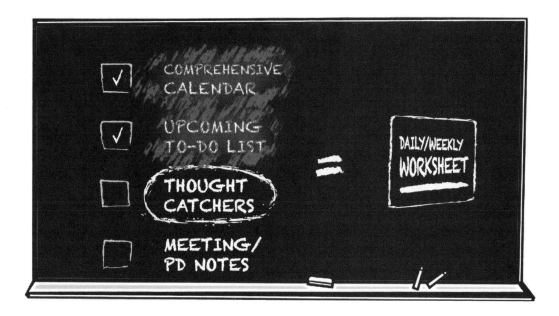

SETTING THE SCENE

It's 2:00 PM on Thursday and you have just taught your social studies lesson and transitioned your kids to physical education. While teaching the American Revolution, you had an idea for an end-of-year field trip. After class you walk over to your colleague's room and notice that she is also on her prep period, while her students are at music. Although she is engrossed in grading tests, you stop in to see what she is up to and to share your idea. She tells you about her interest in an end-of-year trip to Boston. You discuss the possibility of taking your kids biking on the Minute Man trail to Concord. By the time you check the clock it's twenty minutes later—time to pick up your kids. What just happened here? Despite your best intentions, you killed someone else's desperately needed prep with an important but nonurgent brainstorming session. You also lost a good chunk of your own prep period.

Reflection Question:

What do you currently do when you have a thought you want to share with someone?

My guess is that you do anything you can to get that thought out of your head. You shoot them a quick e-mail or immediately pop by their classroom for fear that the thought will otherwise be forgotten. The downside of this approach is that it leads you to interrupt colleagues or to launch ideas into cyberspace with no guarantee of getting a reply. If you *are* disciplined enough to write down your idea, it often lands on a to-do list in a notebook that is never reviewed. So, what is the alternative?

A CLOSER LOOK AT THOUGHT CATCHERS

Now that we have discussed how to manage time through the Comprehensive Calendar and how to outline tasks via an Upcoming To-Do List, it's time to deal with another set of things that can clutter our brains and litter our in-boxes—our thoughts. What do we do with those great ideas about teaching fractions that pop into our heads while we're in the shower, or that fleeting lightbulb that goes on about a book we want to share with our grade team when we're walking down the hall? For most of us, these things are either scrawled onto the agenda of a professional development (PD) session or found later littering a to-do list. Or we forget about them all together. This chapter is about a third tool, the *Thought Catcher,* which is designed to help you capture your thoughts so you can return to them at the appropriate time without creating unnecessary urgent matters for others, firing off a half-baked e-mail that may or may not come back to you, or forgetting your good idea. We will see how some Together Teachers note these thoughts in various locations so they can return to them as needed.

Thought Catchers: Provide you with a space to track nonurgent ideas that you can refer to whenever you have sufficient time to talk them through or take action. You can also have Thought Catchers for things you need to write regularly, such as parent updates, team updates, or a student newsletter. Let's look at a Thought Catcher template (Figure 4.1). You will notice that this is a very simple template organized with boxes to categorize your thoughts—nothing more!

Thought Catcher

Person _____ Literacy Coach	Person _____
More resources to test fluency	

Figure 4.1 Thought Catcher in Microsoft Word

So, how would this work? Let's say you meet with a literacy coach once per week to help design lessons to support your struggling readers. You frequently have thoughts you'd like to share with her when you are moving around the school or even *while* you are teaching lessons. You do not want to barrage her all day long by busting into her office or firing off ten e-mails to her per day. Instead, you should create a Thought Catcher for her by writing her name in the top of a box on the template (or if you use a Web-based system, at the top of a section in an electronic tool) and then write down your thought for her—which in this case is, "More resources to test fluency." Throughout the week you may catch more thoughts for your literacy coach—potentially as many as six to ten discussion items. When you sit down to meet with her at your appointed time, you simply pull out your Together Teacher System and—voila! You have a neatly created agenda and the meeting time is used productively.

You can take a similar approach by having Thought Catchers for notices or memos you write, clustered ideas for the future, or even fun personal items. Each of those approaches is discussed later in the chapter. The overarching point is that you should have a separate location to capture those good thoughts, ideas, and brainstorms that pop into your head throughout the day, and a way to refer back to them later. Let's move ahead and look at some examples from teachers who use Thought Catchers in a variety of ways. As in the previous chapters, a number of tools are presented from which you can choose, but the practice of recording your thoughts in a different place than you record your time and to-dos holds firm.

TOGETHER TEACHERS' THOUGHT CATCHERS

In this section we will look at a variety of Thought Catcher samples. Remember: currently these are just thoughts you will return to later; your return will be triggered by a meeting you need to attend coming on your Comprehensive Calendar or something you have to write or plan showing up on your Upcoming To-Do List. As you review the various samples from Together Teachers, please note the following:

- Are the Thought Catchers paper, electronic, or Web-based?

- Are they typed in advance or handwritten on the fly?

- What categories of Thought Catchers are used?

Thoughts for Colleagues

First let's look at some sample Thought Catchers from Kate, a third-grade teacher, that she uses to jot down nonurgent thoughts to share with her colleagues when the opportunity arises (see Figure 4.2).

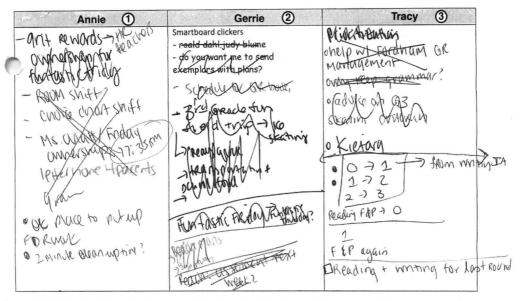

Figure 4.2 Kate's Thought Catchers for Her Co-Teacher, Principal, and Instructional Coach

Kate has Thought Catchers for three people with whom she interacts regularly:

1. Annie is her co-teacher, with whom she shares a classroom. Kate wants to mention something to Annie about grit (character) rewards for their students.

2. Gerrie is Annie's principal. You will notice Kate had a thought for her about "Smartboard clickers" and "Moving Funtastic Fridays to Thursdays."

3. Tracy is Kate's instructional coach. You can see that Kate has important topics to discuss with Tracy, such as support for guided reading classroom management and questions about student reading levels.

When Kate has a thought for one of these people in the midst of her busy day, she writes it in the appropriate box on her Thought Catcher and saves it for the meetings she routinely has with each of these people. As you can see, her captured thoughts range from straightforward questions about her shared classroom, such as where a good place is to put up the FDR assignments, to deeper conversation topics such as shifting a choice chart. Teachers are often guilty of inundating their school leaders with one-off questions that would be more easily addressed during face-to-face time. If Kate wants to ask her principal, Gerrie, about getting a Smart Board clicker, she is going to wait until they have a regular meeting, *or* she is going to compile that clicker inquiry with a few other quick questions in an e-mail so that Gerrie can review all of Kate's thoughts at once.

What if I do not have standing meetings with some of my administrators or colleagues?

If you do not have a regularly scheduled meeting with some of your colleagues, you have a few options. The first option is simply to ask for some regular time with your instructional coach, co-teacher, or other individuals. If this is not possible, then consider saving up ideas until you have three or four and then set up a time to meet, or bundle those ideas into a single e-mail.

Let's look at another example, from Nilda, a middle school writing teacher and teacher-leader. Nilda uses her Thought Catchers to capture notes for other teachers she coaches at her school (see Figure 4.3). Her Thought Catchers help her keep all of her observation notes in a single location.

While she was observing in Esme's classroom, she took two notes—"Strong Voice" and "Marathon Mile Push"—about Esme's lesson delivery. (The first is one of the techniques for effective teaching in Doug Lemov's book, *Teach Like a Champion*.) She wrote these thoughts in her Thought Catcher for Esme, and then, when she sat down to meet with this teacher, she used the Thought Catcher to guide their discussion. The benefit to this approach is that Nilda did not have to search through various notebooks or just remember what she wanted to cover with Esme. After Nilda discusses each item on the list with Esme, she simply crosses

People Boxes

	Esme
~~feedback on (som) tactics~~ ~~looking at directions~~ ~~GN for next week~~ ~~MM~~ ~~Progress reports~~ Exit interview	~~Plan 2 by 2 feedback~~ ① ~~Strong voice (obs: Keri, me, Desiree)~~ ~~Marathon Mile push~~ ~~Bulletin Boards / Break work~~ ~~Putting packets 2 into 1 for small group~~ ~~AR as repeatedly do assessment~~ ~~time Diary exam~~ MM prizes J&R project Plan trip to library for June (Grand Army Plaza)

Figure 4.3 Nilda's Thought Catchers for the Teachers She Supervises

them off. If you are wondering what happens when your Thought Catchers fill up, we will discuss that after we review additional samples.

Now let's review a third example of a teacher coach. Anna uses electronic Thought Catchers to write instructional feedback for other teachers at her school (see Figure 4.4).

As you can see, Microsoft OneNote is an electronic notebook (often packaged with the Microsoft Office suite of products), and Anna keeps a tab for each person she coaches (see the horizontal tabs across the top) and a list of all past interactions (see the dates that run vertically down the right-hand side of the page). In this way, her notes for all of the teachers she supervises are all in one place and she is easily able to refer to them. Of course if she promises one of her coachees a resource, she makes sure to get that action where it needs to go in either her Comprehensive Calendar or Upcoming To-Do List, mentioned in previous chapters. The benefits of keeping her Thought Catchers electronically is that Anna can maintain a running record of conversations over the course of the year and easily refer back to them over time.

Reflection Question:

Who are some individual colleagues with whom you meet, speak, or interact regularly?

Thoughts for Groups of Colleagues

Thought Catchers can also be an effective way to prepare for group meetings or to capture thoughts for entire groups of people. Let's look at how Nilda records thoughts for her writing team in her Thought Catcher for that particular group (see Figure 4.5).

Nilda was in a PD session about assessment when she realized she had a thought for the writing team about "aligned scoring and rubrics." Although she could have just scribbled that thought on the agenda of the PD workshop, she instead noted it in her Thought Catcher. The benefit to this additional layer of intentionality is that when Nilda goes to plan her writing team's meeting agenda, she can refer to her Thought Catcher and have half the work completed already!

Reflection Question:

What are some groups with whom you regularly meet? Departments? Grade levels? Committees?

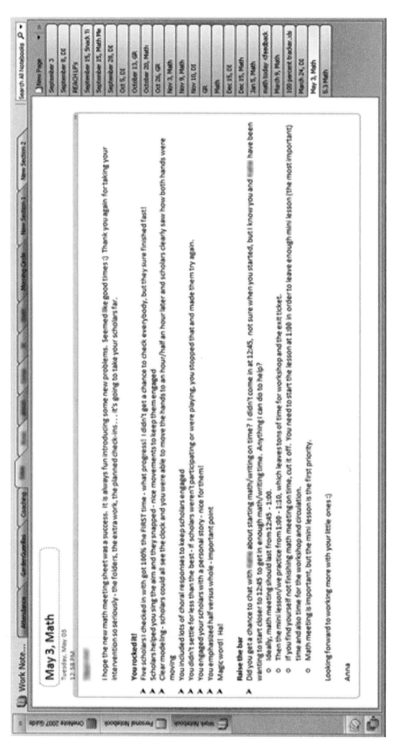

Figure 4.4 Anna's Thought Catchers for Her Coachees, Using Microsoft OneNote

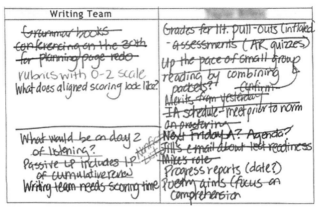

Figure 4.5 Nilda's Thought Catcher for Her Writing Team, Kept in Microsoft Word

Teacher Leader Tip: This tool is particularly helpful for teachers who are juggling leadership roles. For example, you may realize during your weekly staff meeting in February that you want to talk to the science department in April about aligning end-of-year assessments. Rather than forgetting that thought or shooting a panicked e-mail out to your team, you capture it in the section for the science department on your Thought Catcher and put "April" in parentheses beside it. This thought would sit on your Thought Catcher until April, when you build the agenda for April's meeting. You can even encourage other members of the science department to brainstorm topics (for predictable known items) in advance of the meeting and maintain a shared list of meeting topics and ideas for the year.

Could I just use the Upcoming To-Do List for the example just presented because it is something I want to deal with *later*?

Great question. Yes, you could actually put "aligning end-of-year assessments" in April on your Upcoming To-Do List. The way I make the distinction between what lands in a Thought Catcher and what lands on an Upcoming To-Do List is to consider the Thought Catchers as the place for thoughts that neatly cluster under a particular person or group, and consider the Upcoming To-Do List as a place for "unconnected" thoughts. Ultimately, either tool can work for such thoughts as long as you *record* and *review* your tools regularly.

Thought Catchers for Written Updates

Many teachers and teacher-leaders create a written update for parents or students to keep them informed about important notices or initiatives within the school. Let's look at a sample from a school leader of how he keeps track of announcements for his weekly staff update (see Figure 4.6).

This principal, Morgan, writes a lengthy and informative weekly memo to his staff. At the beginning of the week, during his Weekly Round-Up, he already has some thoughts written down, and then as the week goes on he "picks up more thoughts" as he zooms around the school. (Morgan uses an executive padfolio and his tools are in hard-copy in the inside pocket.) He realizes that he needs to share more with his staff about morning messages and he jots down that thought while walking down the hall to say good morning to students in the cafeteria. Relief! When Morgan goes to write his weekly staff memo, he opens his Together Principal System and has a starting point. The thought process of capturing and using your thoughts is summarized in Figure 4.7.

Reflection Question:

What regular updates do you write to colleagues, parents, or others?

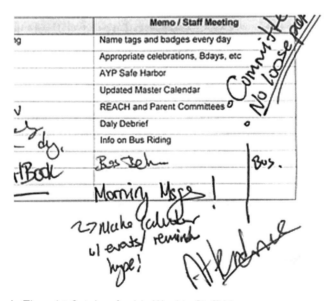

Figure 4.6 Morgan's Thought Catcher for his Weekly Staff Memo

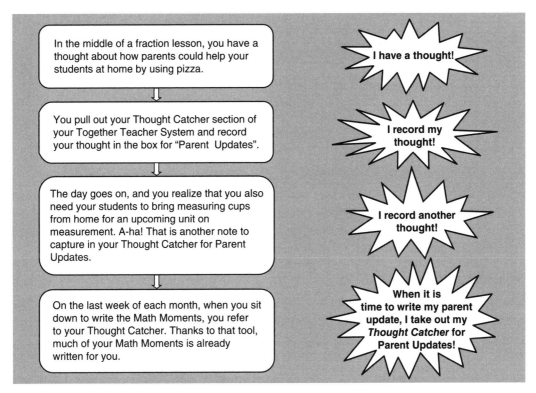

Figure 4.7 Flow Chart: Capturing Thoughts for Written Updates

Thought Catchers for Future Ideas

The beauty of teaching is that we often get to repeat lessons, either the same day, if you are a departmentalized teacher, or the next year, if you continue in the same grade level. Often, in the midst of teaching a lesson you have a great idea about how a lesson introduction might be made stronger, or you realize that you could have explained a concept in a different way, or you are in the middle of disciplining a student and you have a *vision* for improving your student incentive system for the next year. I recommend creating separate Thought Catchers for every topic on which you might want to capture ongoing thoughts that you will want to remember in the future. Let's look at an example of how Joy, a teacher leader, did this during her busy teaching days (see Figure 4.8).

As you can see, Joy had ideas for the *next* school year that she didn't want to lose, so she jotted them down during the swirl of the school day. For example, she noted that "classroom libraries need to have books with pockets." As her boxes filled up, she typed up her list during her Weekly Round-Up, printed it out, and put it in her Together Teacher System. Then, when it is time to plan her classroom physical space for the following year, she has a starting point.

Student Behavior	School Physical Space
Norms for pulling scholars into small intervention groups during the day: Never pull kids during core subjects Daily e-mail with kids kept for homework redos	Classroom libraries: books with pockets and index cards with names of books on them Rename hallways by grade level

Figure 4.8 Joy's Future Thought Catchers

Reflection Question:

What are some ideas you want to capture that should be grouped together?

Thought Catchers for Students

Although you may not have Thought Catchers in use already, many of you may already use this tool with your students without even knowing it. When I was teaching fourth grade I used to start each week with a sheet of adhesive mailing labels with each student's name printed and pre-populated on the label. Throughout the week I would jot down observations about each student to capture the teaching point of the reading or writing conference. For example, if Ferman was struggling with making predictions in his independent reading book, I would jot down that observation on Ferman's label.

This system ensured that I gave each of my students direct feedback on their work each week, and it held me accountable for closely monitoring my students' mastery of the material we were covering in class. At the end of the week I would peel off each label and transfer it to a binder that contained a section for each student, each of which was filled with pages of the previous weeks' labels. Each section was essentially a huge Thought Catcher for each student, and the sticky labels were simply where I jotted down my thoughts when I was on the move each week. I referred to these Thought Catchers when I was writing progress reports and preparing the next week's lessons.

Anna gets even more specific with the student Thought Catchers she uses during writing conferences. She takes the main learning objectives for the week and bakes them into her Thought Catcher template. Let's look at how Anna did this when she was preparing her lessons for the week (see Figure 4.9).

As Anna conferences with her students during writer's workshop, she aims to meet with at least four students per day. The checkboxes on her template before phrases such as "sentence fluency" and "conventions" remind her what the aims of the writing unit are. This method ensures that Anna meets with every student each week for an individual conference—and keeps her focused on her instructional aims!

Elsa

☐ Ideas +Content_____

☐ Organization_____

☐ Voice_____

☐ Word Choice_____

☐ Sentence Fluency_____

☐ Convention_____

Dolores

☐ Ideas +Content_____

☐ Organization_____

☐ Voice_____

☐ Word Choice_____

☐ Sentence Fluency_____

☐ Convention_____

Eli

☐ Ideas +Content_____

☐ Organization_____

☐ Voice_____

☐ Word Choice_____

☐ Sentence Fluency_____

☐ Convention_____

Leo

☐ Ideas +Content_____

☐ Organization_____

☐ Voice_____

☐ Word Choice_____

☐ Sentence Fluency_____

☐ Convention_____

Alberto

☐ Ideas +Content_____

☐ Organization_____

☐ Voice_____

☐ Word Choice_____

☐ Sentence Fluency_____

☐ Convention_____

Adrian

☐ Ideas +Content_____

☐ Organization_____

☐ Voice_____

☐ Word Choice_____

☐ Sentence Fluency_____

☐ Convention_____

Chris

☐ Ideas +Content_____

☐ Organization_____

☐ Voice_____

☐ Word Choice_____

☐ Sentence Fluency_____

☐ Convention_____

Alexis

☐ Ideas +Content_____

☐ Organization_____

☐ Voice_____

☐ Word Choice_____

☐ Sentence Fluency_____

☐ Convention_____

Lisa

☐ Ideas +Content_____

☐ Organization_____

☐ Voice_____

☐ Word Choice_____

☐ Sentence Fluency_____

☐ Convention_____

Figure 4.9 Anna's Student Thought Catchers

Reflection Question:

What tool will you use to capture anecdotal thoughts about your students?

Personal Thought Catchers

The Thought Catcher concept can also extend to your personal life—an idea popularized by David Allen in *Getting Things Done.* For example, I often struggle to think of thoughtful gifts for important people in my life. By keeping a Thought Catcher for gift ideas, I can easily jot down a thought if I read a review of a book or product that might be good for a future gift or if I see a Web site or store to which I may want to return. I can then refer to this list when I am trying to buy my mother-in-law a birthday gift! You can also keep personal Thought Catchers for things like books you want to read, restaurants you want to visit, and movies you want to watch. Let's review the sample in Figure 4.10 to see how I keep track of gift ideas—including gifts I want people to purchase for me!

Reflection Question:

What personal Thought Catchers would be helpful in your life? Books? Movies? Gifts?

PICK YOUR TOOL: WHERE WILL YOU KEEP YOUR THOUGHT CATCHERS?

You can keep your Thought Catchers in a number of different locations. Let's review the various choices and what works and doesn't work about each of them.

Paper Thought Catchers

Most teachers prefer hard copies in their Together Teacher System so they can jot down thoughts throughout the day, such as during a staff meeting or when just walking down the hall. Many teachers print out their Microsoft Word Thought Catcher documents and store these pages in their Together Teacher System. When the pages fill up, they simply throw them away after all the thoughts have been dealt with, or they type up the information and reprint new versions if the thoughts need to be carried over into the following week. Even if you are biased toward electronic options, it is helpful to have a paper backup of your

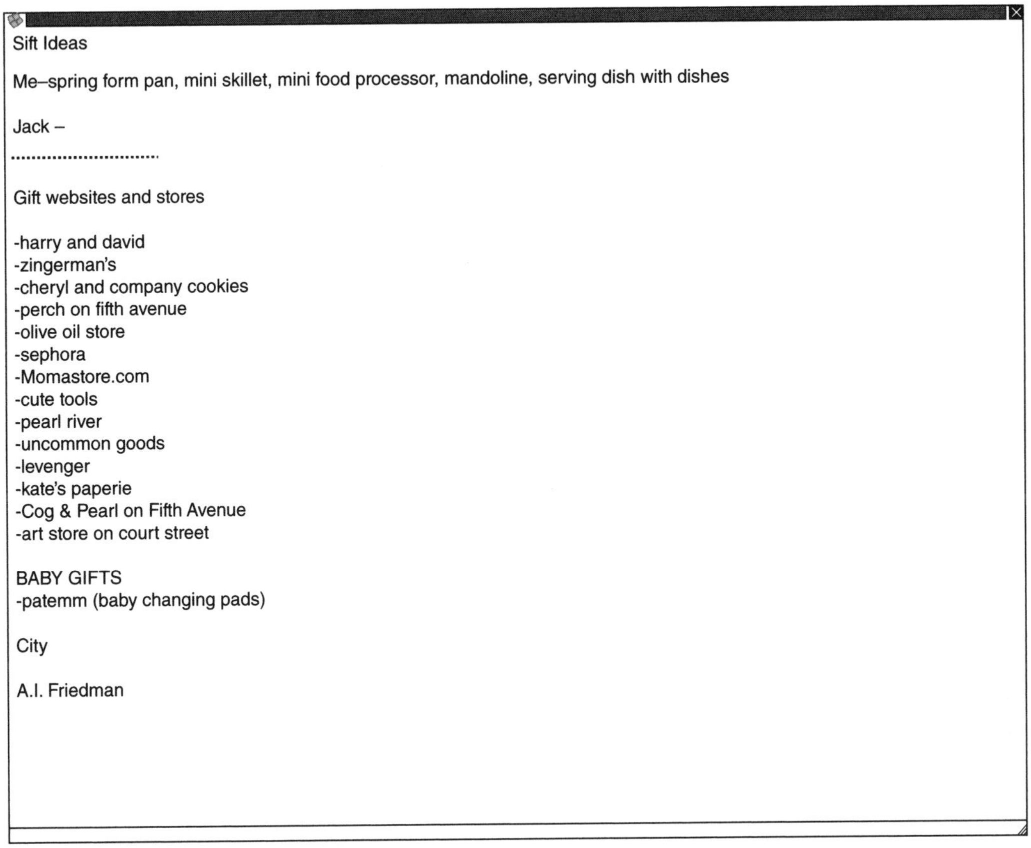

```
Sift Ideas

Me—spring form pan, mini skillet, mini food processor, mandoline, serving dish with dishes

Jack –
..............................

Gift websites and stores

-harry and david
-zingerman's
-cheryl and company cookies
-perch on fifth avenue
-olive oil store
-sephora
-Momastore.com
-cute tools
-pearl river
-uncommon goods
-levenger
-kate's paperie
-Cog & Pearl on Fifth Avenue
-art store on court street

BABY GIFTS
-patemm (baby changing pads)

City

A.I. Friedman
```

Figure 4.10 Maia's Personal Thought Catcher for Gifts, Using Outlook Notes

Thought Catchers because it is often cumbersome or inappropriate to pull out your iPhone, iPad, or laptop in the middle of class or a meeting.

Electronic Thought Catchers

For the more electronic among us, there are a few other ways to maintain your Thought Catchers. You may want to use an electronic option if your Thought Catchers tend to get really full. Some teachers like to use the printed-out Microsoft Word version to capture their passing thoughts during the day and then update them by typing any new thoughts into Word during their Weekly Round-Up and then reprinting the pages. This process requires diligent weekly updating at your computer. We will discuss how to do this in the next chapter.

Here are the options that I have seen teachers like best:

- Microsoft Outlook Notes or Tasks, which synch easily to a BlackBerry or other devices

- Microsoft OneNote
- Microsoft Excel (some teachers like to make a tab for each person)

Web-Based Thought Catchers

Some teachers prefer a Web-based tool (meaning a system they can access only when online), such as online Sticky Notes or any of the many other electronic applications that are available. My only suggestion for teachers who prefer this Web-based approach is that you try to use something that is already connected to your school's e-mail system so you don't create yet another place to house to-dos.

Reflection Question:

Which tool will you use to keep your Thought Catchers?

THE INITIAL INVESTMENT: SETTING UP YOUR THOUGHT CATCHERS

To get your Thought Catchers up and running, you should start by listing all of the Thought Catchers you may need and then taking out your chosen tool and filling in the headers of your Thought Catchers. Review any reflections you gathered as you read this chapter's lessons on the following Thought Catcher topics:

- Individual colleagues
- Colleague groups or teams
- Written updates
- Ideas for the future
- Students
- Personal fun

Is there a limit to the number of Thought Catchers I can have?

No, there is really no limit. You may end up with five to ten for individuals, one or two for colleague groups, two to three for future ideas, and two to three fun ones. You may also realize that some people need a whole *page* rather than just a box on a page filled with other boxes. That is totally fine. Of course, if you start reaching upwards of fifty, you may have gone too far!

MAKING YOUR THOUGHT CATCHERS WORK FOR YOU

Following are a few tricks for making your Thought Catchers work well for you. It would be easy to record your thoughts and never look back at them again, but we don't want your thoughts to get "stuck" in the Thought Catchers!

They must not be time sensitive. First of all, items you capture in your Thought Catchers should not be time sensitive. If a thought is a to-do item with a hard deadline, it should land in your Comprehensive Calendar. If it is a thought you want to consider in the future, it should go onto your Upcoming To-Do List.

They must have a trigger. Second, you must have a trigger to get you to refer back to your Thought Catchers. For most people, the trigger is a standing meeting that prompts them to review this tool. For example, if my husband, a middle school reading teacher, has a Thought Catcher for the fifth-grade teaching team, he can refer to it each time he attends a meeting to see if he has anything to bring up. If you write a monthly parent update, you can review the appropriate Thought Catcher before you start writing. On the personal side, when it is time to start holiday shopping or if you're looking for the perfect restaurant in New Haven, Connecticut, you already have a starting place.

You should choose Thought Catchers over e-mail. This is not to say you should *never* e-mail other people at your school. E-mail is indeed an efficient way to communicate, but we are all guilty of dashing off a sloppy, rambling idea to our peers or managers, and then ending it with the dreaded closing, "Thoughts??!!!" Realistically speaking, what happens to this e-mail? It becomes buried in someone else's to-do list and you have no way of knowing if it will ever emerge. E-mail is good for quick questions or information sharing; it is *not* good for big, ambiguous decisions involving a lot of people. Using your Thought Catchers will help you determine what might be best by e-mail and what should be discussed in person. More will be said on this in the next chapter.

Take advantage of extra minutes in each day. Thought Catchers will enable you to take advantage of spare minutes in your day. For example, if Kate was sitting beside her co-teacher, Annie, in a grade-level meeting that was late to start, she could utilize that otherwise wasted time to review the items listed for Annie in her Thought Catcher.

If you are capturing your ideas as you have them, you will be more prepared to meet with people and write regular updates, and you will avoid those slapdash visits and e-mails that often prove so ineffective.

WHY DO WE NEED THOUGHT CATCHERS, AGAIN?

Picture a world in which you have a place to capture the many, many thoughts that pop into your head as you are teaching, walking down the hall, or in a staff meeting. No longer will they be quickly forgotten, or scrawled on a piece of paper, distracting your colleagues, or creating an e-mail collision course for others. You will calmly jot your thoughts in your Thought Catcher, and then wait for a good time to raise them, or handily refer to them when you need to reference something.

The beauty of Thought Catchers is that they allow you to capture separately the thoughts that rattle around in your head instead of having them clutter up your to-do list, launching them in a scattered e-mail, or simply forgetting them. In fact, as I was writing the draft of this chapter, I had a fleeting thought about items for this very book that I needed to discuss with my writing and research assistant, Emily. If I sent Emily an e-mail immediately, my focus on my writing would dissolve because I would have to log on to the Internet to send her the message, and then I would promptly get absorbed by my online shopping habit. Instead of heading down that very slippery slope, I flipped open my equivalent of the Together Teacher System and recorded the idea for Emily in her section of my Thought Catcher. That way, when we have our regular Monday meeting, I will simply go to her section and be reminded of the items I wanted to discuss with her. This habit takes a ton of practice, but I promise it will pay off.

Nilda, introduced earlier, reflects on how the use of Thought Catchers helps her not only with her personal time management but also with the time management of others. "Thought Catchers have allowed me to free up my 'brain space' on that random yet brilliant idea that my principal doesn't necessarily need to hear from me during Monday's breakfast rotation! I can safely tuck it into my Thought Catcher and know that it will be waiting there to remind me during our weekly check-in. I also use Thought Catchers to avoid e-mail abuse with those one-off messages and that folks just don't know if or how to respond to. I've noticed those don't usually lead to action either. When I'm face-to-face with a colleague, sharing my thoughts on a particular school initiative seems to resonate more and we can have a dialogue about it that results in next steps!"

GET STARTED: NEXT STEPS

- Select the Thought Catcher tool that best fits your preferred work style (and keeps your system simple).

  ◦ Paper

  ◦ Electronic plus paper backup

- Microsoft Word
- Microsoft Outlook Notes
- Microsoft Outlook Tasks
- Microsoft OneNote
- Google Tasks
  - Web-based applications
    - Evernote
    - Toodledo
    - Remember The Milk
- Create Thought Catcher headings for individuals, groups, written communication, and future topics.
- Populate each Thought Catcher with thoughts about the various topics.
- Print it out and carry it in your Together Teacher System, or ensure that it is available to you electronically to record thoughts as you move around your school.

Gilbert
A Day in the Life

Name: Gilbert Cardenas

Years teaching: 3

Grades/subject: Pre-K

Professional goals: To work toward educational leadership

Personal commitments: Full-time teacher, education advocate, active in church and church activities, full-time fiancé to my wonderful future wife!

Proudest teaching moment: I continually teach my students our three classroom rules, which is also the basis of our classroom culture. Jesus, one of my quietest students, didn't utter a word during large groups and rarely spoke with teachers one-on-one. Then there was one day where the kids were running around, yelling, and crying. My students, co-teacher, and I sat down on the carpet to calm everyone down and gain control of the emotions in the room. We sang a song to soothe the atmosphere. Then, at the very end of the song, from the back of the carpet, Jesus said the three rules for the entire class to hear: "We are good, we are nice, and we learn all we can." Everyone, teachers and students alike, was shocked to hear Jesus speak—and we were also very appreciative. He firmly stated the standard we must hold ourselves to and that the way we were behaving was not okay. I was never more proud of Jesus than that day—to step up and take control. For the rest of the year Jesus talked more and became a leader in the classroom.

How he is working to become even more together: Organizing paperwork! I have so much paperwork from so many entities, I'm not sure what to do with all of it. Some of it has moved with me to five different apartments! I have also learned that I'm also not organized whenever I have large amounts of free time. For some reason I just get lethargic and slow down. I'm more productive when I have something to do (usually when it is for someone else).

A Day in the Life

7 AM: I groggily hit the snooze button three times before I wake up at 7 AM. A quick shower helps me get my wits together and I'm fully awake. I check my cell phone for any text messages or e-mails. If there is anything urgent, I'll send a quick text message back. I get dressed, grab my health drink and bag, and I'm out the door.

7:40 AM: Along my drive to work I stop by a gas station for a cup of caffeinated goodness (that is, coffee). I listen to the radio—and sneak peeks at my Weekly Worksheet at stoplights. I arrive at school and, before I get out of the car, I send a quick "I love you" text message to my fiancée.

8 AM: I sign in and get updates from my center director. I head into my classroom and greet my co-teacher. I review the important points of the day. My classroom door is opened and I happily greet all of my wonderful students and their parents. I have my Together Teacher System ready in case I need to jot down any important information I hear from parents (usually upcoming doctor appointments or future absences).

8:15 AM: Students walk into the classroom and play games. I review my Weekly Worksheet and look for any students I need to focus on for the day (assessments, screenings, and so on). I review the student sign-in sheet and document any absences. Then we sit down for breakfast and have delightful conversation about toys and cartoons. Afterward, our class has our morning circle and I teach the lesson for the day. Next, students have an hour of free choice where they can learn in any of the classroom interest areas (their favorites are the block and dramatic play areas). I carry out small-group lessons on thinking and reasoning skills and jot down student observations.

10:45 AM: My fifteen-minute break! I go to the lounge, drink my health drink, and review e-mails. I quickly respond to any important e-mails. I'll leisurely surf ESPN.com and Yahoo News. Before I head out, I quickly review my Weekly Worksheet for any tasks I need to complete.

11 AM: Students are outside playing. I'll run around playing tag and pretending to be a monster gobbling up kids. Students then come inside and eat lunch. Tired, exhausted, and tummies full of food, the

students take their afternoon nap. During nap time I'll get materials for activities, and lessons for the next day.

1:45 PM: I head out to lunch at a nearby pizza parlor and have a pizza slice. ESPN is playing and I take a couple of minutes to relax, refocus, and regroup. I review my Weekly Worksheet and spotlight any observations or paperwork I need to complete by the end of the school day. I'll also spotlight any parents I need to talk to during pickup time.

2:15 PM: Students groggily wake up from their nap time and have their afternoon snack of [crackers] and string cheese. After a short free-play session, parents come at 3:45 to pick up their children. I make sure to talk to parents, sharing good news about their kids and how much they are learning.

4 PM: The last student is signed out and I start cleaning my classroom. I walk into the office and check my e-mail. I talk with other teachers and staff about the happenings of the day— usually the crazy and funny things the students did that day.

I do a final check of the school and lock every door. I sign out, turn out all the lights, and head home.

4:30 PM: I head home and take a short nap. I wake up and start responding to e-mails. If there are any e-mails with attached documents or presentations, this is the time I review them. I update my Weekly Worksheet and Google Calendar.

7:00 PM: I head to my fiancée's place and have a late dinner. We catch up on the memorable parts of the day and have a good laugh. Then we crash on the couch and watch movies and our favorite TV shows.

9:30 PM: I drive back to my place and pull out my Weekly Worksheet. I respond to any other e-mails I received that day. I review my Weekly Worksheet and start working on lesson plans and inputting student data. The late evening is the best time for me to work because it is the time I have the least interruptions.

12 AM: I set my alarm for the next day and fall asleep watching TV.

CHAPTER 5

Beware the Notebook Vortex: Take Great Notes at Meetings and Professional Development

Learning Objectives

■ Determine effective note-taking templates for meetings and professional development.

■ Create methods to file and store your professional learnings so they can be used in the future.

SETTING THE SCENE

One of the benefits of being teachers is that we get to participate in great professional development (PD) opportunities as part of our jobs. We get to stay current in our practice, and we have the opportunity to try out ideas immediately. However, we *know* it doesn't always work out that way. We return to school the next day, enter the swirl of our daily teaching life, and BAM! a student gets really sick or a big curriculum change is made at the district level! Or you get really good observation feedback on your classroom instruction—and then forget to implement it. These good intentions and wonderful ideas you have when you are in learning mode get shoved into the proverbial drawer, and it is rare that they see the light of day. This chapter shares ideas and tools from other Together Teachers on how they keep track of learnings and ideas from staff meetings, coaching sessions, and PD.

Reflection Questions:

How do you currently follow up on PD ideas, department or grade-level team brainstorms, or staff meeting to-dos?

Why is it important to follow up on PD and meetings?

BEWARE THE NOTEBOOK VORTEX

What *do* you do with those copious ideas you gather in great staff PD? In an unscientific study I conducted I found that even those of us who are intentional about this sort of thing—diligently taking notes in a beautiful notebook purchased just for the purpose of capturing

Meeting and PD (Meeting/PD) Notes—simply don't have the time to go back and review that notebook regularly. Or we eventually gather *so many notebooks* that it becomes impossible to remember which notebook contained the idea we wanted in the first place!

This chapter proposes some alternatives to common practices such as taking notes directly on PD agendas, scribbling ideas in a notebook, or writing them on ever-present Post-it Notes. As hard as it can be to abandon the notebook, this chapter can help you access your ideas and materials much more efficiently moving forward. It takes a little bit of discipline and preparation, but this habit will be worth it when you can easily put great ideas into practice in your classroom!

THE EXPLANATION: WHAT ARE MEETING/PD NOTES?

 Meeting and Professional Development (Meeting/PD) Notes: Methods for organizing your professional learnings so they can be useful in both the short and the long term.

Let's look at a few examples of templates that are often used in Together Teacher Systems. It is important to point out that because we are trying to minimize the number of "things" you carry around your school, most often these templates will sit in a section of your Together Teacher System. You can also download the templates from the accompanying CD and use them on your laptop, tablet, or desktop PC to take notes electronically. We will review methods for taking notes at professional development workshops, individual meetings, and group meetings.

BACK FROM THE DEAD: DOING SOMETHING WITH OUR PD NOTES

We are all guilty of it: we sit in incredible PD sessions scribbling important notes and great ideas on a legal pad, then shove that legal pad in the bottom of our teaching bag and unearth it only when it is so crumpled that we actually cannot tell anymore what is recorded on it. Who has the time to go back and write up their notes? Let's discuss how to put those great learnings to use by being more organized about the notes we take. It will take a little bit more planning, but I promise you that it will be worth it.

Taking PD Notes

The first step is to be very thoughtful about how you take notes. Many of us think and process information through writing, which is helpful in the moment. However, it is *not* helpful when we return to those notes six months later and find ourselves sorting through a lot of jibberish. Let's look at a few ways to make this process easier on ourselves—ways to actually take action on those good ideas. We will talk through the ways in which Together Teachers

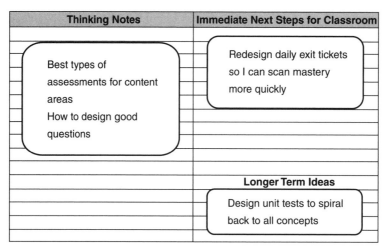

Figure 5.1 A Professional Development Note-Taking Sheet

take notes during PD workshops, graduate school courses, coaching meetings, and observational feedback sessions.

The Word template in Figure 5.1 is designed for you to take to a PD workshop or to graduate school courses and use to take specific notes related to a topic. Essentially you will create a "cover sheet" for all of the information, papers, and tools that come your way during the workshop or class so that you save yourself the time of having to dig through the materials later to find *that one thing* you wanted to be sure to remember! For example, if you were attending a PD workshop on strong student assessments and really wanted to make sure you did something with the knowledge you gathered, you could organize your notes under "Thoughts," "Immediate Next Steps for Classroom," and "Long-Term Ideas." In the note-taking sheet in Figure 5.1, the teacher noted that she wanted to adjust her exit tickets immediately, and in the long term she wanted to fix her unit tests. Let's look at a few more examples of various ways in which teachers take notes at PD sessions.

Let's start with Julie, an elementary special educator, who attended a professional workshop to learn how to help students with attention challenges. For note-taking she chose to use a simple legal pad but took the key step of drawing a line down the middle, essentially creating a handmade version of the Meeting/PD Note-Taking Sheet shown in Figure 5.1. Although Julie took lots of notes about student memory function and kids who struggle with organization, she got very disciplined about what she was going to do as a result of attending the workshop. You can see in Figure 5.2 that she noted the next classroom steps she would take immediately:

1. Research three different types of memory

2. Look up "Type to Learn" and "Typer's Deluxe"

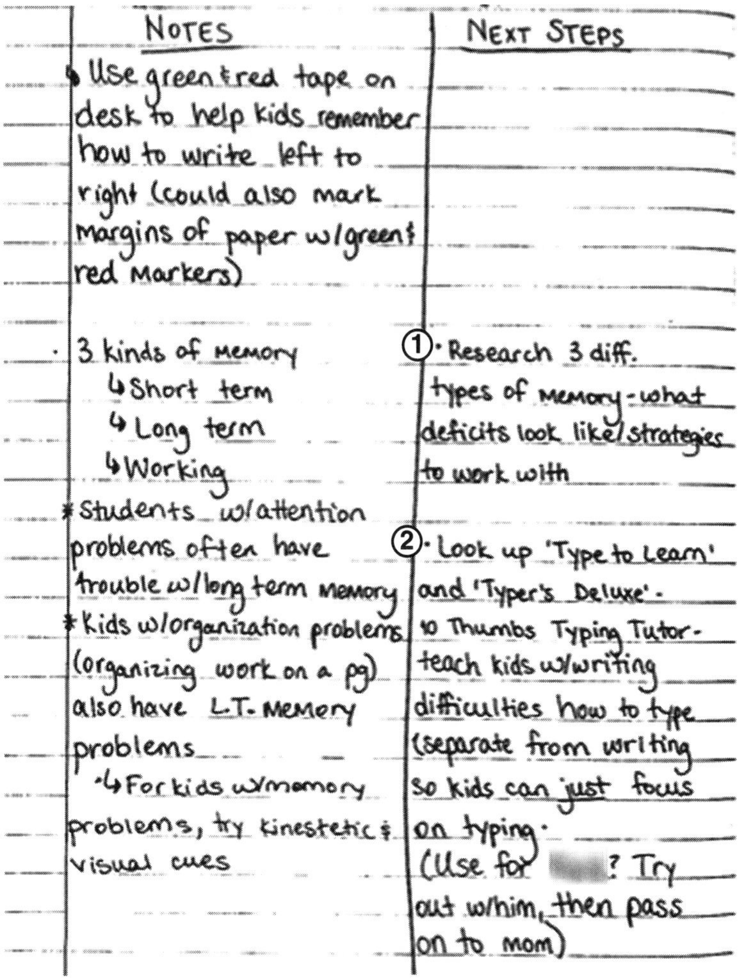

Figure 5.2 Julie's Professional Development Notes Separated by Thoughts and Actions

The trick here for Julie is ensuring that these great ideas get rolled up to her Comprehensive Calendar or Upcoming To-Do List so that she doesn't just end up with notebooks full of good intentions. She can then scoop out her next steps during her Weekly Round-Up.

Now let's review Jacqueline's example. Jacqueline is a first-year teacher who is attending a workshop on classroom management and culture systems. She keeps a few copies of the Meeting/PD Note-Taking Sheet in her Together Teacher System (a small binder) so that they are easily available wherever she goes. When the PD workshop started, Jacqueline took out a Meeting/PD Note-Taking Sheet and began taking notes on it. She took notes about everything from "procedures" to "cold calling" to "foundational tools" (see Figure 5.3). However, she knew she had to pace herself, so she wrote down some Immediate Next Steps for Classroom:

Professional Development Notes

Topic: _____ Date: _____ Presenter: _____

Thinking Notes	Immediate Next Steps for Classroom

- procedures
  - explicit directions
	① add
	  - cold calling procedure

- cold calling	② decide on year novel studies - books
- parent involvement	- resources

- resource exchange
  - MTLD group
  - learning teams
	- Mr ▓▓▓▓▓
	
	- VBG → 12pm Sunday

- Sponsor a teacher → external relations	**Longer Term Ideas** ③ - explicit directions - support from LTL

- foundational tools
  - VBG - 8/21
  - Summative 8/21
  - Unit plan 8/24
  - Unit assessment 8/24
  - Unit tracker 8/25	

	Questions - 7th grade novels ④ - 6th v. 7th curriculum

Figure 5.3 Jacqueline's PD Note-Taking Sheet

1. "Add cold calling procedure"

2. "Decide on year novel studies"

She also noted both Longer Term Ideas and Questions to deal with later:

3. "Explicit directions"

4. "6th v. 7th curriculum"

By categorizing and organizing her thinking and next steps, Jacqueline is better equipped to actually implement the knowledge she gathered in her PD sessions.

Whether you take notes on a legal pad with a clear line drawn down the middle as Julie did, use a categorized template as Jacqueline did, or take notes directly on your laptop or iPad (in which case similar categorization ideas should be used), the overall point is that we all need to do more than scribble the presenter's ideas in the margins of handouts or draw stars around ideas we particularly like. When we reenter our classrooms, we won't have any time to revisit our scribbling!

Storing Your Professional Development Notes

This is where it gets tricky. It can be extremely easy to get buried under notebooks to which we may never return. But imagine the happiness you will feel when you are wracking your brain to figure out the best way to teach that science concept, and then you remember: "Ah ha! I went to that amazing weeklong hands-on science seminar last year! Let me open my binder that has those resources in it!" You will have saved yourself time—and likely gotten some great lesson ideas.

You have a few options for effectively storing your PD workshop and graduate school resources.

Simple method: Create binders ordered by topic or content area, hole-punch all materials and handouts, and put your Meeting/PD Note-Taking Sheet on top of all the materials. Jacqueline, for example, after transferring her Immediate Classroom Next Steps to her Upcoming To-Do List or Weekly Worksheet, would take all of the materials she received in the classroom management workshop, put her Meeting/PD Note-Taking Sheet on top of them, and put all of it into a binder. Store these binders near where you do your lesson planning. (We discuss this method further in the Teacher Workspace section of Chapter Twelve.)

Complex method: Scan all materials from the workshop or course and store them electronically with your other lesson planning resources, arranged by topic. Jacqueline, for example, would scan each item received in her classroom management workshop into a folder on her computer and name the documents so that she could easily recall them. She might want to call the folder "Classroom Management 201108" and put it in another electronic folder titled "Classroom Management." By putting the date in this order—201108— her materials will sort chronologically on her computer, which will be helpful over a long career of teaching. Jacqueline would include her Meeting/PD Notes in the scanned documents.

Reflection Questions:

Where will you take notes and record next steps from PD workshops?
Where will you file the materials received at the workshops?

Taking Individual Development Notes

As teachers, most of us hopefully are getting frequent and high-quality feedback on our lesson design and execution. Unfortunately, most of this feedback happens during brief sit-downs while on lunch duty, or quickly as we are racing out the door. Then we lose the ability to follow up on the rich feedback we receive from peers or supervisors. To maximize our learning, it helps to keep a running set of notes about our own learning and development.

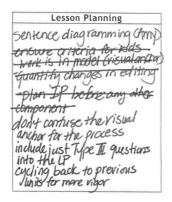

Figure 5.4 Nilda's Individual Development Instructional Feedback Thought Catcher

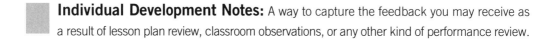 **Individual Development Notes:** A way to capture the feedback you may receive as a result of lesson plan review, classroom observations, or any other kind of performance review.

Many Together Teachers keep all of the feedback they receive in one location so that they can easily refer to it in the future. Let's look at how Nilda captures her lesson feedback (see Figure 5.4).

When Nilda has a lesson observation debriefing with her instructional coach, she takes a Meeting/PD Note-Taking Sheet out of her Together Teacher System and records all of her notes on it. When her handwritten Meeting/PD Note-Taking Sheet is filled with her own learning and development notes, she transfers the content to a document in Microsoft Word, discussed in further detail in the next section.

Storing Your Individual Development Notes

There are a few ways to approach storing your individual development notes. Many Together Teachers type notes directly into a Meeting/PD Notes template or into a cumulative document. Nilda writes her personal development notes on paper during a coaching session. Then, during her Weekly Round-Up, she types them into a cumulative Word document and throws the handwritten notes away. These are the best ways to ensure that you have an ongoing professional record of what is working and what could be better in your classroom.

 Reflection Questions:

Where will you take notes and record next steps from individual development feedback?

Where will you store the individual development notes for future reference?

What Was I Supposed to Do? Taking Clear Meeting Notes

Another place we teachers often take notes is in staff, grade-level, or department meetings at school. It is also at such meetings that a lot of short- and long-term to-dos emerge. However, all too often we ourselves emerge from staff meetings thinking something to the effect of "That was a great discussion, but what will really happen next?" Or we leave a parent meeting unclear about what everyone agreed to make happen. However, we can make meetings better and stronger by having great systems to ensure that we follow through on our great ideas. Let's look at a few ways to do this using various methods to capture notes.

Many teachers use the template shown in Figure 5.5 when taking notes at staff meetings, department or grade-level meetings, or parent meetings. The template is designed for putting your "thinking" notes ("Thoughts") on the left and your actual to-dos ("Next Steps") on the right. This recording process at least saves you the time it would take to scan through a notebook to figure out what you need to do!

Let's say you are taking notes during a staff meeting where your principal is reviewing the procedures for Back-to-School Night. Likely you are taking a lot of notes, but what I suggest you do is separate those notes into *Thoughts* and *Next Steps* so that you can easily refer back to them later in your Weekly Round-Up. In the example presented in Figure 5.5, when the teacher returns to his notes he can very easily scan for *exactly* what he has to do, which in this case is to create a PowerPoint presentation for the parents of his students.

Now let's look at two examples from Kate's and Sue's notes from staff meetings at their respective schools (see Figures 5.6 and 5.7).

Kate was in a staff meeting about grading interim assessments and, as a first-year teacher, she was quickly taking notes in her Together Teacher System. She works in a school where laptops are not used in group meetings, so she took handwritten notes. As she was recording her thoughts, she was careful also to capture her next steps, such as "write model responses."

Meeting Notes

Meeting Topic: _____ Date: _____ Participants: _____

Thoughts	Next Steps
-Back to school night coming -Parents joining on rotation schedule -Whole school presentation first	Create PowerPoint for classroom presentation to parents

Figure 5.5 A Note-Taking Sheet for Meetings

Meeting Notes
Meeting Topic: Grading LAs Date: _____ Participants: _____

Thoughts	Next Steps
• figure out place for error analysis	- figure out place for error analysis
• fill in all bubbles/use rubric	- Write model responses
	- find proposed passage for extended responses

Figure 5.6 Excerpt of Kate's Meetings Notes from a Staff Meeting

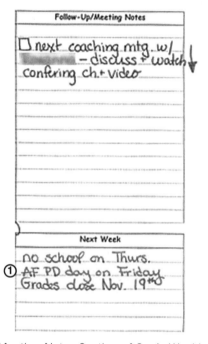

Figure 5.7 Excerpt from the Meeting Notes Section of Sue's Weekly Worksheet

When Kate reviewed her Meeting/PD Notes during her Weekly Round-Up, she could decide when she wanted to complete these to-dos.

Sue, a middle school English Language Arts teacher with fifteen years of experience, takes a superefficient shortcut with her Meeting/PD Notes. She skips a template entirely and includes her Next Steps into her Weekly or Daily Worksheet (covered in Chapter Six)! This method works if you really don't have any thinking notes or any notes you need to share with others. If you were to look at the Next Week section of Sue's Weekly Worksheet (item 1 in Figure 5.7) you would see how efficient she is:

- Sue notes when the next Achievement First's (AF) Professional Development Day is and when grades close.

During her Weekly Round-Up she will simply transfer that information right to where it belongs: in her Comprehensive Calendar as an FYI information date and as a due date.

Reflection Questions:

Where will you take notes and record next steps from meetings?

Storing Your Meeting Notes

Assuming that you have pulled out the to-dos, I recommend throwing away your handwritten Meeting/PD Notes (unless you need to maintain them for record-keeping purposes, particularly notes from parent meetings or from any student situations you are required to document). If you cannot *bear* to part with your Meeting/PD Notes, you have two options:

- Throw them into a manila folder labeled "Meeting/PD Notes XY Year" and just put them in your file cabinet. Of course, if you have a ton of meeting notes, you can create separate files for parent meetings, staff meetings, department meetings, and so on.
- Scan them, label by date and topic, and keep them as electronic files on your computer.

Reflection Question:

How will you store your meeting notes, from large staff meetings, one-on-one meetings, and small-group meetings?

Now let's summarize what happens to your Meeting/PD Notes, whether you choose to use a specific template in your Together Teacher System, to use a notebook, or to take all your notes electronically. The flow chart in Figure 5.8 summarizes the process of how to take and then refer to your notes.

PICK YOUR TOOL: WHERE WILL YOU KEEP YOUR NOTES?

You can keep your Meeting/PD Notes in a number of different locations. Let's review the various options and what works and doesn't work about each of them. As you review the options, consider whether you prefer to handwrite or type (probably depends on how fast you are!), how often you are online, and what feels more comfortable to you.

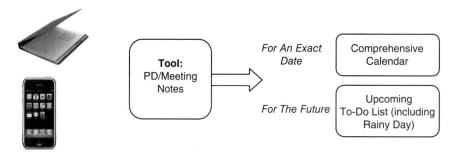

Figure 5.8 How to Get Your Meeting/PD Notes into Your Together Teacher System

Paper Tools

Most teachers prefer to have a hard copy in their Together Teacher System so they can jot down thoughts throughout the day, during a staff meeting, or when walking down the hall. If you keep multiple copies of a note-taking template in your Together Teacher System, they are available to you at all times. When a sheet has been used and all relevant information has been dealt with, you simply throw the sheet away! Even if you tend toward the electronic side, it is helpful to have a paper Meeting/PD Notes option available, because it is occasionally cumbersome or inappropriate to pull out your electronic device in a staff meeting or professional development workshop.

Electronic and Web-Based Options

For the more electronically inclined among us there are a few other ways you can maintain your Meeting/PD Notes. Here are the options I have seen teachers like best:

- Microsoft OneNote (available in most Microsoft Office Professional suites)
- Evernote (http://www.evernote.com)

Hybrid Options

Some teachers like to use the hard-copy version of a template to capture their notes by hand during the day, and then rewrite them into an electronic file, such as in Microsoft Word, when they are in front of their computer. This practice requires diligent weekly updating during your Weekly Round-Up.

Reflection Question:

Which tool(s) will you use to keep your Meeting/PD Notes?

MAKING THE MOST OF SMALL-GROUP MEETINGS

Most likely you meet regularly with your department, content area, or some other kind of working group. These meetings can quickly take a downhill turn because people tend to plan less for meetings with smaller groups. However, these meetings are often the lifeblood of the school and they are really an opportunity to make things happen. The template shown in Figure 5.9 is for group meetings in which follow-up steps are established for multiple people (rather than for just you who are recording your own to-dos!).

We want to be sure that our departments, grade levels, and committees are having strong meetings with consistent and transparent follow-through. For example, if the third-grade team were in a meeting focused on an upcoming field trip, one person would be appointed the Notetaker. He or she would either record all of the next steps on the meeting notes template or cut and paste the table from the template into an e-mail and type the meeting notes directly into it. Immediately after the meeting, the Notetaker would send all the notes to everyone on the team, who would then revisit them at the next meeting. The beauty of this process is that if you receive next steps from a colleague in this format, it is very easy to quickly transfer them right onto your Comprehensive Calendar or Upcoming To-Do List.

Let's look at an example of how a Together Teacher and grade-level lead, Stephanie, planned, led, and followed through on a grade-level meeting to prepare the third-grade students for Funtastic Fridays (a positive rewards system at her school) (see Figure 5.10).

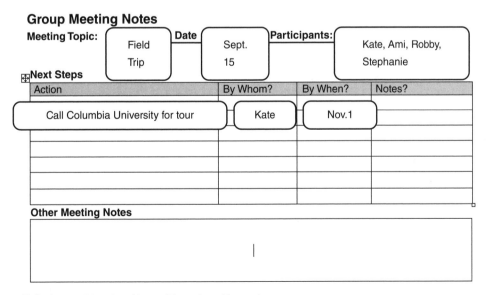

Figure 5.9 Group Meeting Notes Template Example

<table>
<tr><td colspan="4">Wednesday's Morning Outcomes
◊ Team Exceed will understand the Funtastic Fridays (FF) timeline and have action steps to be completed before our first Funtastic Friday
◊ Team Exceed will divide and conquer all materials needed for Week One.</td></tr>
<tr><th>Time</th><th>Topic</th><th>Owner</th><th>Outcome</th></tr>
<tr><td>8:00-8:05</td><td>Warmer- If you could have any super power what would it be?</td><td>Steph</td><td>get to know each other better. ☺</td></tr>
<tr><td>8:05-8:10</td><td>Agenda/AIMs</td><td>Steph</td><td>understand the outcomes for today.</td></tr>
<tr><td>8:10-8:30</td><td>FUNtastic Friday ☺
• What's this?
• Timeline
• LP for Fri. Aug. 26</td><td>Steph</td><td>understand the FF timeline and have action steps completed before our 1st FF.</td></tr>
<tr><td>8:30-9:00</td><td>Days 2-5 Materials Check-in
• Owners
• Create/Fill out intern request forms</td><td>All</td><td>review days 2-5 to see if there are any additional materials that need to be made.</td></tr>
</table>

Figure 5.10 Wednesday's Morning Outcomes

In this example, Stephanie set the stage for a very productive team meeting (and you can too, using the Group Meeting Notes template on the accompanying CD). Let's break down what Stephanie did to prepare.

Set outcomes. She clearly set the goals of the meeting by defining the outcomes. It is very clear to participants that they will leave with a plan for Funtastic Fridays and will know all they need to prepare for Week One.

Aligned the topics and time to the outcomes. Stephanie then created the meeting topics and allocated time to each topic.

Assigned a facilitator. To keep meetings moving, someone has to be in charge! Although Stephanie often has other members of the team facilitate, in this case she led most of the meeting herself.

Distributed agenda in advance. Stephanie e-mailed this agenda to the third-grade team in advance of the meeting so that they all knew what to expect and how to prepare.

During the meeting Stephanie took notes on what the team agreed to directly on her laptop. Immediately following the meeting she e-mailed the next steps to everyone so that it was very clear what was happening moving ahead. Let's keep following this meeting by reviewing the next steps that were sent out (Table 5.1).

Stephanie will start the next grade-level meeting by reviewing the status of the next steps she distributed. This will ensure that there is accountability for the entire grade team, and clarity on who is doing what. Although this level of preparation and follow-up takes an extra ten to fifteen minutes before and after the meeting, the time saved by having a very focused and productive meeting, by consistently explaining behavior expectations and rewards to

Table 5.1 Follow-Up Notes from a Grade-Level Meeting

Action	By Whom?	By When?	Notes
Create a PowerPoint presentation for the introduction of Funtastic Fridays and distribute it to the team.	Heath	Monday, August 21	
Introduce Funtastic Fridays to the kids and get them all pumped up.	All grade-team members	Friday, August 26	
Post the number of days until Funtastic Fridays in the grade's hall.	Alex	Thursday, August 25	
Monitor and track student behavior weekly against criteria.	All grade-team members	Through October 7 (first Funtastic Friday)	

students, and by clearly dividing up the work will pay off later when the team is not scrambling to create their own behavior system.

Describing her approach to meetings, Stephanie said, "I prepare so much because the grade-level meeting goes astray if I do not. We wouldn't end up getting through everything and would be unable to create solid, clear outcomes. It's also important to prepare so that the team feels it is worth their while. I need a plan for how I want each topic discussed to look. For example, am I giving them think time? Do I need everyone's voice? I also spend time doing a detailed follow-up because it just solidifies whatever plan the team came up with and reduces any confusion."

GET STARTED: NEXT STEPS

- Select the tool that best fits with your working style for Meeting/PD Notes. You might need different methods for PD, one on one, small group and large group meetings.
  - Paper
    - Notebook
    - Templates available on accompanying CD
  - Electronic/Web-based
    - Evernote
    - Microsoft OneNote
- Ensure you have a way to always carry your Meeting/PD Notes, and that you have enough copies available.

- Record Meeting/PD Notes during PD and meetings, and clearly denote short- and long-term action steps.

- Review Meeting/PD Notes during Weekly Round-Up.

- Determine how you will store your Meeting/PD Notes. (You may use different systems for Meeting Notes and PD Notes.)

PART 3

Narrow Your View

CHAPTER 6

A Week's Worth of Readiness: How to Look Ahead

Learning Objectives

- Extract your To-Dos for *this week* from your Comprehensive Calendar Upcoming To-Do List, Thought Catchers, and Meeting/PD Notes.

- Maximize a week and a day by plotting your time and to-dos in advance.

- Utilize the small bits of free time you have during the teaching day to advance your weekly and daily plan.

We have made it through the four tools that all Together Teachers need! It is *finally* time to make that list we all crave—the list for this week *only*. We will do this by carefully sorting through all of our tools and scooping out what we need to do *this week only*. This chapter contains a way to take your Comprehensive Calendar, Upcoming To-Do List, Thought Catchers, and Meeting/PD Notes and scoop out the work for this week. This process will create a clear view of your week or day that allows you to plan ahead, get stuff done, and capture incoming work. This is really where it all comes together. We are going to discuss how to take your appointments, teaching time, and meetings, *plus* your to-dos and put them in one place: on your fancy-schmancy list for—you guessed it—this week only! We will create a Weekly or Daily Worksheet, which are key tools we will use as Together Teachers.

 Reflection Question:

How do you decide what to do with your preparation period(s)?

THE TOTE BAG CALLS TO YOU FROM THE CORNER OF THE ROOM

It's 4:30 PM on a Friday afternoon. Your kids have left the building and your fellow teachers are pressuring you to join them at a much-needed happy hour. You look at the bottomless pile of papers to grade and the incomplete lesson plans and think: *I'm exhausted, but there's no way I'm going to make progress on this stuff in an hour.* So you shove everything into your tote bag and pray you will get to it all on Sunday.

Now let's return to the scene of what typically happens to most of us. Sunday comes around and by the time you eat breakfast, go to the gym or spend time with your family (or both), do laundry, and grocery shop, it is past 3:00 PM. The tote bag taunts you from the corner of the living room. Eventually you open it and try to comb through its contents. You have no idea where to begin. It takes an hour just to sort everything into piles—papers to grade, scraps of paper with scribbled notes on them, graded papers that need to be recorded in your grade book, agendas from staff meetings with notes scrawled across the page, and graphic organizers to copy for next week's lesson plans. By the time you have sorted through everything, it's 5:30 PM. By the looks of it you still have about five more hours of work left and your alarm will go off at 5:15 AM tomorrow. For most teachers this is the weekly challenge: How on Earth do I get it all done?

This is not because you are doing anything wrong, but for most of us teachers our preparation periods allow us to take a breather, deal with an unexpected kid situation, or catch up on e-mail. Given that prep periods are often the *only* bit of discretionary time within our professional day, it is a constant challenge to determine how to use it wisely. However, I would encourage all of us to think about that little chunk of time as an opportunity to get more done at school—so you can take less work home! Now it is time to get more specific and talk about how to prepare for a week.

I don't want you constantly looking through all of these tools throughout the week: too much on there, too overwhelming, not efficient. To get through a busy teaching week, we must put on blinders and narrow our view. Now that we know where we need to be and when and what we have to do with both hard and soft deadlines, we need to fit carefully what we can into the 168 hours available to us to use in any given week.

A CLOSER LOOK: WHAT IS A WEEKLY OR DAILY WORKSHEET?

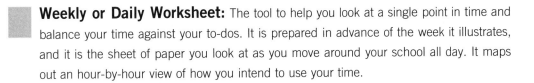

Weekly or Daily Worksheet: The tool to help you look at a single point in time and balance your time against your to-dos. It is prepared in advance of the week it illustrates, and it is the sheet of paper you look at as you move around your school all day. It maps out an hour-by-hour view of how you intend to use your time.

There are probably lots of things you instinctively do to get ready for a week of teaching. You plan lessons, make photocopies, create charts, make phone calls, and so on. Preparing your Weekly or Daily Worksheet is not about *doing* the work; it is about *defining* the work and planning your week so that you can maximize your time and *make the best choices* to move things ahead. For *most* teachers, this task requires a *highly* portable and constantly reviewed tool that gives a view of your time rather than of your to-dos.

The Process Matters More Than the Product

What I want to be clear about here is this: the *process* matters more than the product. Depending on whether you are biased toward paper products or toward electronic systems, your output may look very different. The point is that I want you to go through the same thinking process each week. Your Weekly or Daily Worksheet should allow you to do the following:

- *Plan* the week or day in advance by mapping out how you will spend your time.
- *Look* ahead at what is coming and map backward toward deadlines.
- *Do* the work by ensuring it is clearly organized.
- *Capture* incoming to-dos and thoughts.

Let's start by examining how the various tools used for this purpose are set up.

The template in Figure 6.1 is designed to give you a full view of your work each week—your time mapped against your to-dos. Let's walk through the specific pieces of this template.

Sections of a Weekly Worksheet

Although you can title the sections of the worksheet with whatever categories you would like, I encourage you to start with a basic template that works for many teachers (available on the accompanying CD). It contains the following sections:

Priorities. This is where you fill in the priorities for the week for both work and home. For example, if improving your classroom culture is important for this week, that priority will land in this section. If hosting a bachelor party for a close friend is important personally, you will note this here too. These are high-level priorities, not specific to-dos (at this time). The best way to come up with your priorities is to review the overall goals for your classroom for the year and simply close your eyes and ask yourself, "What could I do that would have the *highest* level of impact on me both personally and professionally?" You will later write specific to-dos associated with your priorities. For example, if a classroom priority was student culture, one action might be, "Create a Student of the Week recognition system and criteria." My hope is that your time and to-dos will be aligned with these priorities, and you can perform your own check later when you tailor this template to your own needs.

Schedule. This is where you write any appointments and meetings for the week. You do this by checking your Comprehensive Calendar to see what you have recorded and scoop that into your Weekly Worksheet. Your staff meetings, coaching meetings, and dentist

_____ 's Weekly Worksheet, Week of _____

PRIORITIES

Classroom	School	Personal

SHAPE OF THE WEEK

	M	T	W	R	F	Weekend
APPTS						
DEADLINES						

Lessons to Prep	E-mails / Calls	Meeting Notes

Errands/Home/Personal	Copies to Make	Next Week

Figure 6.1 A Blank Weekly Worksheet

appointments will land here as well. It is also wise to note your discretionary time, such as before school, after school, and preparation periods, and create a plan for how you will spend that time. Some teachers prefer to make the schedule take up the entire Weekly Worksheet so they have more room to write in how they want to spend their preparation periods. You can view several variations on the accompanying CD.

Deadlines. Again, these are pulled from your Comprehensive Calendar. Your deadlines are the things that *must* be completed on a particular day. This could include standard due dates, such as lesson plans each Thursday, and one-off due dates, such as when progress reports are due. This is also where you will record items that come up for that *day*, such as a parent phone call that you must return on the same day, or a professional development resource that you promised to bring from home for your co-teacher.

Upcoming To-Dos. After filling in the top portion of the worksheet with your time and to-dos for the week, it is time to revisit that Upcoming To-Do List and scoop out some of the other work that has to get done that week and figure out which day has the most time. If it is something that *must* get done, I would give it a proposed time in the Schedule section.

Bottom Sections. This is where other to-dos are filled ins, such as personal stuff, meeting notes, and incoming work for the following week.

Most likely you will start each week with some items pre-populating your Weekly Worksheet, and then collect additional to-dos and meetings along the way. You will record them with a pen in the appropriate section of your Together Teacher System as you move around your school, and you will review the items regularly as part of your Weekly Round-Up.

TOGETHER TEACHERS' WEEKLY WORKSHEETS

Now that we have reviewed the templates and tools in their blank form, it's time to see them in action. In this section you will have a chance to see exactly how other Together Teachers plan for a week to really maximize every moment. You will notice that each teacher has created his or her own personalized template from the model shown in Figure 6.2—which is exactly what I encourage you to do! As you review the examples, please consider the following questions:

- Are they totally paper, hybrid, or electronic systems?
- What is typed and what is handwritten?
- What sections have the teachers created to customize the template for themselves?
- What level of detail do they use?

Weekly Worksheet - Week Of: January 16 - January 22

"Start by doing what's necessary; then what is possible; and suddenly you're doing the impossible."

	S 16	M 17	T 18	W 19	R 20	F 21	S 22
Appointments / Meetings		o MLK Day do o Mom Sick	o Marilyn Out o Candice In	✓ Joncho's B-day ✓ Performing Arts Workshop @ 10am • Candice In	6pm Academy of Sciences ①	5pm De Young Museum ① 2pm-4pm Teacher Network	Kait's B-day Weekend for me.
Deadlines	☐	☑ Jog (20) ⑤	☐ Lesson Plans (Ne)	☑ Teacher Network ☐ LP to (Ne) ② ☑ Workout (30)	☑ LP to (Ne)	☑ Lesson Plans (Isabel)	☐

	Work		Personal		Calls-Emails-Notes
☐	1/24	Phone Interview @ 5pm 1/24 G's	☑ 1/18	Planning visit back home to Bako	☑ 1/18	CM's about where they are with the year
☑	1/16	Sponsor a Teacher Letter [1/18]	☑ 1/18	Looking up weekend retreat for men.	☒	Mom:
☐	1/29	TFA ELA Event Candice training ③	☑ 1/19	Joncho's Birthday (facebook)	☒	"Dead Copy" weekly worksheet
☐		12pm - 3:30pm @ LPS · Hayward	☐		☒ 1/20	"Action Planner" document and
☐		28000 Calaroga Ave	☐			"Dead Copy" as well
☐		Hayward, CA 94545	☐		☑ 1/18	Andy mens retreat
☐	1/22	Susan Dambroff meeting for Gran	☐		☑ 1/19	Teacher Network Email
☑	1/19	Lesson Plans for Ne [1/19]	☐		☐	
☐			☐		☐	
☐			☐		☐	

	Me		Reading			Next Week
☐	Jogging (20) M	☐	Purpose Driven Life ④	S M T W R F S	☐	Field Trip to Ocean View Library ⑥
☐	Workout (30) W	☐	Bible	S M T W R F S	☐	TFA ELA event
☐		☐	Not the Problem	S M T W R F S	☐	Volunteering at Reality SF
☐		☐	Reading Games for Young Children	S M T W R F S	☐	Susan Meeting
☐		☐		S M T W R F S	☐	Phone Interview

Week of: Jan 16 - 22

Figure 6.2 Gilbert's Weekly Worksheet: A Paper Tool Reflecting an Entire Week

Gilbert's Weekly Worksheet

Let's start with Gilbert's example (Figure 6.2). Gilbert is a pre-K teacher with three years of teaching experience and a lot of outside interests. He is a hybrid paper-electronic organizer. He uses Google for his Comprehensive Calendar, keeps a paper Upcoming To-Do List, and a paper Weekly Worksheet.

As you can see, Gilbert has gotten incredibly intentional with how he uses his time as a teacher.

Top Section

1. **Appointments and meetings.** Gilbert has marked anything out of the ordinary on his Comprehensive Calendar and scooped it into his Weekly Worksheet. You can see where he has noted a teacher's birthday and a Friday night museum visit. He keeps all of his events and meetings in the calendar section.

2. **Deadlines.** Gilbert has also taken his hard deadlines from his Comprehensive Calendar and transferred them to the relevant days on the worksheet. For example, he has noted that his "lesson plans are due to Ni" on Thursday.

Bottom Section

3. **Work.** Gilbert has an upcoming hard deadline to complete a training on January 29. Because he has looked ahead on his Comprehensive Calendar during his Weekly Round-Up, he knows he cannot wait until January 29 to start writing this training, so he has blocked time this week to get a head start on the work. Gilbert has also taken all of his work and tentatively assigned it a due date.

4. **Reading.** Gilbert is a big reader, and he wants to make sure he is current and consistent in his reading practices. As you can see, he created a list of daily readings he tries to do and he has circled the days he has accomplished this reading from the Bible or *The Purpose Driven Life*.

5. **Personal time.** You can see that Gilbert has also blocked personal time on Monday and Wednesday to work out and jog. It may feel funny to block "personal time," but on the flip side, it can feel amazing to know that you have a block of time that is yours to do with whatever you wish—without that nagging feeling that you *should* be doing school work. This is where Gilbert's *ideal* week aligns with his very practical version of the *real* week.

6. **Next week.** This is an invaluable category because this is how Gilbert manages to look ahead. As items come up during the week, Gilbert jots them down here so he can allocate

time to them the next week. For example, he planned a field trip to the Ocean View Library for his students and he didn't want to be taken by surprise so he is keeping it on his radar throughout the week.

Now, picture how Gilbert can maximize his prep period by going through this process. He has an incredible level of intentionality about how he enters a week and a day, he no longer stresses that he may have forgotten a key item, and he can see his whole world in one place. Let's look at another example.

Reflection Question:

What is important to you personally each week?

Sue's Weekly Worksheet

Let's see how Sue, an English language arts teacher with fifteen years of experience, uses this tool to help her manage the demands of teaching and raising a family. Sue is exclusively paper-based in her Together Teacher System, so she has a paper monthly Comprehensive Calendar, a paper Upcoming To-Do List, paper Thought Catchers, and paper Meeting Notes.

You can see what is most important to Sue. Let's walk through her Weekly Worksheet (Figure 6.3) piece by piece.

1. **Priorities.** Sue has placed a high priority on sixth-grade classroom culture and on taking good care of her family.

2. **Schedule.** She has carefully baked her hard commitments (both externally and internally imposed!) into the calendar portion of the Weekly Worksheet, so her time is aligned with her priorities. Also typed into her Weekly Worksheet are times for what Sue values, such as taking care of her family. Hence the to-dos of meeting her son at the bus stop and meeting with Rosie for co-coaching are permanently part of her weeks.

3. **Catching additional to-dos for the week.** Other stuff is recorded as it comes up in meetings and through e-mail. For example, "E-mail why I love AF ELA to team recruit" came up during the week, so Sue jotted it down right in the moment as she was going through requests in her e-mail in-box.

4. **Upcoming items.** Like Gilbert, Sue also notes upcoming work, such as "Grades due Nov. 19th," and she will record this in her Comprehensive Calendar when she does her Weekly Round-Up.

Sue's Weekly Worksheet, Week of <u>Nov. 1 – 7</u>

PRIORITIES

Classroom	School	Personal
Grade papers and put into grade book!	6th grade culture…drink the Kool Aid ①	Take good care of ▩ and ▩ ☺ ①
		Crossfit 2 or 3 X every week

SHAPE OF THE WEEK

	M 1	T 2	gym! W 3	R 4	gym! F 5	Weekend
Schedule		election day ▩ @ school w/ mom —Meet w/ ▩ Bl. 3—	Meet w/ Rosie Bl. 4 for co-coaching ②	CT Reading Assoc. Conf. Observe ▩ Bl. 3 Debrief ▩ Bl. 4	F+P Friday	Sat: 6 ▩ Judo @9:45 Brkfst. w/ the ladies @ 9:00
②	▩ off bus @ 3:45	▩ theatre class @ 3:45	▩ data debrief @ 4:00 Stay late and catch-up make lesson plans for Thurs!	Stay late and catch-up		Sun: 7 Church 9:30-11:30 Day w/ ▩ @ 9:00 Boston?

WORK

☐ transfer grades to I.C.
☑ find How's it Going
☐ put LTP on B.L.
☑ begin planning V.V. unit
☐ grade literary essays
☐ admin. survey

E-mails / Calls

☑ Friday - call ▩ mom to schedule mtg.
☑ Flex ▩ to ▩ by Thurs. → Friday
☑ call parents of all F+P tested kids
☐ email why I love AF ELA to team recruit by Friday ③

☐ log calls, emails, etc. into I.C. (▩)

Follow-Up/Meeting Notes

☐ next coaching mtg. w/ ▩ – discuss + watch confering ch.+ video

Errands/Home/Personal

Visit/call ▩ ✓
call ▩ ✓

☐ get flu shot

Glows / Grows

Next Week

no school on Thurs.
AF PD day on Friday
Grades close Nov. 19th ④

Figure 6.3 Sue's Weekly Worksheet: A Paper-Based Plan That Includes Time for School and Family

What is so thoughtful about Sue's planning is her deliberate approach to what choices she makes throughout her week. She has prioritized her son's after-school activities on two days, and she knows she will have to stay later at school to "catch up" on two others. This decision illustrates an incredible level of intentionality. Instead of worrying about whether she will fall behind in work because of the days she accommodates her son's after-school activities, Sue has anticipated the extra work she needs to accomplish and has blocked time to get it done. Sue's method ensures that she has focused on what is most important to her at any given time, and that she is completing the right tasks throughout her week. The peace of mind that accompanies this approach allows Sue to be more present with her students and her family, and alleviates a tremendous amount of stress that she'd otherwise encounter at home and at work.

Reflection Question:

Are there nights or mornings that you could allocate to get the bigger work completed?

Anna's Weekly Worksheet

Let's look at another example (Figure 6.4). You have met Anna already. She uses a paper Comprehensive Calendar, paper Thought Catchers, and electronic Meeting/PD Notes kept in Microsoft OneNote.

1. **Schedule.** Similar to Sue and Gilbert, Anna begins her week with all of her known commitments already typed onto the page. She then handwrites in additional details and appointments as they arise. She creates a detailed breakdown of each day before her week has begun, and plugs in how to use her discretionary time.

   What I love about Anna's example is that she has intentionally blocked time in her ideal week for students who need additional love and support. She simply plugs in the names of the students who need extra attention so she can be mindful of meeting with each of them. This time reflects a priority of Anna's that is key to her role in the school and reinforces her belief that students come first.

2. **Deadlines.** After deliberately outlining her appointments in the top half of her Weekly Worksheet, Anna articulates her work in its bottom portion. As you can see, Anna is training for a marathon during this week and has carefully mapped out her running schedule on her worksheet, as well as her strength training and speed work. She has also inserted her routine work, such as collecting tardies and absences, so that she does not fail to record this critical information; and she has left room on her worksheet to capture to-dos as they arise throughout the school day.

	Monday 25	Tuesday 26	Wednesday 27	Thursday 28	Friday 29	Sat 30 Sun
①	7:15-7:30 Arrival	6:45-7:10 Coach A/S 7:15-7:30 Arrival	7:15-7:30 Arrival	7:15-7:30 Arrival	7:15-7:30 Arrival	SATURDAY
	7:30 Tardies	7:30 Tardies	7:30 Absences	7:30 Absences	7:30 Morning Circle Prep.	9:00 Prospect 18 miles
	8:00-9:10 Attendance 9:15-10:05 GR	8:00-9:10 Attendance 9:15-10:05 GR	8:00-9:10 Attendance 9:15-10:05 GR	8:00-9:10 Attendance 9:15-10:05 GR	8:00-9:10 Attendance 9:15-10:05 GR	
	10:05 Math LP -finish-	10:05 ▓▓-GR	10:05 ▓▓-GR check GR LPs	10:05 JK-DI	10:55 Lunch w/ 1st Gr. MATH	5:00 Teacher U Graduation
	11:15-11:35 Recess	11:15-11:35 Recess	11:15-11:35 Recess	11:15-11:35 Recess	11:55 ▓▓▓▓▓	9:00 Halloween
	11:35 Lunch	11:35 Lunch	11:35 Math w/ ▓▓	11:35 Lunch		
	12:00 Culture Blast	12:00 CB	12:00 Lunch	12:00 CB	12:45 Read Aloud	SUNDAY
	12:30 ▓▓, ▓▓	12:30 ▓▓, ▓▓	12:30 ▓▓, ▓▓	12:30 ▓▓, ▓▓	1:00 CB	
	1:00	1:00 ▓▓-Math	1:00 CB	1:00 ▓▓-math	2:30 PD	12:00 Rock Climb ▓▓
	1:50 Lunch	1:50 Lunch	1:50 Lunch	1:50 Lunch	MAKE-UP	
	2:30 Math	2:30 Math	2:30 Math	2:30 Math	▓▓▓	
	3:35 Issa/Ron-Math	3:35 ▓▓/Ron-Math	3:35 ▓▓/Ron-Math	3:35 ▓▓/Ron-Math	▓▓▓	
	4:00 Elijah P-Writing	4:00 ▓▓ P-Writing	4:00 ▓▓ P-Writing	4:00 ▓▓ P-Writing	▓▓▓	
	4:20-5:00 TLM SNACKS	4:30-5:30 GLM	4:20-5 Coaching Pod		▓▓▓	

② DEADLINES	SEND GIFT ☑		Send LPs ☑	★CALL MOM★ MOM'S B-DAY ☑		
			Permission Slip ☑	★★ ★	Call parent chaperones ☑	
	5 miles ☑	5 miles ☑ / weights ☑	8 miles ☑	5 miles ☑ / weights ☐	2 miles ☑	

	Lesson Plans		Materials to Prepare		Emails/Calls/Follow-Ups	
	Math ☑		Parent letter -Culture Night ☑		Ms. ▓▓ - reading ☑	
	MM ☑				Ms. ▓▓ - tardies ☑	
	GR ☑		Permission Slip ☑		Ms. ▓▓ - attendance ☑	
					Ms. ▓▓ - stay after ☑	
					▓▓ - Garden Guerillas ☑	
			Saturday ☑☑			
			-oreo truffles - dip/pepper			
			pumpkin bread - veggies			

	Errands/Home/Personal		People		MUST DO!	
			▓▓ - $		◉ ◉ ◉ Run	
					◉ ○ Weights	
			Thank You Notes- Dad		◉ Speedwork	
			Erica			
			Emily			
	Fresh Direct ☑		Coach			

Figure 6.4 Anna's Weekly Worksheet: A Paper Version of Time and To-Dos

Anna also remembered to send her Mom's birthday gift and call her on her birthday!

TOGETHER TEACHERS' DAILY WORKSHEETS: A DIFFERENT OPTION

Some teachers find it challenging to keep one week of their whole lives on one page, so they choose to split their Weekly Worksheet into five Daily Worksheets (one for each day), either by creating their own hard-copy version (a template is provided on the accompanying CD) or by printing out a daily view of their electronic calendar. Although most teachers prefer the Weekly Worksheet, a few prefer the extra level of detail and the additional room to write in the Daily Worksheets. This is *totally* fine; just don't do both a Weekly *and* a Daily Worksheet. That is overkill. Let's look at a paper template in Figure 6.5.

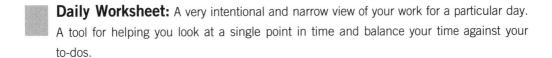

Daily Worksheet: A very intentional and narrow view of your work for a particular day. A tool for helping you look at a single point in time and balance your time against your to-dos.

Sections of the Daily Worksheet Template

- **Meetings/Appointments.** In the upper left-hand quadrant of the template there is a place to note your daily schedule. The hour-by-hour section allows you to note all of your meetings and appointments. You may mark your discretionary time, such as arrival in the morning, prep periods, and evening times, and determine what you will accomplish during these times.

- **Daily Priorities.** Review your deadlines at the top of your Comprehensive Calendar and assign time in the upper right-hand quadrant to accomplish them. These are the *most* important items to complete this day. You now have a view of your time relative to your to-dos. At this point many teachers actually assign a time to complete each to-do.

- **Quick Stuff: Two-Minute Tasks.** The bottom right-hand section usually starts the week empty and fills up with a lot of small to-dos that you catch on your walk down the hall, reading your e-mail, or checking your messages.

- **Captured Thoughts.** The bottom left-hand quadrant is where *everything* else from the day lands; it can capture any random idea that pops into your brain. The reason this section is deliberately different from the right-hand side of the paper is that we do not want to mix

Daily Four Square Planning Page

Date: _____

MEETINGS / APPOINTMENTS		DAILY PRIORITIES	
7:00 a.m.		Location	
:30			
8:00 a.m.			
: 30			
9:00 a.m.			
:30			
10:00			
:30			
11:00			
:30			
12:00			
:30			
1:00 p.m.			
:30			
2:00 p.m.			
:30			
3:00 p.m.			
:30			
4:00 p.m.			
:30			
5:00 p.m.			
:30			
6:00 p.m.			
:30			
Evening			

THOUGHT-CATCHER		TWO-MINUTE TASKS (TMTs)	
Where?	Action	Where?	Action

Figure 6.5 A Daily Worksheet Template

up our immediate to-dos with a lot of clutter. This section must be cleaned out during your Weekly Round-Up and the random items should get put back into their proper tool.

Sections of Electronic or Web-Based Daily Pages

You can also create Daily Worksheets electronically. The most common electronic calendars I have seen teachers use are Google, iCal, and Outlook. Regardless of your choice of program, almost all of the functionality is similar. New versions come out all the time, so I encourage you to experiment.

- **Meetings and Appointments.** This is where your meetings and appointments, and likely all of your teaching schedule, prep period, and so on, would be kept.
- **Deadlines.** These would already be entered at the top of your Comprehensive Calendar using the All-Day Appointment feature to bump it up to the top of the page. At this point I would recommend *also* assigning it a time to be completed, being careful to consider your energy levels, motivation, and chance of interruption.
- **Upcoming To-Dos.** This is where you would note other to-dos from your Upcoming To-Do List that you would like to accomplish. If you are using an accompanying to-do feature of Google or Outlook, there are ways to just see those side by side. If you choose to keep your to-dos in another system, such as Remember The Milk, then you will want to write them in the space that shows up when you print out the daily view.
- **Thought Catcher.** This section is where you would capture anything else that came up during the day that you needed to assign later to another location.

There are two cautions when you use Daily Worksheets:

- You must be careful to take a moment to step back and think about your biggest priorities, because the templates or electronic tools don't prompt that kind of thinking.
- If you use electronic tools, you should make sure you use a printable version that allows you to have room to capture incoming work.

Susan's Daily Worksheet

Susan, a middle school math teacher with five years of experience who is also a teacher coach, chooses to create five daily pages rather than a weekly page. She prefers the extra level of detail and the additional room to write. This is *totally* fine; just don't do both a Weekly *and* a Daily Worksheet.

Susan has carefully laid out her day with an incredible level of detail (Figure 6.6). She keeps five Daily Worksheets in her Together Teacher System (a binder with tabs for each section). Let's review what Susan did in her example.

Daily Four Square Planning Page　　　　　　　　Date: 12|3

MEETINGS / APPOINTMENTS		DAILY PRIORITIES	
7:00 a.m.	→ Thurs HW/PS – create	Location	
:30			
8:00 a.m.	→ Breakfast w/Brown	2²⁵	Observe MG
:30			
9:00 a.m.	→ Brown Math: IA#2, Pt 2	3¹⁵	Mtg O
:30			
10:00	→ Call Mr. ▮▮▮ / Thurs CW/HW/PS	Prep #¹: Thurs CW/HW/PS	
:30	↳ 5th grade snack – copies		
11:00 ①	→ Friday CW – copy	11am: • Fri CW/HW/ Test ②	
:30	Test – create	• IA2 Part 2	
12:00	→ Wash U Math: IA#2, Pt 2	• PGP	
:30			
1:00 p.m.	→ 5ᵗʰ lunch – Mult. Showdown		
:30	↳ SGI		
2:00 p.m.			
:30	Observe MG – PS (Brown)		
3:00 p.m.			
:30	→ Mtg O		
4:00 p.m.	→ 3⁵⁵ – Dismissal		
:30	⌐ leave w/ ▮▮▮		
5:00 p.m.	⌐ gym – 45 min		
:30	⌐		
6:00 p.m.			
:30	Dinner w/ ▮▮▮		
Evening			

THOUGHT-CATCHER		TWO-MINUTE TASKS (TMTs) ③	
Where?	Action	Where?	Action
	S.S. Gift ??		Call Mr. ▮▮▮
			Email Team 5 re: ▮▮▮
			Timeframe for Content Day?
		7-8 am	Pencil cases – ▮▮▮, ▮▮▮
		During IAs:	✓ Exit Tickets for Brown & Wash U

Figure 6.6 Susan's Daily Worksheet Giving a Detailed Overview of a Day

1. **Schedule:** Susan spelled out exactly what she needs to do during her prep period: "Friday CW [Classwork]—copy, Test—create." She has also named exactly when she is going to leave school, and made time to go to the gym and have dinner with a friend.

2. **Deadlines:** Susan spelled out exactly what she was going to accomplish during her preparation period, right down to the detail "Friday CW / HW [Homework]/ Test [creation]."

3. **Two-Minute Tasks:** Susan recorded quick calls and e-mails in this section. She will tackle this stuff when she has less energy.

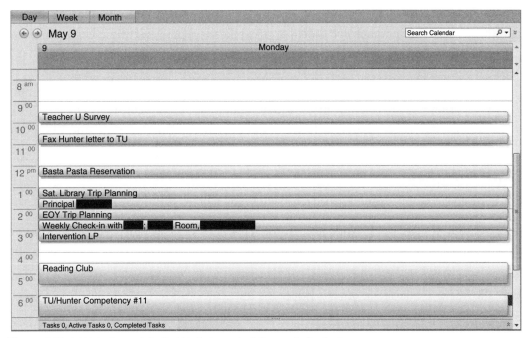

Figure 6.7 A Web-Based Daily Worksheet in Microsoft Outlook

As you can see in Figure 6.7, the process is similar whether you go with a paper or electronic calendar. (Those of you who keep electronic calendars may have more detail because it is easier to input.)

CHOOSE A PRODUCT THAT WORKS FOR YOU

Your Weekly or Daily Worksheet can follow an inordinate number of formats. Some teachers prefer to draft their worksheet in Microsoft Word (there are several templates on the accompanying CD), others prefer Excel. Other teachers prefer to print daily or weekly copies of their Google or Outlook calendars. If you do this, make sure you use the print view, which allows you to (1) always have it with you and (2) write on it during the day. Other teachers prefer to modify their commercial planners (such as Uncalendar, Moleskine, or others) to get them to accomplish the same goals. In this book's Recommended Resources for the Together Classroom section I share some opinions on commercial planners that I like best. Remember, the *process* matters more than the *tool*. Let's walk through the options for how you can keep your Weekly or Daily Worksheets.

Options for Weekly or Daily Pages

There are several options available for keeping your Weekly or Daily Worksheets. Your choice depends on your appetite for detail, your fluency with technology, and what other tools you might wish to blend with your Worksheet.

For the Paper Lovers

If you use a paper Comprehensive Calendar or a relatively spare electronic Comprehensive Calendar, you will likely prefer one of the following options:

- A one-page paper-only Weekly Worksheet on which to see your whole week
- Five paper-only Daily Worksheets on which to see your whole week a day at a time. This method is preferred by people who want more room both to see to-dos and to capture what comes at them.

For the Technophiles

If you use an electronic Comprehensive Calendar you will likely prefer the following option:

- A printout of your Daily Worksheet in the daily view to ensure that you have room to plan and capture.

Particularly for the Weekly Worksheet, most electronic productivity systems out there don't allow you to take stock of your priorities, time, and to-dos.

 Reflection Question:

What tool or template will you use to create your Weekly or Daily Worksheet?

Can't Choose a Version?

Just get started. This is a case where the habit matters more than the tool. If you are stuck figuring out the perfect categories or just can't settle on a version, then *try* one and see how it works. You will find yourself scribbling in the margins, and when you end a week, additional categories will likely emerge on their own. In fact, many people continue to adapt their worksheet over the course of their careers as they assume varied responsibilities.

GET STARTED CUSTOMIZING: NARROW YOUR VIEW

Let's discuss how to make this narrow view of your week or day work best for you. For many of us, this process feels fantastic because it offers us the opportunity to clear our brains.

Download a Template or Practice Viewing on and Printing from Your Computer

Review the Together Teacher examples in this chapter and the next and see what appeals to you. There are also multiple templates for a day or a week on the accompanying CD. Note that nothing will be perfectly designed to meet your needs, but that is the point. We are on a careful customization journey together. If you find yourself hating what you select, remember: you are not getting married to it. You can always decide to switch later.

Personalize Your Weekly or Daily Worksheets

No matter how it is laid out—whether on paper or electronically—all Weekly and Daily Worksheets should contain certain essential elements: Priorities, Schedule, Deadlines, Work, E-mail and Phone Calls, and Upcoming Work. As you develop this routine you will begin to customize your Weekly or Daily Worksheet to include your own sections, such as Personal Priorities, Errands, and so on. You may want to refer back to your Ideal Week.

- **Put in the standing meetings or events.** This may include lunch duty, staff meetings, and prep periods.

- **Insert standing personal commitments.** This may include church, exercise, time with family and friends, and simply nonworking time.

- **Insert recurring deadlines.** This may be lesson plan due dates or completing attendance reports.

Rule 8: No Tool Is Forever

If you are searching for *the* perfect template to use for the rest of your life, you may as well just buy a sleeping bag and move into the local Office Max. It doesn't exist. What *does* exist is a tool that is good for a period of time in your teaching life. This tool will need to be adapted and modified over the course of your teaching life. For example, there may be a time when you need a section for your graduate school or certification responsibilities, and then there may be a period a few years later when you need a section for your department head role. Your iPhone may crash and you may revert to paper for a year. The point is that you *want* to evolve your system over time.

Now, that was the easy part of customization. Let's talk about how to maximize that limited amount of time you have during the school day.

WHY DO I NEED TO NARROW MY VIEW?

Certainly not everything can be anticipated in a school environment. This is not the point. There are the inevitable fire drills (literal and figurative), the last-minute staff meeting, and the student who requires additional time and support. By planning for what we can, we can *better deal with the unexpected* because we are consciously making the choice to deal with the emergency and we know what balls may drop. Jennifer shares the story of how very careful weekly planning helped her personally and professionally.

TEACHER VIGNETTE
Jennifer's Story

At the beginning of her second year of teaching, Jennifer became grade-level chair for fifth grade. She immediately felt crushed by the increased workload. "I lost control of my schedule," Jennifer says. "I was coming to school at 6 AM and my nights were consumed with parent phone calls, and my lesson planning and other academic preparation would spill into the next day. When I was an individual teacher I had greater control over this because anything I spoke with parents about was in my own classroom. Now, as the grade-level leader, I'm accountable for following up and communicating what happens in other classrooms, and it takes time to track down that information. Add to that the fact that I cannot predict what is coming my way in the way I can in my own classroom, and I was just drowning."

Jennifer threw herself a life raft and requested her principal's help. Together they tracked her time and realized that she was routinely committing more than three hours per day to phone calls! To remedy this, they determined that she should devote two of her prep periods exclusively to parent phone calls. The reason behind this decision was twofold. First, like Jennifer, many parents are in the workplace during the day and share her desire to keep calls to the point. Second, she could batch process. It is much easier to sit down with a phone, your laptop, your parent contact list, and other necessary information and make a bunch of phone calls at one time rather than scattering them throughout the day. Now that call time is blocked into Jennifer's Comprehensive Calendar (she currently uses Outlook) on a daily basis.

To save her even more time, Jennifer and her principal brainstormed ways to make the execution of parent phone calls more efficient. For example, if Jennifer has just a few minutes left before she begins teaching again, she will often start a call by saying, "Hi, Mrs. Smith. I'm returning your call about X and I believe we should do Y," or "I have ten minutes before my students return from orchestra but I wanted to get back to you right away. How can I help you?"

After getting parent phone calls under control, Jennifer became incredibly disciplined with her discretionary time at night. During this intense period, Jennifer was writing her graduate school thesis, planning her wedding, and applying to business school. Although it wasn't ideal to be working as much in the evening, she determined how to use that valuable time down to the minute. Relying heavily on Time Blocks and efficiency-building strategies, Jennifer has been able to find time to apply to graduate school, complete her master's thesis, regularly eat dinner with her fiancé (she cooks on Sundays and he on Tuesdays, and they eat leftovers on Mondays and Wednesdays), and attend a Zumba class or schedule hair appointments on Friday nights!

GET STARTED: NEXT STEPS

- Determine which tool you will use to keep your Weekly or Daily Worksheet.
- Customize your Weekly or Daily Worksheet Template to have categories and sections you need.
- Insert standing items (such as lunch duty), Deadlines, Upcoming To-Dos, and Time Blocks into your Weekly or Daily Worksheet template.
- Print multiple copies.
- Insert the copies into your Together Teacher System.

The mechanics of assembling your together teacher system:

By this point you have selected the tools for your Comprehensive Calendar, Upcoming To-Do List, Thought Catchers, Meeting/PD Notes, and Weekly or Daily Worksheets. For many teachers, now is when they pause and put everything together. For almost all teachers this means inserting your tools (even if you are electronic) into a small binder or folder. In the Recommended Resources for the Together Classroom section I recommend a few of my favorite binders for purchase at any major office supply store. For more detailed information on assembly of your tools, please visit http://www.thetogetherteacher.com.

Those of you starting totally from scratch will likely customize and print out each of the templates and put them in a small, five-tabbed, flexible binder. If you have a combination of some paper-only tools and some electronic tools, you can still print out the electronic ones and insert them here (replacing them weekly during the Round-Up).

Those of you who are converting a previously purchased paper planner may need to find a place for Thought Catchers or find a way for your weekly view to contain a more detailed schedule.

Those of you who have gone almost completely electronic should make sure that those applications or systems are adjusted to allow you to enter data easily, that your smartphone is synchronized, and that you have a good electronic notebook up and running. Remember: you may still need some kind of paper backup for your system when you do not have your device with you.

Most teachers like to add a reference section to their Together Teacher System to include important information they always want at their fingertips, such as state standards, student phone numbers, colleague phone numbers, and student reading levels.

Jeff
A Day in the Life

Name: Jeff Vasquez

Age: 32

Years teaching: 12

Grades/subject: Middle school math

Other school responsibilities: I'm thinking of starting a chess club that I funded by from DonorsChoose to build on math life skills application after school, but I generally leave work pretty close to dismissal.

Professional goals: I want to push myself to become a master at my craft. I want to consistently strive to have 100 percent of the students I teach achieve proficiency or greater on any given assessment. I want families to rejoice when they hear their children will be in my class, and I want to inspire my students to think outside their math abilities and consider how they will impact the world around them for good. I want to finish this year with high attendance rates across the school, and strong classroom culture in each classroom.

Personal commitments: I want to continue practicing the guitar and I want to continue running. Both bring a sense of release and channel my energy in a productive manner over time. I'd

also like to see my blog grow as a resource for parents and educators as I continue to archive lessons, articles, and anecdotes I want to pass on to my sons.

Proudest student moment: Recently a former student (whom I haven't seen in eleven years) posted to my Facebook wall: "I'm in my second year of teaching. . . . I teach seventh and eighth grade social studies in East Harlem. It's a really great place to be. I get lots of support. I want to thank you for being such an influential person in my life. I still have the Dr. Seuss book you gave me during graduation. I still read it and find it completely relevant and inspiring, especially when the going gets tough. Thanks for believing, which in turn allowed me to believe."

How he is working to become even more together: There are a few things I think would make my teaching better and my life easier. I've got to figure out how to clean things up on my laptop so that I know what's useful and what's not. Along the same lines, I'd like to organize the standards I teach in a way that's accessible to students. A colleague of mine has a crate full of folders labeled by

standard. Each folder contains work that is specific to that standard. As soon as a student is done with independent practice and has extra time, they assign themselves to the standard-specific work on the basis of their own needs.

A Day in the Life

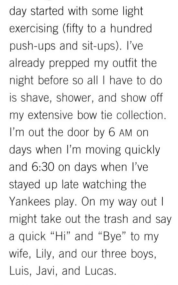

5 AM: I get the day started with some light exercising (fifty to a hundred push-ups and sit-ups). I've already prepped my outfit the night before so all I have to do is shave, shower, and show off my extensive bow tie collection. I'm out the door by 6 AM on days when I'm moving quickly and 6:30 on days when I've stayed up late watching the Yankees play. On my way out I might take out the trash and say a quick "Hi" and "Bye" to my wife, Lily, and our three boys, Luis, Javi, and Lucas.

7:30 AM: I've set up the board space (aims and homework assignments) in the classrooms I'll be teaching in and I've set up whatever materials I'll need for the day on my teacher cart.

[Jeff's cart is also featured in Chapter Ten.]

9:00 AM: I'm in the middle of my first class. Daily routines and rituals carry the momentum of the class, so before you know it, it's already noon.

12 PM: By midday I'm teaching my third section and I will already have had my first prep. During that prep time I'm usually grabbing a quick snack (usually something the school is offering or a granola bar from home), making final preparations for my last two classes (making adjustments to the lesson plan for the day or revising plans for the following week) or writing for my blog (thecraftoffatherhood.com).

2:15 PM: I get my only true lunch break. I may have snacked some more on the school lunch during lunch duties, but now is when I get to eat that peanut butter and jelly sandwich my wife prepared with loving hands. As I eat, I may also decide to update my grade book, grade last night's homework, or make copies for the following week. I usually like to interact with our temperamental copiers once or twice a week. I make that moment count by copying for the entire upcoming week.

4:00 PM: I pride myself on running a tight afternoon homeroom. Students come in, pack up, and are dismissed to afterschool groups or detention within seven minutes. By 4:05 PM I'm being texted by my wife, Lily, who's just picked up two of our sons who are in elementary school and is letting me know she's on her way to pick me up.

6:00 PM: The only thing I've brought home is some homework that I want to grade while watching the Yankees (or anything the boys are watching on Cartoon Network). By now I've checked Luis's and Javi's homework and helped give the boys a bath, and I'm getting my gear together for an evening run (I've been running five miles three times a week for almost a year now) or using some of the exercises I picked up while doing some P90X.

8:00 PM: After my evening run I might practice my guitar as I put the boys to bed and catch up on some prime-time TV with Lily. I'll check in with how the Yankees are doing, update my Facebook page, and check how many hits my blog is getting while picking out the right bow tie and shoes combination for the following day.

10 PM to midnight: Bedtime happens a little later than I would like because I want to make sure I see my wife! A typical late evening has us laughing at the television, making decisions about the weekend, and convincing each other that a desired online purchase is really worth it.

CHAPTER 7

Automate: Create Routines for Planning

Learning Objectives

■ Prepare systematically for a week and a day by creating a Weekly Round-Up agenda.

■ Create Opening and Closing Routines to maximize time before and after school.

■ Define how you will use your preparation periods.

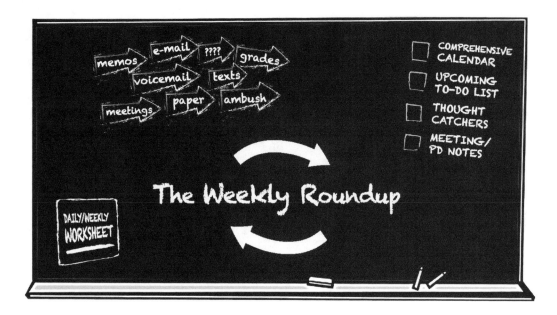

Congratulations! You are the new owner of five key tools to help you do the following:

- Meet your deadlines (Comprehensive Calendar)

- List your to-dos (Upcoming To-Do List)

- Track your ideas and thoughts (Thought Catchers)

- Follow up from meetings and PD (Meeting/PD Notes)

- Plan your schedule (Weekly or Daily Worksheet)

Now it's time for us to discuss *how* to actually use all of these tools together on a regular basis, and how to keep them current and working for you! This chapter is about the habits of creating and maintaining your organization system through the establishment of daily and weekly routines. Once you have articulated what those routines are, you must determine how much time to allocate to them, which specific tasks you must complete to get through them, then build them into your Together Teacher System. You will want to ritualize your planning routines so that they become automatic and your brain is freed to think about the harder work of teaching kids. As teachers we have a very, very limited amount of discretionary time available to us. Basically we have the time before school, preparation periods, the time after school, and the evening. These amounts of time will vary depending on your school, your personal commitments, and your habits. This chapter discusses how to plan ahead and make the greatest use of your limited discretionary time—all in the interest of your taking home less work!

THE POWER WORKOUT: THE WEEKLY ROUND-UP

Much like training for a marathon, once a week we need to take a longer run. This run requires planning, and it will really exercise your organizational muscles. Let's be honest: the process of planning for a week is not particularly fun. It is fulfilling in that you know what is coming, and your stress may decrease. However, it is certainly not as exhilarating as designing an innovative geometry lesson. Regardless, it *must* be done, and it must be done routinely. After meeting with yourself each week, we want you to emerge with a relatively detailed plan for how you will spend your time in the upcoming week: your Weekly or Daily Worksheet. (David Allen discusses a similar routine for busy professionals in *Getting Things Done.*)

 Weekly Round-Up: The time to take stock of the week that just happened and plan ahead for the upcoming week. I sometimes think of it as the convergence of your time and your to-dos. This activity doesn't require tons of brainpower, but it must be systematic in order to be effective.

Now let's take a closer look at how to go through your Weekly Round-Up, piece by piece. Each week we want to take all of the millions of things flying at us and incorporate them into one or more of our four tools. Throughout this book we have already been noting that we want to review these tools during the Weekly Round-Up. This process is *essential* to becoming a Together Teacher, because *as* teachers we have such limited free time. Although the Round-Up will take an hour or so, it will be worth it because you will head into the week with an accurate picture of what is happening when, what work you have to do, and what free time you have. You will be a better teacher for your students, your students' families, and your colleagues because *you* will be the person your students can count on to get those graded essays back when you said you would, *you* will follow up with the parent concerned about their child's homework completion, and *you* will bring those shared lesson plans to your grade-level colleagues. By very carefully plotting your time commitments and your to-dos (both personal and professional), you will find there is more free time in the week than you thought there was, more time you can save by being efficient when it counts, and more time to relax and rejuvenate because you are not worried about "when will I get all this work *done?!*"

Your Personalized Weekly Round-Up Agenda
- Name your priorities (you may want to review your Ideal Week Template from Chapter One).
  - What is *most* important, personally and professionally, this week?

- If one of your personal priorities is "Train for marathon," you will want to block time in your schedule to run.

- If one of your professional priorities is "Get guided reading groups on track," you will want to find time to speak with your literacy coach during the week. By naming a priority, you are reminded to add Time Blocks for achieving this priority to your schedule.

  ○ Review any classroom data you have. Are there any important areas on which to focus this week?

- Create your schedule: review your Comprehensive Calendar.

  ○ Enter time that is already "spoken for".

    - When are you teaching?

    - When do you have meetings?

  ○ Make time to meet important deadlines.

    - What deadlines do you have this week?

    - Check your Comprehensive Calendar. Do you need a Time Block in your schedule to accomplish any of the deadlines?

    - What deadlines do you have in the next three weeks? Do you need Time Blocks in your schedule to work toward these deadlines?

  ○ Sketch out your instructional planning routines.

    - What will happen during your Opening Routine, Closing Routine, and preparation periods? (More on this later in the chapter.) Spell them out in detail in your schedule. (After doing this once, you can just leave them typed into the template or leave space to write what you will do in your preparation periods each day.)

Instructional Planning Routine: The ritualized ways in which you use your preparation periods over the course of a week to complete high-impact instructional planning and grading work.

Opening Routine: A ritualized set of to-dos that you complete each and every morning upon arrival at school. It may be short or long, but it matters that the routine is planned into your day.

Closing Routine: A ritualized set of to-dos that you complete each and every afternoon before departing from school. It may be short or long, but it matters that the routine is planned into your day.

- Block time for routine work (at low-energy times).
  - When will you enter grades, make or return parent phone calls, make copies, and answer e-mail?
- Block time for rest and rejuvenation.
  - When are you *not* working?
  - You do not *have* to plan what you do with this time. Simply leave it blank. However, if you have specific priorities, such as "keep in touch with friends," scheduling a meal with them in advance makes sense.
- Leave some wiggle room for the inevitable changes that can happen in a school. That unexpected yet mandatory evacuation training exercise can certainly throw off our best intentions!
- Fill in your basic physical needs and necessities:
  - When are you eating? Sleeping? Showering?
  - When are you commuting?

- Define your To-Dos.
  - Review your Upcoming To-Do List for soft commitments and deadlines for the current month.
  - Are there any events or deadlines that require Time Blocks to prepare?
  - What else do you *want* to do this week, if time allows?
- Review your Thought Catchers.
  - Is there anything recorded that needs to be typed into a Microsoft Word document?
  - Is there anything that cannot wait until a meeting with someone this week?
- Review your Meeting/PD Notes.
  - Do you need to type up or transfer any PD Notes into documents on your computer? Do you need to scan in any materials from PD?
  - Did you take any Meeting Notes this week that need to be transferred to your Comprehensive Calendar or Upcoming To-Do List? Once you have transferred them, throw the Meeting Notes away.

At this point, your Weekly Worksheet is likely to be pretty full. You may find that you have very little time left after you have filled in all of this. Remember: things will *never* go exactly according to plan. That is *okay*. The idea here is that we want to head into each week with a clear view of our time—both professionally and personally. Let's keep going on our Weekly Round-Up.

- Review any loose scraps of paper you have gathered this week.
  - Are there any calendars or notices in your teacher mailbox that you need to transfer to your Comprehensive Calendar?
  - Are there any student data you have gathered on your clipboard that you need to add a Time Block to deal with?
- Review any communications that will take time to respond to.
  - Are there any phone calls to return? At what time in your schedule will you do this?
  - Are there any e-mails that need longer replies? What time in your schedule will you answer them?

When should you have your Weekly Round-Up? Ideally, you should prepare your Weekly or Daily Worksheet on either Friday morning or Friday afternoon, in preparation for the following week. But it can be nearly impossible to evaluate sufficiently what's ahead after an exhausting workweek. If you cannot map out your next week on Friday during school, the next best time is over the weekend. However, I have heard from *multiple* teachers who work on weekends that establishing what must be accomplished over the weekend *prior* to Saturday reduces the feeling of being overwhelmed.

- Tess, a middle school ELA teacher, describes her process: "I do my Weekly Round-Up on Fridays at 3 PM. It is honestly one of my favorite times of the week. I chose Fridays because my school is empty, it is quiet, and I'm not thinking about what I need to plan for tomorrow morning. I can really be focused on what I want to accomplish next week. Heading into the weekend, I feel really good. Before having this routine I was spending thirty minutes on Monday morning making a to-do list that I couldn't even find on Wednesday!"
- Brendan, a special educator, says, "I get ready for my week on Sunday morning with a friend. We actually go out for pancakes at IHOP! I bring my Weekly Worksheet, my Comprehensive Calendar, and my Upcoming To-Do List, and I go through everything, updating all of it in my laptop. Then I comb through my e-mail and record any new deadlines or appointments."

How long will the Weekly Round-Up take me? For most of us, this weekly planning process takes between thirty and ninety minutes, depending on how much work we need to process from the previous week.

What to Have at Your Weekly Round-Up

- Computer (laptop or desktop)
- Recycle bin

- Together Teacher System, including your
  - Comprehensive Calendar
  - Upcoming To-Do List
  - Thought Catchers
  - Meeting/PD Notes
- Any data you need to review regularly (objective mastery, attendance, homework completion, and so on)
- Any loose papers that may have come in that week from any direction
- Clipboard, notebooks, your binder or whatever contains your Together Teacher Tools
- Printer
- Unit and lesson plans

Where **should you conduct your Weekly Round-Up?** Some Together Teachers conduct their Weekly Round-Up at school, others at a coffee shop, and others at home on the couch. Whatever location you choose, you want to make sure you can spread out your materials, be relatively uninterrupted, and have access to a printer.

Rule 10: Pause to Plan

The Weekly Round-Up process makes a huge difference in the life of Jennifer, the middle school English teacher we profiled earlier. During that time, Jennifer assesses her calendar and creates Time Blocks for classes she teaches, each of her preparation periods, lunch periods, and grade-level meetings. Then, as she prepares for a week, she assigns specific tasks into the blocks she has available. Jennifer says, "Microsoft Outlook became helpful. I decided I simply had to get faster at certain things, because there are only twenty-four hours in a day—and Outlook almost blocks off your sleeping hours for you! This forced me to say, look, I have this time chunk allocated to parent calls and this time for graduate school work. I had to look at my Outlook calendar and the critical question was, 'Does this activity get that much time?' Doing that at the beginning of the week forced me to prioritize—and ensured that I was building in time to take care of myself."

My own husband, Jack, a middle school language arts teacher, keeps blank copies of his Weekly Worksheet at home, fills one out each Sunday morning, and inserts it into his Together Teacher System. His worksheet also captures the many things that come up on the fly in our lives. He will frequently write down things we discuss in a weekly family meeting—such as e-mailing the building superintendent about getting the overhead track lighting fixed. Jack's weekly planning helps us carefully coordinate who gets to go to the gym when, who is on baby duty, and when to prepare for visits from our respective parents!

Let's look in detail at how Jenny, also profiled earlier, conducts her Weekly Round-Up. Jenny says, "I try to make my Weekly Round-Up as relaxing as possible. I generally do food shopping on Sunday morning, and then on Sunday afternoon I sit down and create my Weekly Worksheet. I review my Comprehensive Calendar (kept in Outlook) a few weeks in advance, plan out how I will use my preparation periods, and carefully plot out the work I need to do as a teacher and as a grade-level leader."

Jenny has customized her Weekly Worksheet to include categories for Teacher Tasks and Grade-Level Tasks. When she created the Weekly Worksheet shown in Figure 7.1, it was the end of the school year and Jenny was overseeing the kindergarten step-up (graduation) day and managing the closeout of the year for her grade level—all while maintaining her regular full-time teaching responsibilities.

Block time for priorities. This week Jenny has prioritized planning kindergarten graduation, organizing a genre library, and running. Note: Jenny borrows the term *Sharpening the Saw* from Steven Covey's *The 7 Habits of Highly Effective People* to define her personal priorities section. You will see that Jenny built time into her schedule to accomplish her deadlines for the week.

Review your Comprehensive Calendar to build your schedule and deadlines. Jenny pulled the week's appointments and deadlines out of her Comprehensive Calendar and added them to her Weekly Worksheet. For example, her Data-Driven Plan was due on Tuesday, so that is marked in her Deadline section. Additionally, Jenny's standard weekly personal and professional time commitments, such as gym time, coaching responsibilities, and grade-level responsibilities, remain typed into her Weekly Worksheet template.

Jenny also takes care of herself personally. You will notice that she has carefully blocked time for dinner with friends on Friday night and a date night with her boyfriend on Saturday night (she also squeezed in a manicure!). Knowing that she has those rejuvenation and relaxation times built in can often be a welcome thought during a very busy week of teaching. By treating these events with an importance equal to her professional activities, Jenny ensures that her teaching career is sustainable.

Next Jenny looks even further ahead on her Comprehensive Calendar so she can be prepared and start getting ahead. She realizes that it is the end of the school year and that the parents of the kindergarten students need an explanation of final reading levels (F&P). She writes a to-do to write an "F&P parent letter," even though it is not due until the following week.

Review your Upcoming To-Do List. Jenny also pulled out from her Upcoming To-Do List to-dos that don't have hard deadlines but need to be done that week, such as "Update Site Word Wall and Ring" and guided reading planning for Hawks—both of which are listed

Jenny's Weekly Worksheet, Week of _6/6_

PRIORITIES

GLL	Classroom	Sharpening the Saw
-email Mr. ▓ about graduation	-organize genre lib -organize leveled library	-Run outside in the park (2) days -Date night

SHAPE OF THE WEEK

	M	T	W	R	F	Weekend
	Gym	Gym	Gym	Gym	Gym	Gym
APPTS	-SS meeting with ▓ 12:45	12:40 Planning GL Appreciation gll 4:30-5:20 -Maia call 7:15PM	12:40 Coaching 4:00pm Email final writing plans	12:40 Writing Planning GL Appreciation Email Draft writing plans -talent show 6-8	7:30pm dinner w/ ▓	Mom + Dad's anniversary dinner
DEADLINES		-Email DDP -Email ▓ reflection template	-Email GL Agenda -call Ms. ▓	-Print GR sheets -Organize lib @ 12:45		-dinner @ 8:00pm

Teacher Tasks	GLL Tasks	Meeting Notes/Follow Up
-Update Sight Word Wall and Ring -GR planning Hawks -GR planning Lions -sight words stamps -refill center papers (lions) -refill IP pages (hawks) -copy writing papers -Lions sw papers -DP take-home (131-141) -F+P parent letter -Math parent letter	-GL Agenda -discuss moving up ceremony with ▓ -Reach scholar temp. -email ▓ about reach plans from LP -Email ▓ a/b HW for next week -Dress up party GL letter -talk w/ team a/b HW for last week	GLM: -email ▓ a/b moving up ceremony -leadership speech -email ▓ about PLC email -email ▓ about speech -Set appt. w/ Ms. ▓ about reten- tion Other Meetings: -email ▓ a/b K diplomas -email ▓ w/ SS outcomes
Coaching Meeting Priorities: -Reach scholar temp. -Email ▓ → reflection		

Personal Errands	Sharpening the Saw	Looking Ahead→Work
-coop food shopping for the week -email Aunt ▓ a/b anniversary party -Drop off Laundry -call + get gift card for Dad	-date w/ ▓ (fri.) -Manicure (wed/thurs?) -talk w/ Mom + Dad → wed	-EOY checklist -level the class library -Math parent letter -GR for summer school

Figure 7.1 Jenny's Weekly Worksheet, the Result of Her Weekly Round-Up

Table 7.1 Plan Your Weekly Round-Up

Routine	When will you have your Round-Up?	Where will you be?	What materials do you need to have on hand? (*You can use the preceding list as a starting point.*)	What is *your* personal agenda for this time?
Weekly Round-Up				

under Teacher Tasks. She can review those to-dos each day, see what discretionary time she has, and then determine when to do them. She also notes her Personal Errands that week, such as "coop food shopping for the week" and "call & get gift card for Dad." In fact, Jenny may be able to group those two errands together and accomplish them during the same outing.

Leave room for your Meeting/PD Notes. For Jenny, this section starts the week empty and gets filled up during her various meetings. For example, she was taking notes at a grade-level meeting and noted some next steps for herself directly on her Weekly Worksheet (thus avoiding a notebook all together, as suggested in Chapter Five): "email about PLC [Parent Leadership Council] email" and "email about speech."

Leave some time for the unexpected or opportunities. Jenny is not going to start the week with every hour mapped out. She knows that stuff will come up, so she has wiggle time built in. Whenever she has an ounce of time, however, she can make smart choices about how to use it based on the planning she has already done for the week.

Complete the Routines table in Table 7.1. It may help to flip back through your Reader's Guide.

Rule 9: Own Your Schedule

At this point, many teachers begin to think that I'm some kind of robot who simply generates to-do lists but never has an ounce of fun. In fact, it's just the opposite! The point is that if you don't plan time for yourself, you will find yourself always half working and half not working, worrying about all the stuff you need to do rather than enjoying time in which you're truly relaxed. Have you ever noticed how much more efficient you are during the school day when you know you have an evening event and cannot drag your grading home with you? Although it may feel like a waste to spend this kind of time preparing with this level of detail, it pays off to have a clear view of your week—to know when it is busy and when it is light; to know what you have to accomplish and what is coming up. If you have a point of view about how you want to use your preparation periods at the start of the week, you are less prone to distractions and "emergencies."

DAILY ROUTINES: MAKING THE MOST OF OPENINGS AND CLOSINGS

Similar to the ingrained morning and evening rituals you likely conduct at home—guzzle coffee, take shower, pack lunch, eat breakfast, brush teeth—you also need clear rituals for those times at school. Each day when you arrive at school, there is a set of things you must do to prepare, and each day before you leave, there is a set of things you must do to close out. The objective is to standardize these actions and eliminate all guesswork so that you can accomplish these necessary tasks in a way that most positively benefits you and your classroom. These routines may be no more than ten to fifteen minutes each, but having them ingrained will save you countless minutes that you may otherwise have spent planning inefficiently for your day. It also lets you own your schedule rather than reacting to the crisis of the day. When you head into school with a clear plan for how you will use your prep, you will find you are more likely to be protective of the time.

Opening Routines

Many of us already conduct an informal set of rituals when we arrive at school each morning. We check e-mail, say hi to our colleagues, write lesson aims on the board, ensure that all copies are in place, and so on. Much of our morning routine depends on how our school is run. It also depends on our own energy, the availability of classrooms, and other personal obligations. For example, if the copier is routinely broken, making photocopies should not be part of your morning routine. If you frequently receive e-mail updates that require action, checking e-mail should be a part of your morning routine. Your school may also have some specific requirements, such as submitting attendance or administering reading tests during off-hours, that affect when you do what. In my third year of teaching, an after-school program run by other instructors limited my access to my classroom after school and forced me to lesson plan at the incredibly early hour at which I decided to arrive at work. There is no one right way to have a morning routine; it is just important that you have one that is clear to you. Now let's hear how a few different Together Teachers utilize their mornings.

Nilda's morning. "I arrive at 6:15 AM and I always start by rereading that day's lesson plans. This is necessary because I plan a week in advance, so I occasionally forget details. On Monday I print out all lessons for the week and put all lesson plans in my Together Teacher System. As I'm making coffee, I highlight stuff to remember and write additional questions to ask within the lesson. After that, I look at e-mail one quick time to see if there is anything that will impact the day, like a student absence."

Anna's morning. "I arrive at 6:40 AM, say hi to other teachers, and then go straight to set up my desk area. I pull out my Together Teacher System, turn on my laptop, review my Comprehensive Calendar (I keep a higher-level view in my Weekly Worksheet, and room locations for meetings in Outlook), and generally make sure I know what I'm doing that day. I've been trying to leave my computer at school, so I usually have between five and ten e-mails to take care of and respond to. I do have a fair amount of time in the morning, so I try to get work done. I try and tackle a project, such as something big with attendance, guided reading stuff, any number of things. I have found if I do the heavier lifting in the morning, I get more done and faster. I learned the hard way that if I save the bigger projects for the afternoon, they take much longer. Because I oversee math instruction, I review math lesson plans and exit tickets, to make sure the team is on track."

Both Nilda and Anna are incredibly purposeful with how they use their morning hours to get work done and be ready for the day of instruction. I want you to be similarly purposeful and to have the same level of focus heading into the school day. Although it might seem silly to write down in a twenty-minute period everything you want to accomplish, this will ultimately help prevent you from taking more work home!

Sample Opening Routine for a Morning Person

- Arrive at school, coffee in hand, say hi to other early arrivers.
- Sign in, put lunch in refrigerator, turn on classroom lights, put on soft music.
- Return garbage cans tipped over on your desk by custodian to their proper location.
- Double-check that all lesson materials and copies are laid out for the day.
- Set out any materials needed for any early-arrival student jobs, such as papers to hand out, homework to return.
- Scan e-mail for anything urgent; leave the rest for later.
- Review your Weekly Worksheet for what you outlined to accomplish for your Opening Routine.
  - Make progress on aims of unit plan.
  - Create end-of-unit assessment.
  - Grade half of the reading journal responses.
- Greet students at door.

Sample Opening Routine for a Nonmorning Person

- Arrive at school, stagger to coffee machine, grunt to other early arrivers.
- Hope there is something good served in the cafeteria for lunch.
- Double-check that all lesson materials and copies are laid out for the day.
- Greet students at door.

Reflection Questions:

Consider your own classroom and Opening Routine. Are you someone who arrives early to get in some quiet lesson planning time? Or do you stroll in as late as possible to squeeze in a few extra minutes of sleep?

Depending on the answer, what do you need in your morning routine?

Closing Routines

Whew. Your students are all safely out the door after a good day of learning. If you are lucky, your classroom is in relatively good physical shape after the madness of the instructional day. What next? If you are like many teachers, your energy is hitting a low and you are scrounging through your pockets or purse to see if you have change to get a much needed jolt of caffeine from the soda machine in the teachers' lounge. On the way to the soda machine you pop into a colleague's room so you can debrief each other about the day. The rundown of the day reminds you of a question you had for your co-teacher, so you go back to your classroom to see if he is still there. He has left already, so you open your e-mail and start drafting a message to him. Arg—twenty new messages! It's too stressful to review them all now. You close down your computer and wander around the classroom—picking up a few stray pieces of paper, erasing the lesson objectives on the board, and before long an entire hour has flown by. Drat! Now you have to grade all of your exit tickets at home. So much for relaxing after dinner! Why does this keep happening?! You give up, throw the exit tickets in your bag, glance at the board and think, "I *should* write up my lesson objectives for tomorrow and check my copies," but ultimately you decide to call it a day and save those tasks for the morning.

Now, this is very, very normal, and it is amazing how much time can pass when we stay after school, feel like we are working, but in fact are getting little done of importance or impact. We might as well just go home and take a nap. However, if you take the time to get very clear about what specifically you want to accomplish each afternoon, you will likely find yourself speeding more efficiently through your work, less prone to distractions, and out the door at an earlier hour. This is called a Closing Routine and is simply a standard list of things you try to accomplish before you leave school every day. Following is an example of my own Closing Routine when I was teaching fifth grade, all subjects.

Ms. H-.M.'s Closing Routine

- Take a deep breath, refill water bottle, quickly check-in with my fourth-grade colleague (we shared a teaching trailer) to decompress.

- Check e-mail and take note of any deadlines that have come my way, answer any short e-mails, and block time to deal with longer e-mails.

- Review reading and math exit tickets quickly and jot down any reteaching points.

- Answer five reading response journals. (I wrote personal responses to all students each week, five per day. I did this at school so I would not have to lug the heavy five-subject notebooks home.)

- Clean out the in-box on my desk and note any to-dos, file any papers, throw as much away as possible.

- Distribute homework assignments to my students' individualized mailboxes. (This practice was eliminated after I figured out a student could do the job.)

- Erase dry-erase board. (This too was eliminated after I figured out a student could do this job.)

- Write next day's teaching objectives and agenda on my Anchor Board. (The Anchor Board is a classroom station discussed in Chapter Ten. This task was also eliminated after I figured out that a student could do this job!)

- Review next day's lesson plans and double-check that all teaching materials are available.

- Note any parent phone calls to make from home that evening.

This is clearly an example of a longer Closing Routine. Other teachers close down their days in shorter ways, some of which involve alone time, some of which involve meetings with colleagues or small-group work with students. Jenny literally posts her short Closing Routine on her desk so she doesn't forget anything. Let's look at what Jenny does to close out the day:

Jenny's Closing Routine: End-of-Day Checklist

- Write guided reading aims (Lions and Hawks)
- Post math meeting information
  - Problem of the day
  - Word problem
- Post writing aim
- Post morning message
- Vacuum carpet

Jenny refers to this checklist that is taped onto her desk to quickly prepare her classroom for the next day. She gets her guided reading aims, math meeting board, and morning message posted, quickly vacuums the carpet, then heads out the door. Whatever your approach, the reliable routine you follow each day should take into account your energy levels and work in the best possible way for you.

Reflection Questions:

Consider your own classroom and closing routine. Are you someone who needs to race out the door for personal commitments, or can you reserve a good chunk of time after work to complete some key routines?

Depending on the answer, what do you need in your Closing Routine?

USE THOSE PREPS TO THEIR FULLEST

Now that you have a routine for planning out your time each week, and a good way to open and close your day, it is time to talk about how to maximize those preparation periods. As you are well-aware, a whole set of to-dos needs to be completed each week to get ready for the next week of teaching—planning, grading, copying, assembling materials, creating charts, writing student paychecks, and so on. The idea is that we need to articulate how we want to use our "free" time, and then record these routines right into our Weekly or Daily Worksheets.

Ahhhh, the preparation period—a blessing and a curse. On one hand, it feels luxurious to have forty-five to sixty minutes *without* children in the middle of a school day. However, for many of us, preps are only an excuse for pointless meetings, an open invitation to disruptions, and a chance to *maybe* tick some smaller things off a list. What's more, if we do not head into our preparation periods with a very clear intention about what we want to accomplish in this short burst of time, we spend those precious minutes figuring out what we have to do, and then BAM!—our kids are back in the room! Similar to how we spelled out exactly what we want to accomplish in an Opening and a Closing Routine, we want to be as purposeful about how we plan to use our preparation periods. We will do that by actually mapping out all of the preparation time we have in a week and determining what we will do with that time. Similar to creating your Ideal Week Template, it will *of course* not always play out exactly as planned, but that is not the point. The point here is that we are taking time to spell out what we aim to accomplish, and when we get a last-minute request to cover a class, have a student requiring additional attention, or get pulled into a committee meeting, we can at least be aware of what we are *not* accomplishing and find other time to deal with it.

Now let's look at how a few teachers approach their instructional planning time.

Alice, an experienced elementary school teacher who is now a principal, was incredibly intentional about how she used her preparation periods—and because of this her entire teaching staff is equally as intentional. Alice had a hundred minutes of preparation time each day, so she worked hard to maximize that time, knowing that anything she did not complete would need to be done at night and on the weekends. Let's look at how she spelled

UNC To-Do list	Week of: _____				
Monday	**Tuesday**	**Wednesday**	**Thursday**	**Friday**	**Weekend**
Miscellaneous work for this coming week: € write upcoming first grade mini-lessons € Call parents:	**Get ready for next week:** € Plan next week reading ML (select books) € Plan next week writing ML (make anything) € Plan Math € Plan next wk LW € Print next week ML € Print next week math lessons ① € Print next week LW € Copy math papers € Copy LW € Copy morning work € Copy HWT € Call parents:	€ Plan Word Study for next week ② € New word study materials € Plan interactive writing/HWT € Copy sort € Plan morning meeting € Prep. vocab words on cards € Call parents:	€ Select and plan SR books € Plan poetry € Poem on chart paper € Prep. counting packets € Plan SS/Sci € Make copies for SS € Call parents: ③	€ Select and plan RA books € PAT time materials € Grade book € Print next week LP € Call parents:	€ Read teaching books

Figure 7.2 Alice's Weekly Preparation Plan

out what she wanted to accomplish during her preparation periods each day of the week (Figure 7.2).

Let's take apart Alice's use of her preparation periods throughout the week.

1. **Blocked time for printing and copying.** As you can see, Alice planned to do most of her printing and copying on Tuesdays to prepare for the following week.

2. **Time to plan for each subject.** As an elementary school teacher, Alice had a lot of lessons to plan and materials to prepare. She carefully spelled out when she would plan for each of those subjects, and when materials were subsequently copied and prepared.

3. **Blocked time to call parents.** Alice kept a space on her Weekly Worksheet to note parents she wanted to call.

Rule 5: Keep Like Items with Like Items

Whenever possible, complete as much of the same type of work all at once. I'm sure you all have heard the news that shifting gears and multitasking actually slows us down. Try to get in a lesson planning groove and crank out as much as you can. Get comfortable in a grading groove and complete a whole set of papers. This way you can be surrounded by the right materials at the right time, complete what you start, and not divide your time by checking e-mail, calling parents, grading, planning, and procrastinating!

Let's look at another example. Kate has established a professional and personal routine for Sundays that has enabled her to reduce her anxiety heading into the weekend and allows her to enjoy her "off" day on Saturday. Figure 7.3 shows the detailed checklist she has made for herself to prepare for the week of teaching. We should note that this is in addition to very good use of her morning, afternoon, and preparation periods.

There are a couple of things that make Kate's instructional life easier:

1. **Categories.** Kate has categorized her work and put it into buckets so that she can see what to tackle when. For example, her personal Sunday work is separate from her school planning work.

2. **Bite-size.** She has also gotten incredibly specific about what she has to accomplish.

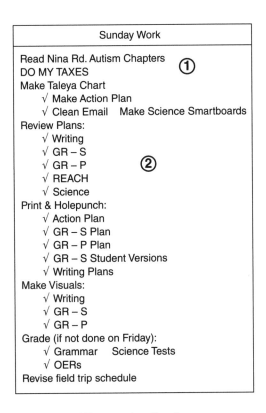

Figure 7.3 Kate's Weekly Instructional Preparation Routine

Although Kate's list in Figure 7.3 may initially look overwhelming for a Sunday (remember, Kate is in her first year of teaching!), it is super clear what Kate needs to accomplish. This clarity makes it much easier for her to do a few of these things—those that require greater brainpower—while she is fresh in the morning. Then she can devote a chunk of her day to running and to calling her family. Later she can complete some of her lower-energy but necessary work, such as creating visual anchors (which could likely be done while enjoying an episode of her favorite TV show).

By automating this process, Kate is no longer stressed going into the weekend. Yes, it is a *lot* of work to complete on a Sunday, but at least it is all spelled out and not some mystery blob called Work that lurks in the back of her head during her days off. None of the weekend work that Kate needs to complete is unknown; it is all completely predictable and immediately actionable. After you articulate your planning routines, you can insert this checklist right into your Weekly or Daily Worksheet.

Now Kate is completely ready to use the limited amount of discretionary time she has throughout the school week (Figure 7.4). If you find that this level of detail is too much for your Weekly or Daily Worksheet, simply staple it to the back.

Kate's example shows that very carefully planning for the limited amount of time you have in the school day can mean that you are more efficient with small bits of time and end up taking less work home with you each day. You can see that Kate left room to be flexible and wrote in other items that came up during the day and week.

Reflection Question:

What things do you need to do to get ready for a week of instruction?

Complete Table 7.2 for your preparation periods. Your to-dos will likely take place from Thursday through Sunday. Some items may be small, others may be big.

> **Teacher Leader Tip:** If you write any kind of regular communication or prepare for any meetings, you should make note of it and assign it a time during the week.

CREATING ROUTINES: WHY DOES THIS MATTER, AGAIN?

Sue, profiled in Chapter Six, describes her teaching life before she deliberately implemented a weekly planning routine: "It was day-by-day. I would show up at school each morning and hope that Joe (a colleague) wasn't hogging the copier as usual. I had a rough sense of where

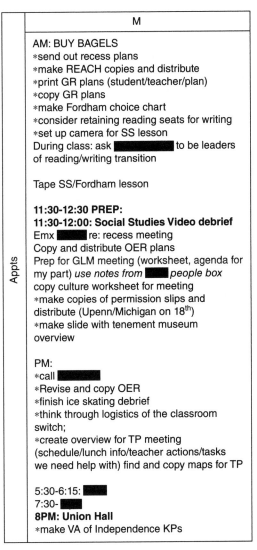

Figure 7.4 Kate's Monday Opening, Closing, and Prep Period Routines Baked into Her Weekly Worksheet

Table 7.2 Prep Period Instructional Preparation Routines

	Weekend	Monday	Tuesday	Wednesday	Thursday	Friday
Morning						
Preparation Periods						
Evening						

things were going, from point A to point B, because of our interim assessments, but it was not a cohesive vision. It was a constant search for time, like, When am I going to find ten minutes to make this chart? When can I copy these assessments? I felt frantic and unprepared."

When I met Sue, she was initially skeptical about the time that the Weekly Round-Up would take and how it would help her teaching. However, after watching some of her colleagues, Sue has now built the habit of religiously planning both her personal and professional weeks. Her tools have varied over the past few years, but the discipline of looking ahead to the next week is now something she cannot live without. Sue says, "I am at my happiest place if I can look ahead each Friday, at the end of the school week, but sometimes my time or mental capacity doesn't allow this to happen." If Sue cannot make the time on Fridays, Sunday nights are the default alternative.

Sue starts by doing her instructional planning for the week. She looks at her six-to-eight-week plan, which is a loose sketch of what she wants to teach. She then prepares her lessons to a greater level of detail using her lesson planning book. She puts the lesson aims into the plan's pages and then writes out the lessons more thoroughly, making notes along the way about where she needs to create additional materials or what portions she would like to share with other teachers at her school.

After that, Sue conducts her Weekly Round-Up for the upcoming week. As you saw in Chapter Six, her Weekly Worksheet is customized to include her commitments that do not change. She adds any meetings listed on her Comprehensive Calendar or on the family calendar hanging in her kitchen, notes what phone calls she needs to make, decides what meals she must prepare that week (using a handy dandy meal planner worksheet she made!), and takes stock of when she has commitments for herself, her son, or her partner. By carefully looking ahead and mapping out her time, Sue is able to exercise at the gym near her school three mornings a week before school (she showers at school), to pick her son up from the bus a few days per week, and to participate in a fun book club. Both of these planning routines take Sue between sixty and ninety minutes per week (she does the heavier lifting of her instructional planning during the school week when she has an extended prep period). By going through this process, Sue is able to be a great teacher *and* do other things that are important to her.

Jacqueline, a teacher in her first year of teaching, describes how this process helps her: "My Weekly Round-Up takes place on Sunday afternoon. This allows me to have enough time to do anything I may have forgotten I need to do for Monday. It also allows me to enjoy my weekend and still be prepared for the week. I like to send any pending e-mails or make any phone calls at this time as well. I usually try to synthesize and get rid of anything I can from my Thought Catcher. By meeting on Sunday afternoons, I allow myself to see the scope of the upcoming week and the following week."

The process of establishing routines is beneficial whether you are in your first year of teaching or your fifteenth. Having clear and established routines allows us to plan for what is predictable (in a world that often is *not* predictable!) rather than worry about *when* we will fit things in, and to make the most of the limited amount of personal and professional "free" time we have. Although it does take some additional time (anywhere from ten to sixty minutes each day, depending on your Opening and Closing Routines, and at least sixty minutes weekly), that time will pay you back with the ability to get more done and have less stress.

GET STARTED: NEXT STEPS

Now that you have created routines to help prevent to-dos from sneaking up on you, let's make sure you have time blocked on your Comprehensive Calendar to make those actions happen. Here is a summary of planning routines that effective teachers use. This template is also available on the accompanying CD.

- Map out your Weekly Round-Up agenda, including the what, where, when, and materials needed.

- Determine your Opening Routine and write it into your Weekly or Daily Worksheet.

- Determine your Closing Routine and write it into your Weekly or Daily Worksheet.

- Carefully list how you will utilize your preparation periods and write it into your Weekly Worksheet.

- Insert all of your Routines into your Weekly or Daily Worksheet.

Ward Off the Demons: Keep Those Organizational Muscles Strong

---

CHAPTER 8

Learning Objectives

■ Test your Together Teacher System's ability to stand up to the pressure of your job.

■ Identify why to-dos get stuck and what to do when this inevitably happens.

■ Name typical human behaviors that hold us back and how to circumvent them.

Now that we have discussed four tools you can use to manage your time, your to-dos, and your thoughts as teachers (the Comprehensive Calendar, the Upcoming To-Do List, Thought Catchers, and Meeting/PD Notes), plus a set of routines (Opening Routine, Closing Routine, and Weekly Round-Up), let's pause to discuss some normal human behaviors that can get in our way. Having the right tools and knowledge is one thing. Actually creating those tools and reviewing them regularly is another. Similar to trying to eat healthy, being incredibly organized is a process, and no one person is ever perfect twenty-four hours per day, seven days per week. This chapter articulates some common pitfalls you may hit on your journey to becoming a Together Teacher and, if you do, how to find your way out.

KEEPING THOSE ORGANIZATIONAL MUSCLES WORKING: YOUR DAILY EXERCISE

Now that you have created your customized Together Teacher System let's talk about how to keep it in use all day long to manage the daily deluge. The longer you practice the habits, the more natural they will feel. Like trying a new exercise routine, initially it feels a little awkward, it is potentially painful, and it is easy to hit the snooze button. But if you keep it up, you start seeing the benefits of more consistency and better planning for your teaching, plus the side benefits of less stress, which incentivizes you to keep it up even more! Let's discuss a few common bumps on the journey to becoming Together Teachers.

Common Bumps on the Journey

Bump 1: We forget to carry it with us! There are few rules with regard to your Together Teacher System, but one is that it must be easily accessible and highly portable. One Together Teacher I know prints his Weekly Worksheet on purple paper so that it never gets lost among his other papers. Whether you want to go that far or not is up to you. What I care about is that your system allows you to enter items easily and that you can physically carry it around your school and between school and home.

Bump 2: We forget to look at it! A Together Teacher System does you no good unless you *look* at it. Mary, a special educator in her third year of teaching, describes when she actually looks at her Weekly Worksheet. "I review it first thing in the morning, whenever there is a shift in schedule, whenever I have a few spare minutes, and again at the end of the day. Reviewing it this often helps me get little things done that I would have otherwise had to take home."

Bump 3: We don't write everything down! Imagine you are running down the hall to make a few last-minute copies and are stopped by your school's literacy coach, who asks you to e-mail her your guided reading plans so she may share them with other teachers. Typically this situation plays out in the following way: we quickly agree to accommodate the request, keep running, make our copies, return to our students, and promptly forget whatever promise we've made. Instead of attempting to store these requests in your head and running the risk of forgetting them, you can simply jot down a note on your Weekly or Daily Worksheet, and then follow up on it whenever you have a spare moment.

Bump 4: We forget to look beyond *today*! The beauty of your entire system is that it allows you to plan ahead more sufficiently. If you notice on your Comprehensive Calendar that progress reports are due on Friday, you may allot thirty minutes per day on your Weekly or Daily Worksheet to devote to them over the course of the week. Alternatively, you can list the bite-size steps needed to complete those reports on your Weekly Worksheet and move through them gradually—a tactic that will prevent last-minute work.

Bump 5: We choose the wrong tool! Sometimes we see our friends with these very cool electronic systems and are convinced such a system will work for us—even though we simply love pen and paper. Or conversely, your colleague has an awesome commercial paper planner that you just have to have, and your fingers fumble with the pencil. Although changing habits is entirely possible, it is helpful to remember to embrace your personal inclinations.

Reflection Questions:

Have you ever experienced any of these common bumps when trying to implement a new habit of any sort?

Are there any learnings for you in this new process?

If you are struggling in your implementation, check this list of common challenges to see if you are falling prey to one of them.

I'M ROUTINED, I'M PLANNED, BUT THE WORK STILL ISN'T GETTING DONE

In spite of our best intentions, clear lists, and commitment to an organization system, sometimes things still don't move ahead and we find ourselves re-copying the same dratted to-do week after week. For many of us, particularly if we judge our success by the ability to cross *everything* off a list, this situation can cause us to feel less than successful on a daily basis. Over the years, many teachers and clients have admitted to me that although the planning routines make sense, they still find that some to-dos get stuck and fail to move off the list. In my experience, to-dos can get stuck for a few reasons—some of which are very good reasons to get stuck! Let's talk about this common issue and discuss what to do when this happens.

Why To-Dos Get Stuck and What to Do About It

1. **You don't feel like doing it.** I can't do much to help you here if it *truly* has to be done. Let's face it: there will always be things that you should do but just don't feel like doing. Ever. For some teachers, it may be completing attendance reports. For others, it may be entering grades into the online system. And for others, it may be detailed lesson planning. If it truly has to be done, then you have to figure out a way to incentivize yourself *and* make the action more efficient. However, there are a few ways to get yourself started!

   - The first (and admittedly my favorite) way is to give yourself a present. There's nothing like old-fashioned extrinsic motivation.

   - The second way to unstick yourself is to set up an interim deadline, such as a meeting with your co-teacher about the topic, or some other way of publicly holding yourself accountable.

   - The third option that folks find helpful is to actually complete the task *first* thing in the morning, before you do anything else. Even completing a small portion of dreaded tasks can make doing the rest of it easier to bear.

Reflection Questions:

What are some things you never, ever feel like doing?

What are some ways you might reward yourself for completing them?

2. **It may not need to be done.** We are all guilty of carrying over the same tasks week after week after week. In these cases, I often ask people to question whether the work they've avoided doing even needs to be completed. There are certain to-dos that initially have a high-level of importance but whose significance diminishes as time goes by and the context around them changes. In fact, you may arrive at a point where such tasks may not even have to be completed at all. For example, let's say a grade-level team commits to researching new science curriculum ideas to address gaps found in their student assessments. Weeks go by, yet the to-do remains uncompleted. The students deliver a much stronger performance on their next science assessment, but we still feel pressure to unearth new curriculum ideas. For whatever reason, we tend to hang on to to-dos. We feel that if we wrote it down, then we are committed to completing it. *This is not the case.* Trust me, some tasks were meant to die. This is the beauty of the Upcoming To-Do List. Unless it has a hard deadline, you can roll the to-do over to another month or use one of the strategies listed earlier to encourage yourself to complete it.

Reflection Question:

Is there anything that you have been carrying around that you can cross off your list?

3. **Make it bite-size.** This is the number one reason that to-dos get stuck. Most teachers put items on their Weekly Worksheets that are simply too big to accomplish in the limited period of discretionary time they have available. David Allen calls this making things "actionable," which means being very clear about precisely what the next step is. When I review Weekly Worksheets, one to-do I see over and over again is the term *unit plan*. As all of you know, creating a unit plan is no easy task, and it often takes research, comprehensive consultations with others, reviews of state standards, and assessment design.

Let's say you have a forty-minute prep period. By the time you talk to one student after class, refill your water, and use the restroom (and maybe peek at your e-mail), you have about twenty-five minutes left. Let's say you still need to write your aims on the board and post the warm-up—and knock your break down to twenty minutes. You look at your Weekly Worksheet and you see the term *unit plans* and you balk. Why? Because your brain has to translate that term into a series of actionable to-dos that you will need to complete in order to cross it off the list. Let's say you translate *unit plans* as "Design the end-of-unit assessment." At this point you have fifteen minutes left. You open your laptop at your desk and then review the last unit assessment—and your first student comes into the classroom. Zap. Prep period gone. No movement on the unit plan. And you are too tired to write good unit plans at night.

Reflection Question:

What are some big tasks, such as unit planning, that forever weigh on your list? Choose one. Now break it down into actionable to-dos.

Rule 4: Make It Bite-Size

Figure 8.1 is Emily's Weekly Worksheet. Emily is a high school history teacher in New Haven, previously introduced in Chapter Two. She is the queen of making to-dos bite-size. As you can see, instead of just writing "Unit 3" on her Weekly Worksheet, Emily has broken it out into several steps: "Calendar," "Objectives," "Assessments," and "Materials." Some of these to-dos require certain materials or a certain energy level. By carefully considering that, Emily will make more progress on Unit 3. All of a sudden, tackling Unit 3 doesn't feel so daunting.

So, let's talk about how this could look in your context. Let's say that this time, *before* you begin your unit plan, you break it down into all of the to-dos it would take to complete it.

Reading/Literature	
Sub Plans for 10/14	☐
Unit 3 calendar	☐
Unit 3 objectives	☐
Unit 3 assessments	☐
Unit 3 materials	☐
Tracking Board	
Student Work Board	☐
Alternate IA's	L
Prove-it Posters	
Work for Devonte,	
Tavis, Otavia,	
Score Process Essays	
Score RTL's	

Figure 8.1 Emily's Weekly Worksheet That Shows an Example of Bite-Size To-Dos

Then you assign each to-do to the schedule for your week. The time you choose for these to-dos will likely revolve around the amount of time you need to accomplish the task, what materials you'll need to tackle it, and the energy level you must possess to achieve it.

What if some of my to-dos have *lots* of steps?

Some of you may have questions about what to do when your to-dos are complex and multistep, such as planning a field trip. Appendix 3: Project Plans for Teachers, located at the back of this book, explains a way to break down complex to-dos that makes them simple to accomplish.

If you find yourself transferring the same to-dos from Weekly Worksheet to Weekly Worksheet, or rolling over the same to-do from month to month in your Upcoming To-Do List, check and see if one of the ideas presented earlier will help you accomplish (or free you from guilt for not accomplishing) your to-do.

FIVE DEMONS THAT HAUNT US: SOME COMMON HUMAN BEHAVIORS

We just discussed three common challenges of personal organization systems—the first was not having a superclear, articulated system for everything that comes your way. The second challenge was not using your system well (in our health analogy, this is like lifting the weights but not doing it properly). The third challenge was having things actually not move off your well-intentioned lists. For the most part, these are *skill* challenges.

However, there are some other issues that can plague us, ones that usually go unmentioned. As some of you may have experienced in the past, there are a few common demons that can get in the way of our becoming Together Teachers, or establishing any new habit. There are five common demons that tend to appear when teachers are establishing their personal and classroom organization systems.

Five Demons That Get in the Way of Becoming a Together Teacher

- **Perfectionism.** If this describes you, you may find yourself fiddling repeatedly with formatting a certain tool. You may hesitate to get started because you just cannot pick a tool that works perfectly for you. The only way to customize your organization system is to *just get started* and see what works for you and what doesn't. Only through this process will you discover that, for example, you need a section for graduate school in your Weekly Worksheet, or that you cannot stand to enter to-dos electronically.

- **Procrastination.** For many of us, this demon means we may be really excited to get started but we just want to wait until we have *four* hours to finally get that e-mail inbox under control. Then we finally find that long chunk of time, and something else more interesting calls our name. We end up never getting started on our personal organization system because *something* or *anything* keeps getting in the way. If this is you, I recommend that you pick one tool and get started immediately.

- **Temptation.** You have a loyalty issue; it is hard for you to remain committed to a Together Teacher System. This is the person who dives in head first, pitches every single Post-it Note, sets up a Together Teacher System after one whirlwind trip to Staples, and then . . . sees a colleague with a really cool planner and becomes tempted to switch systems. This is also the person who starts cheating on *your* system when you find yourself scribbling on Post-it Notes or jotting notes on your arm! You can tell you are prone to temptation if you hear yourself saying, "Well, *that* system didn't work for me. That woman didn't know *what* she was talking about! I better try something else immediately." If this sounds like you, I encourage you to make sure you are actually *using* your tools before you toss the system out the window.

- **Distraction.** If you are distraction prone, you are likely to sit down to start creating a portion of a Together Teacher System and then you remember something else you have to do, so you get up and walk over to your colleague's classroom. You return to your desk, ready to start populating your Comprehensive Calendar, and you remember an e-mail you have to write. You open up your e-mail and start replying to what came in, eventually forgetting about what you meant to write to begin with. Two hours later, your Comprehensive Calendar is yet to be started.

- **Overcomplication.** If you are a systems zealot, you may be salivating by now and eager to dive in. If this describes you, you likely came into this book already having a fancy notebook, at least one gadget, a planner, and a complicated e-mail filing system. Your system might be very complicated and not comprehensive because stuff lives in too many places and you have too many organization systems running. You can tell that you are subject to overcomplication if you have to answer the quiz questions at the beginning of the chapter with seven very detailed sentences per question.

 Reflection Questions:

Do any of these demons visit you?

When have you seen them?

How have you successfully fought them?

If you're haunted by one of these demons, what can you do about it?

The Antidotes to the Demons

I'm going to be honest. This *will* be hard initially. Much like when starting a new workout regimen, you will feel a bit of pain. Staying moderately together takes a little bit of time and a heck of a lot of discipline. There are a few tricks that I've seen Together Teachers, who are as prone to the demons as the rest of us, do to keep the system moving.

Keep it simple. Each Together Teacher I have spoken with has a strong desire to simplify their system. They all try to carry fewer things, look fewer places, and consolidate items.

Remain consistent. As I mentioned earlier in the book, one way to ensure that you can fight those demons is to stay consistent. Any Together Teacher System takes daily and weekly maintenance, as well as an initial investment. Whatever tools you choose to use, try and stick with them at least three months to build a new habit.

Remember the purpose. Each Together Teacher realizes that being organized is a means to an end—stronger student outcomes and more free time. Being organized just for organization's sake gets us nowhere.

Now that we have tested our *personal* organization systems to ensure that they are airtight, discussed how to use our systems most effectively, and named some normal human behaviors that hold us back, we should feel good about our Together Teacher Systems. We should feel confident about planning our time, managing our to-dos, capturing our thoughts, and executing smartly. We will test our systems again in the last chapter just to make sure we feel confident. Let's now turn our attention to our external environment—namely e-mail overload, our physical classroom space, and dealing with piles of paper.

Anna
A Day in the Life

Name: Anna Tattan

Years teaching: 5

Grades/subject: First Grade

Other school responsibilities: Student attendance systems, teacher coach

Professional goals: I want to finish this year with high attendance rates across the school, and a strong classroom culture in each classroom.

Personal commitments: I am training for the New York City Marathon this year. I will also be learning German so I can chat with my German relatives at my cousin's wedding next summer.

Proudest student moment: A first-grade scholar was consistently late to school and he was missing his guided reading class (with me!) every morning. After many concerned yet unproductive discussions with his mother, I finally sat down with my scholar and had a genuine conversation about what happens during reading class that is so important to his future and the consequences of what happens if he never learns to read because he is always late to school. Wouldn't you know it, within the week, Mom came to me and exclaimed, "My son has been waking *me* up every morning because he says

he can't be late to school or he won't be a leader!" He hasn't missed reading group since, and he is turning into *quite* the leader.

How she is working to become even more together: Prioritization: especially when it comes to e-mail. A full in-box is stressful and I want to answer e-mails and respond immediately. If I do that, my in-box is cleaned out and it temporarily feels spectacular, until I realize that I didn't prioritize the tasks that really *needed* to get done that day. I am still working on focusing on my priorities over all else so that my work is primarily proactive versus reactive.

A Day in the Life

5:40 AM: Alarm goes off. I get up, brush my teeth, and am out the door by 6:10 AM.

6:40 AM: I walk into school and greet the few teachers I see. After dropping off my lunch in the kitchen, I make my breakfast (granola and milk, easy!) and look over my Weekly Worksheet and Comprehensive Calendar (kept in Outlook). I ensure that all important to-dos

are in my Together Teacher System, which often means recording a few meetings from Outlook onto my Weekly Worksheet because things have changed through the week.

7:00 AM: I check in with my co-teachers to say hello and offer assistance on any classroom projects.

7:15 AM: As students arrive, I have time to myself to work on my schoolwide attendance project. I run reports to see who is consistently absent and make meetings and set up conferences to combat poor attendance.

8:00 AM: I call families of students who are absent and coerce them to come to school. This typically takes an hour, but if I finish early, I make positive calls to families who always bring their children to school on time.

9:00 AM: I check my Weekly Worksheet and my e-mail, looking for two-minute response e-mails or emergency e-mails.

9:15 AM: I'm teaching a group of the first graders who are struggling with reading.

10:05 AM: I pop into the classrooms of the teachers I coach, take notes, and send out observations to discuss with teachers during our weekly meeting. I don't check e-mail at this time, even though I'm on my laptop.

11:00 AM: I lesson plan for math since I plan for the entire first-grade team.

12:00 PM: I eat lunch while reading *Time* or other newsy magazines. I spend time chatting a bit with surrounding teachers. Lunch is typically fifteen minutes. I quickly check my Weekly Worksheet and e-mail.

2:30 PM: Now I'm back teaching math to my first graders!

3:30 PM: This is fun! I bring perfect attendance awards to classrooms, interview scholars for our daily Culture Blast, or help with dismissal and tutoring.

4:00 PM: I look over my Weekly Worksheet to ensure that I've accomplished my tasks—and if not, I rewrite the tasks on a later date. Often I attend a meeting or finish a project.

6:00 PM: I almost always run and stretch. I usually make dinner and dessert or go out to dinner with friends.

8:00 PM: Nearing the end of the day, I prepare for the next day (pack lunch, lay out clothes, check Weekly Worksheet). I usually just relax, talk on the phone with my sister or other family members, write letters to far-away friends, or just catch up on personal time.

10:30 PM: I am in bed and reading a book before I fall asleep.

PART 4

All That
Other Stuff!

Tame the E-Mail Beast: How to Manage Your In-Box

CHAPTER 9

Learning Objectives

■ Apply effective measures to prevent your in-box from getting out of control.

■ Create simple and efficient systems for responding to and filing e-mail.

■ Determine format and standards for writing clear e-mails.

SETTING THE SCENE

Just uttering the word *e-mail* is enough to send most people—including teachers—running for the door. E-mail is particularly challenging for us as teachers because we are not in front of our computers most of the day. We have limited time to process and respond to the important information that is being shuttled back-and-forth electronically across our schools. On top of this, most of us are managing anywhere from one to five different e-mail accounts: a school account and personal Gmail, Yahoo, or Hotmail accounts. Additionally, if you dabble in social media, you likely have a Facebook in-box, a LinkedIn in-box, and an unending stream of tweets clamoring for your attention. And much like I have mentioned in previous chapters, your e-mail in-boxes are yet another place where your to-dos lurk unaccounted for in your larger Together Teacher System.

Consider, for example, that memo from your principal or a request from a parent. Oh, yes, you know which one I'm talking about—that e-mail you have opened, read, tried to make sense of, and then closed. Typically we check our e-mail quickly between classes, become overwhelmed by what we find in our in-boxes, log out to suppress the anxiety, and fail to capture any important actions or deadlines. By the time we log back in, a new set of e-mails has appeared, making older messages not marked as "new" as good as gone. For many of us, e-mail is an enormous time-suck and procrastination technique, and it becomes the default activity whenever we have a free five or ten minutes. The problem with compulsive e-mail checking is that you rarely have time to deal with e-mail in this short period, so you actually end up only raising your stress level by checking it so frequently. In this chapter, we will focus on habits that Together Teachers use to manage effectively all of the e-mail communication that comes our way from many directions.

 Reflection Question:

Describe the state of your e-mail in-boxes. Say more about your e-mail habits, for example, are you always checking your e-mail? Never checking it?

E-MAIL IS NOT THE ENEMY, BUT . . .

E-mail is not the enemy, but when it is abused, neglected, or not cared for properly, it can become out of control. *Out of control* means that your in-box is full of hidden to-dos not accounted for in your Together Teacher System, thereby causing you tremendous stress and increasing the likelihood of missing something important. Why does this matter? It matters because most of us spend too much time scrolling through our in-box, rereading messages, and figuring out what we need to do with them, rather than systematically deciding how to deal with each e-mail. There are lots of good resources on e-mail clean-out, and even some humorous ones, such as videos called "In-box Zero" started by Merlin Mann, author of a popular blog called 43folders.com. Because we are talking about being Together *Enough* Teachers, I think that getting to zero is unattainable for the average human.

I like to think of it as *Operation One-Screen*, meaning that once per week, each of your in-boxes has been cleaned out to the extent that you can see only *one* screen and you do not have to scroll to figure out what you have to do! In this chapter, we will focus on how to structure our in-boxes, the best ways to sort, organize, and file, and when and how to use e-mail appropriately. Keep in mind that each school has its own unique communication culture, so you may have to adapt some of the ideas to work in your own context. For the sake of this chapter we are assuming you work in a school where e-mail is used as a regular communication device for contact between teachers, between teachers and parents, and between teachers and administrators.

Stage an Initial Intervention (or Declare E-mail Bankruptcy)

Our goal here is to get our in-box as clean as possible. To be clear, this does not mean you are answering every single message every day. Rather, it means you are processing your e-mails by answering quick questions and noting when you need to block out time for longer replies and recording that time on your schedule on your Weekly Worksheet or on your Comprehensive Calendar. Let's start examining our e-mail accounts and getting them set up for a more healthy future. We will take a few small steps to create a simpler, more efficient structure for our in-boxes.

Reflection Questions:

How many in-boxes do you actively maintain? Inactively maintain?

How many messages are in each of your in-boxes?

Limit your total number of e-mail accounts. There are different schools of thought about how many accounts you should maintain. I recommend that you aim for as few accounts as possible. This is because I want you to have to look in as few places as possible. For most teachers, this means a school account, a personal correspondence account, and one account for "junk" e-mail, when you need to give an address to a shopping Web site.

Unsubscribe to any junk or updates you don't bother to read. Unwittingly, we end up signing up for updates we never read, news flashes that cause distraction, and professional newsletters for which we have the best of intentions. Those Gap sale promotional e-mails can be useful, but also distracting, so many teachers have found it helpful to set up filters so that the junk e-mails automatically flow into folders and do not clutter their in-boxes. Although the ASCD's (formerly the Association for Supervision and Curriculum

Development) SmartBriefs are incredibly insightful, if you get fifteen per day you will never succeed in unburying your in-box and your eyes will glaze over and fail to pick out what is truly important. Additionally, you can set your filters to catch the spam that inevitably works its way into our in-boxes.

Get your smartphone synchronization working. If you carry a smartphone, you should set the options so that e-mails you delete never appear in your in-box. This ensures that you don't have to reread the same old e-mail over and over. Once you read the e-mail on your smartphone and write a reply, you should delete it so you never have to read it again. The double read takes way too much time in your already busy day. It is too easy to leave those e-mails lurking around your in-box.

Direct your family and friends to where you want them to go. Direct your family and friends to the e-mail account you prefer them to use. For most of us, this is a case in which separation of the professional and personal is actually helpful. This way, you can avoid looking at the millionth of your great-aunt's political rant forwards during the work day. Also, when you are on vacation or at home in the evening, you can still log into your personal e-mail without getting distracted or stressed by your work in-box. If you are friends with your work colleagues, don't be shy about letting them know that you would prefer they use your personal account for social e-mails.

Turn off the auto notifications. If you are accustomed *or* addicted to hearing a little bell or seeing a little envelope pop up on your navigation bar, I would turn off these options! These seemingly well-intentioned notifiers can divert you from what you are trying to do in the moment.

Get friendly with the delete button. We all have a phobia about deleting e-mails. The underlying issue may be fear of losing an important message, a sentimentality we develop toward the messages we receive, or an uncertainty surrounding what we may need in the future. These possibilities aside, I believe we should all delete as much as humanly possible. Remember: the goal is to make your life simpler, and that starts with getting rid of the clutter. It would be helpful to develop the habit of pressing that delete button after you reply and on anything you don't need. I think you will enjoy the sense of relief!

A drastic approach—Declare e-mail bankruptcy. If you are not sure where to start, you may need to use your one and only get-out-of-jail-free card and declare e-mail bankruptcy. This involves deleting *every* message in your in-box. You can do a quick search on YouTube and find instructions on e-mail bankruptcy declaration! You may want to alert your colleagues in advance, and you should remember that you can declare bankruptcy only one time! It's scary, but you can do it. Close your eyes, take a deep breath, highlight, and drag your deleted messages into the trash mailbox. There—you *did* it! Get used to this feeling and purge your in-box regularly with the methods discussed in this chapter.

Although these small structural tips will not tame the e-mail beast by themselves, they are a starting point for getting things in order.

Reflection Question:

Are there any structural adjustments, such as creating filters or synchronizing your smartphone, that you need to make in your in-box to regain control?

SET UP YOUR IN-BOX FOR SUCCESS

Although I do not want people to go crazy setting up a complex system for e-mail filing and storage, there are some options that can make your in-box easier to get through. This section shares some ideas for filing and referencing information in your in-boxes.

Create Simple Folders for Filing

I don't recommend setting up fancy filing systems, because they are too time-consuming to maintain. Searching is faster than filing these days, and your in-box should not function as a filing cabinet. Constant scrolling to figure out what you have to do is an inefficient use of time. I recommend setting up a few folders: Follow-Up, Projects, Upcoming Meetings, Administrative, and Processed. Let's look at the specifics of each of these folders using Anna's in-box (Figure 9.1). Anna was focused on school-year readiness planning for her school, so she added a special folder (Readiness) for storing all of the e-mails related to that project.

Technology Tip: If you use a Web-based or electronic Comprehensive Calendar, then you can simply drag the e-mail into the calendar onto the day you want to deal with it.

A Simple E-mail Folder System

Follow-up

The Follow-Up folder is where you will put any e-mail that takes longer than five minutes to address. The trick with this folder is that, in order to make it work, you have to record the messages in it on your Weekly Worksheet (if you have to answer it this week) or Comprehensive Calendar (if you have to answer it further into the future by a specific deadline).

If you forget to return to the e-mails in the Follow-Up folder, you run the risk of clearing them out of your in-box (which is a good instinct!) but never referencing those messages again (which is not good!). After you complete the to-do associated with the e-mail, delete it. The Follow-Up folder should store no more than twenty-five messages, and it is the only folder in which you may store any action items. The beauty of this folder is that it creates a space for e-mails that would otherwise clutter your in-box, making it more difficult to focus on the never-ending flow of new messages that arrive there. This system will let you go into your in-box with a specific purpose rather than going in to scan every five minutes.

Projects

The Projects folder is for storing e-mails related to any projects on which you are currently working. An e-mail goes into the Projects folder either if it contains material you need to reference for a project you are actively working on or if it is so important that you need it grouped for future reference.

Example of a Project Folder

For example, if you were working on progress reports, one of your current folders would likely be called Progress Reports. Whenever you receive an e-mail from your assistant principal with details about how to format your progress reports, you simply drag it over to this folder. Then, when it is time to work on your progress reports, all of your materials are in one place.

Testing Whether Something Goes into a Projects Folder

The easiest rule of thumb for the Projects folder is to consider which of your projects would require a manila folder if you were handling hard-copy documents. If it would require a manila folder, it warrants a subfolder in your in-box.

Meetings

This is as simple as it sounds. Anytime you create or receive a meeting agenda, simply drag it over to this folder. Then, when it is time for the meeting, you can simply look in this folder for your agenda or meeting materials. You can periodically clean this folder out, but there is no real need to do this. In general, I advocate downloading any documents attached to e-mails, but most schools create agendas within the text of the e-mail, so it is easier just to file it.

Administrative

Your Administrative folder should contain important e-mails, usually about noninstructional matters, that you will want to reference again, such as e-mails about passwords from your IT team, or a revision to a student dress code policy. Many teachers use subfolders in this section, such as a folder for e-mails about employee benefits.

Processed

This is my favorite folder. Michael Linenberger, author of *Total Workday Control Using Microsoft Outlook,* describes the Processed Mail folder as the place where, after you have replied and acted on your in-box, you drag everything remaining in the in-box. This has the benefit of still storing all your old e-mails, but not wasting your time by nitpicky filing. If you still have a deleting phobia, this is where *everything* else that does not require any action is housed—no subfolders needed! To determine whether an e-mail should be housed in the Processed folder, here are your steps:

1. Consider whether you want to reference that message in the future.
2. If that is a possibility, then move the e-mail to your Processed folder for safekeeping.
3. Then, whenever you need to scramble through your e-mails for a particular message, you can look for it in this folder.

   Thankfully, most major e-mail providers have a useful search feature that allows you to look for e-mails by key words or to sort very quickly.

Additional Folders

If you are a grade-level leader, department chair, special educator, or in any role that has extra responsibility or requires additional documentation, you may find you need to add more e-mail folders. This is totally fine. Just be judicious about what you add so that you don't fall into the "I can never deal with my in-box until I have a half-day to file everything" category. As you can see, Anna chose to make a School Readiness folder because it was a major initiative for which she was responsible.

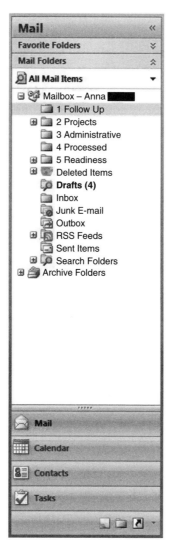

Figure 9.1 Anna's Outlook In-Box with Simple Folders

Technology Tip: Your e-mail folders organize themselves alphabetically by default. You can override this function by doing a few small tricks.

- Put a number in front of each folder (see Figure 9.2). For example, if you want the Upcoming Meetings folder to come first, then name that folder 1–Upcoming Meetings.

- If you want to group particular folders, give them similar first names. For example, if you want all of your instructional e-mails grouped together, you may label them "Instructional—Math," and then "Instructional—Reading."

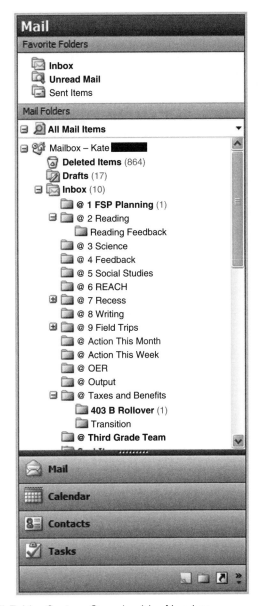

Figure 9.2 Kate's E-Mail Folder System Organized by Number

Reflection Questions:

What e-mail folders will you delete?

What e-mail folders will you create?

Are there additional folders you need?

Rule 6: Create a Trigger for What You Put Away

Occasionally, we become overzealous in our newfound e-mail techniques and start arranging different filters, sending messages into multiple in-boxes, or just moving items quickly into the Follow-Up folder. Be very, very careful with moving a To-Do out of your immediate line of sight. Once items are tucked away (much like that beloved stack of professional development materials in a folder on your desk), it becomes difficult to remember to actually go back. If you do put an e-mail requiring action into your Follow-Up folder or add a great article about literature circles to the stack of professional reading, be sure to make a note of it in your Comprehensive Calendar or Upcoming To-Do List so you have a trigger to return.

Quick E-Mail Quiz

Let's take a quick e-mail quiz to make sure our folder and filing systems are in good shape. What would you do with each of the following e-mails that have landed in your in-box? You are reviewing at 11:00 AM, right before lunch duty.

@ 1. A daily e-mail update from your assistant principal that names the students who are *not* riding the bus.

@ 2. A returned e-mail from your grade-level leader confirming that she can meet with a parent on Tuesday.

@ 3. An urgent e-mail from the office staff asking if you can call a parent ASAP about a "bathroom incident."

@ 4. A lengthy e-mail from your academic coach giving feedback on your literature lesson plans.

@ 5. An e-mail from your after-school coordinator laying out the process for finding additional work time for students in the afternoon.

The answer key for this quiz is located at the end of the chapter.

ADMIT YOU ARE PART OF THE PROBLEM: CREATE BETTER E-MAIL HABITS

Now that we have tackled some structural issues like in-box setup and folders, let's get a little more personal. It is time to face some of those demons discussed previously. If you are like most people, it is unlikely that you have had a focused work session in a long time. Let's talk about ways to curb our own addictions and be more purposeful about when we actually "do" e-mail.

Reflection Question:

When was the last time you sat down to work on something for two hours without checking your e-mail?

Why E-Mail Is Hard to Resist

Reducing the frequency with which you check your e-mail takes an *insanely* high amount of discipline. I'm a moderately disciplined person myself and it's *all I can do* not to check my Android and BlackBerry right now as I write this paragraph. AHHHHHH! I gave in. I checked my work account on my Droid. Now I'm distracted by a new request. Why do we struggle with this? I think there are a few reasons.

Reason 1: Focusing is *hard.* The first reason is that it is incredibly hard to focus these days with so much coming at us from all directions. At any given moment you may have an incoming text from a parent, an urgent e-mail from your assistant principal—and your mom leaving you three voice mails about your great-aunt's fiftieth wedding anniversary. Answering a bunch of e-mails is a way we allow ourselves to feel accomplished—sometimes without moving much of value forward.

Reason 2: E-mail *feels* like a nifty little present. The second reason is that we all secretly hope that what may appear in our in-boxes is actually more *interesting* than what we are doing right at this moment. One of my favorite teacher trainers in the country, Orin from MATCH Charter Public Schools in Boston, said to me, "Each e-mail feels like it could be some sort of little, neatly wrapped gift—waiting there for you in bold font, teasing you with possibility. How could you *not* open it?"

Reason 3: Being Proactive Is Much Harder Than Being Reactive. The third reason is that reacting is easier than acting. Replying is always easier because you get to think less. You can just *do. Oh, someone needs something from me? Let me help them. I am so useful and important.* It is *much* easier to reply to an e-mail from your grade-level chair about a student discipline issue than it is to think about how to crack the nut with your struggling readers.

So, given all of these temptations and reasons to be glued to our in-boxes, how do we fight this habit? The first way is to have designated times that you check e-mail, rather than half-heartedly checking it all day long.

When to Check E-Mail

How often to check e-mail often depends on the culture and practices of your school, but most teachers can get away with checking two to three times per day. Most teachers check e-mail first thing in the morning, at some point in the middle of the day, and again at the end of the day.

Choose When to Answer Your E-Mail

Together Teachers *choose* when they will check their e-mail rather than checking it during every free moment and not having time to actually do anything about it. Jennifer, the middle school literature teacher we met previously, says, "I try not to read e-mail if I don't have time to do something about it. If I receive an e-mail with a deadline that looks like it will take me some time, then I look ahead on my Comprehensive Calendar to determine when I can get to it—and I actually write it into my schedule."

Anna works at a school that uses e-mail to communicate about student issues, so she checks her e-mail more often than some teachers. Anna has set aside particular times of day to check her e-mail so she can focus on bigger projects. She says, "I check my e-mail quickly in the morning, but then quickly shut down so I can focus on student attendance phone calls. I next check at 11:30 or 12 PM, then at the end of the day, around 3:30 PM so I can prepare the Culture Blast (a daily behavior celebrations and information e-mail) to send to the teachers at my school."

A Recap: When to Check Your E-Mail

- *If your school uses e-mail frequently to communicate about urgent issues:* Try to check e-mail briefly every few hours. Ensure that you write down any actions that come up, file anything that needs to be referenced later, and delete anything you do not need to read again. Do not just scan and close. You will be doing double work later.

- *If your school regularly sends e-mails containing important information and deadlines but does not use e-mail for urgent issues:* Choose one to three times per day to read e-mail, and deal with it using the strategies listed in the next section.

- *If your school uses e-mail irregularly:* Choose once per day to read and reply.

You will note that *none* of these options say to check e-mail between every class and at every prep period. This will result in raising blood pressure and getting very little done. By proactively selecting times of day to review and deal with your e-mail (or to delay responses that take more time), you will find that you will move through your in-box much more efficiently and be less distracted by the "gift" your in-box just delivered.

Now that you have learned several ways that teachers manage e-mail in different school contexts, think about when it will make the most sense for you to check your e-mail.

Reflection Questions:

When will you check your e-mail during the day?

Have you given it a time in your schedule?

Are there people who get priority responses, such as parents or administrators?

How to Check E-Mail

Now that we have discussed *when* to check e-mail, let's discuss *how* to check e-mail. As you read, the teachers mentioned in this chapter try to touch each e-mail only one time—and they resist looking at e-mail all day long as a distraction. I have found that most of us need structured choices that will enable us to check e-mail only once. One of my favorite blogs, Productive Flourishing (http://www.productiveflourishing.com), describes a method called STAR that will help you deal with the e-mail deluge.

What to *do* with your e-mail? The STAR method

Scan your in-box for senders and subjects. This step gives you a higher perspective on what's in your in-box: you have to know where you're starting from and where you're going.

Trash everything that's not relevant, useful, or something you want or need. You may see 60 percent of the messages in your in-box disappear at this one step alone.

Archive means "archive relevant reference information." A lot of messages just contain information that you want to keep but don't need any specific action from you at this time. Archiving them clears them from your attention, and this may account for 20 to 30 percent of the messages in your in-box.

Respond to what's left. This is the hardest step, when it comes down to it, because you'll actually have to do more than click on a few buttons. But once you get this far, you'll have a lot fewer messages, and that alone may give you the motivation to start working through these messages that you'll have left.

As you check your e-mail, have your Together Teacher System beside you in case you need to record that you need to return to a particular e-mail. For example, if I saw an e-mail requesting that I give feedback on a math interim assessment and the deadline was two weeks away, I'd Time Block a thirty-minute chunk before school when my energy is highest and then move that e-mail to my Follow-Up folder.

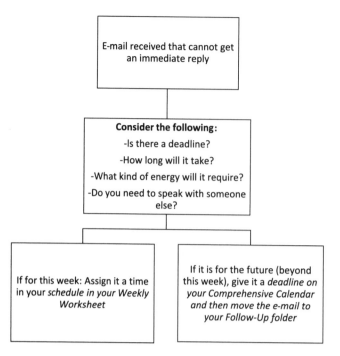

Figure 9.3 Step-by-Step E-mail Flow for E-mails You Cannot Deal with Now

Then, when that Tuesday morning arrives and I review my schedule, I will simply go to my Follow-Up folder, grab the e-mail, and give feedback on the interim assessment. This process ensures that I do not spend valuable morning work time scanning my in-box figuring out what I have to do. The steps to figuring out what to do with e-mails you cannot deal with in the moment are also outlined in Figure 9.3.

The second reason to defer an e-mail is that you actually don't know what to do about it and you may need to think or ask another person. Even in this case you still need to write down what the next step is. Possible options often include the following:

- Does it need to go on a Thought Catcher for your principal?
- Do you need to write an e-mail to someone else to get their opinion?
- Do you just need time to think about it?

CLARITY IS KING

I have frequently seen that the problem can lie with the author of the e-mail rather than with the folks receiving a zillion messages. Many of us unintentionally use our e-mail communication as an opportunity to revisit our college creative writing skills rather than viewing it as a tool to help us complete our work more efficiently. E-mails should be warm, brief, and clear. Let's talk about how to write clearer e-mails. It sounds silly but a clearly written e-mail can make all the difference, because it will spur equally clear (and likely fewer) follow-up replies.

Clean Up Those Subject Lines

I am a bit of a zealot on clear subject lines because I believe they create and clarify the level of priority for your audience. When subject lines are not clear or when they create a level of urgency not intended, it can cause us to feel glued to our in-boxes and respond to everything the second it hits. To combat this, we can use some simple tags to help clarify the nature of the e-mail for our reader. Table 9.1 contains some possible subject lines that are commonly used in schools with strong communication systems.

Now, of course you don't want to start just using these subject lines without discussing them within your department or grade level or with your school community. That would not go over very well. Many schools choose to make a School Communication Agreement. An example is included for you in Appendix Four.

Format Your E-Mails to Get Better Replies

It sounds simple but the way your e-mails are formatted can often be a help or hindrance to your reader. Although it may feel overly formal at first, remember the goal here is to help you get a reply and what you need to move things forward. Here are a few tips for ensuring that our e-mails are clear and easy to read. First, let's look at some e-mails that are less likely to get replies, and how to improve them.

An E-Mail from a Colleague to Others in Her Department

From: Emily Gansworth
Sent: Monday, March 28
To: Maia Heyck-Merlin; Cheryl Walker; Lotoya Grant; Hollis Terrell
Cc: Jennifer Atworth
Subject: Progress Reports 3rd Marking Period

Hey guys!

With Ms. Dormand out, Mr. Robichaux had requested that these be in by COB [close of business] Thursday. Let me know if you have any questions!

Emily

Table 9.1 Sample E-Mail Subject Lines and Examples

Type of Subject Line	Definition	Example
FYI	This stands for *for your information,* meaning the reader should be kept in the loop on the e-mail's subject but *does not have to respond.*	**Subject Line: FYI: Victor's mom has been contacted** Dear Jenny, I have contacted Victor's mom about the missing homework, and she is on top of it moving forward. Maia
Action Requested by X Date	This is when you request that someone else do something but you do not need a reply.	**Subject Line: Parent Phone Calls [Action Requested between 10/7–10/17]** Dear Grade Team, As we discussed in this week's meeting, please make at least five positive parent phone calls between 10/7 and 10/17 and record them in the Google document. Thanks, Jenny
Response Requested by X Date	This means you are expecting a reply from your respondent. Now, you cannot go around saying, "Reply requested ASAP," because that approach is simply unfair to your reader. Your school or team should establish norms for response times so you can be clear what is expected of you. Some schools set up an agreement that you should allow 3 to 4 days for messages that require a 30-minute or more reply.	**Subject Line: Best Approach to Student Holiday Celebration [Response Requested by 11/17]** Dear Grade Team, As you know, it is time to determine our collective approach to student holidays in our grade. We have three options: (1) Class potluck (2) A small Secret Santa exchange within classrooms (3) No celebration but a thematic unit Please let me know your choice or alternative suggestion by November 17. Thanks, Jenny
Quick Question	This subject heading would be reserved for items that are *truly* quick questions, meaning that the receiver can give a yes or no answer to the question. The general expectation here is 12 to 24 hours of response time.	**Subject Line: QQ: "Gloria's Way"?** Jenny, Do you have the book *Gloria's Way?* Maia

Table 9.1 (*Continued*)

Type of Subject Line	Definition	Example
Urgent	Use this one wisely. This likely means you need a reply in less than 24 hours, and you should follow up with a phone call to signal your urgency. If you feel yourself compelled into the world of red exclamation points, remember that most people with whom you work are *not* in front of their computer all day; therefore, a phone call or text *may* be more appropriate.	**Subject Line: URGENT/IMPT: Terrell's missing permission slip** Dear Jenny, Terrell forgot his permission slip for today's trip. Can you please have the office call his family as soon as possible? Maia

This is a very brief e-mail that doesn't give any detail or context for what the teacher is asking of her colleagues. It would benefit from a few lines of context and clarity. Let's rewrite it to be clearer and easier to answer.

From: Emily Gansworth

Sent: Monday, March 28

To: Maia Heyck-Merlin; Cheryl Walker; Lotoya Grant; Hollis Terrell

Cc: Jennifer Atworth

Subject: Reminder: Progress Reports for 3rd Marking Period due Thursday, April 2

Hi Fourth Grade Team,

As you know, Ms. Dormand is out of school at a professional development conference this week. Mr. Robichaux requested your 3rd quarter marking period forms be turned in to the box on his office door by 5:00 PM on Thursday. If you need to refresh yourself on the directions for the online system, please refer to the e-mail sent in February with detailed instructions. I have also pasted it below for your handy reference.

Best,

Emily

So, what did we do to make the e-mail more clear?

Context. We added a context for what the teacher was asking.

Specificity. We named what "close of business" meant and exactly where the forms were to be turned in.

Clarity. We gave a resource where additional information could be found.

Let's look at another e-mail from a teacher to her principal requesting her feedback on an upcoming important decision.

An E-Mail from a Teacher to Her Principal

From: Sarita
Sent: November 2
To: Monica
Subject: Holidays

Good Morning Monica,

How are you? Are you back? We've missed you!

This trimester, I wanted the children to sing holiday songs. I've drafted a letter to parents because I know this subject can be tricky. I've attached the letter and beneath the letter is a list for you of what I would like the children to sing. Please read the letter. Does it sound OK? Is there anything I should add or take out? Do you think I should change the song list? I'd love feedback and suggestions if you have any. Thanks in advance!

Sarita

This e-mail will be really hard for a principal (or anyone) to get through. It has a list of questions embedded in the paragraph, it doesn't direct the principal on where specifically to give feedback, and it doesn't give any context or timeline. Let's rewrite it to make it more likely to get a favorable reply from Sarita's principal.

From: Sarita

Sent: November 2

To: Monica

Subject Line: Holiday Song Parent Letter Review

Good Morning Monica,

How are you? Are you back? We've missed you!

This trimester, I wanted the children to sing holiday songs. I've drafted a letter (attached) to parents that includes a list of proposed songs because I know that this subject can be tricky. I have already run the letter by the grade-level team and they all gave input. You are the last step.

Can you please read the letter and let me know:

- How would you rate the overall tone?

- Is there anything I should add or take out?

- Do you think I should change the song list?

I'd love feedback and suggestions if you have any. It would be helpful to get your reply by November 13. Thanks in advance!

Sarita

So, what did we do to make this teacher's e-mail more clear? This e-mail needed:

- A clearer subject line that included the topic
- A context for why the attachment was created and who had already reviewed it
- Clearer "asks" in bullet points

Write Better E-Mails

- **Put actions at the beginning and context at the end.** All your reader really cares about is what he or she needs to do and by when. Put the action at the top of the e-mail and offer greater context later. Make it *very* easy for readers to do what you want them to do.

- **Avoid text-heavy, prose-like e-mails.** E-mails are not meant to be novels or creative outlets. Use spaces, bullets, and other signposts to help your reader determine what is important. A common error is to embed many questions within one paragraph. What often happens is you get a reply but only to your last question. If you really want to get clear replies to your questions, bullet them.

- **Give or request a timeline or indicate urgency.** Use clear subject lines to help your reader determine when they need to reply.

E-MAIL: USE IT, DON'T ABUSE IT!

In our current digital state we can find ourselves using e-mail for almost everything at all times of day: urgent issues, missives about our complaints, quick questions, complicated student issues, tricky parent situations, and so on. The thing we want to remember is that although e-mail is always convenient, it is not always appropriate. Let's talk about some examples.

Reflection Question:

What do you do when you have a thought you want to share with someone at your school?

When E-Mail Is the Preferred Path

Now that you will ask yourself "Do I need to send this?" before hitting the Send button, let's talk about when it is appropriate to use e-mail and when it is not. The four most common e-mail offenses that all of us commit are as follows:

1. Using e-mail in an emergency

2. Using e-mail to resolve conflicts or disagreements (I have a personal rule on this one: If I find myself irritated by an e-mail, I have to wait at least twenty-four hours to reply.)

3. Using e-mail to deal with complex issues

4. Using e-mail to give unsolicited feedback or to try to initiate major change

Let's explore each of these in more detail and get clear on when it is appropriate to use e-mail and when we may want to make a different choice.

When E-Mail May Not Be the Most Appropriate Choice

- **Using e-mail in an emergency.** For whatever reason, some schools create e-mail urgency addictions on the part of both the teachers and the administrators by using e-mail for urgent situations. If a principal, for example, has to constantly check her e-mail for behavior situations, then that principal is not going to be able to be proactive in approaching other student culture issues. If a teacher has to run to check his or her e-mail every hour to look for urgent updates, he or she cannot be focused on teaching. *E-mail is not for emergencies.* Set up different protocols in your school for emergencies, preferably using the cell phone for communicating urgent issues—or an old-fashioned note sent by student messenger to the principal.

- **Using e-mail to resolve conflict or disagreements.** Just avoid this. You know why. Nothing good ever happens. Set up a time and speak in person. Avoid starting e-mail wars. Or if you receive an e-mail that may be laden with emotions, pick up the phone or have a meeting to discuss the issue.

- **Using e-mail to deal with complex issues.** This is another no-no, unless absolutely necessary. Why? Because complex issues usually involve multiple people and lots of nuance, neither of which lend themselves well to e-mail. For example, I've seen one member of a grade-level team send out a lengthy, winding missive to his team to propose an overhaul to the grade's approach to teaching writing. Within this e-mail there are questions on how writing time is currently structured, how students learn and read and write, and what best practice research says on this topic. Given the scope of the topic (and likely strong opinions!), this topic would be better saved for a department meeting.

- **Using e-mail to give unsolicited feedback or to try to initiate major change.** Let's start from the bottom up. Change is good. Change from teachers is especially good. Writing an e-mail to your principal that is incredibly long-winded and replete with issues, ideas, and an unclear aim is *not* an effective way to use e-mail. Composing such an e-mail will end up being very time-consuming for you—and cumbersome for your principal to respond to—and most likely you will not get a reply.

 Reflection Question:

Look through your sent e-mail messages. Are you using e-mail wisely? Could anything be written more clearly or saved for meetings?

Communicate Better: Moving Beyond E-Mail

Here is a list of ideas for when you can use e-mail to trigger communication on an issue, but you may need to solve the issue through some other means.

- **Propose solutions.** Earlier we discussed the common error often made via e-mail in which the sender throws out multiple thoughts or ideas and ends with the ubiquitous question, "Thoughts?" or "Reactions?" Be the person to offer a few solutions to the challenge you pose in your e-mail. By proposing ideas, you are giving people something to respond to so they don't have to come up with the possible solutions all by themselves. This will ease the load on them and increase the chance that they will respond. You will be amazed at how much more quickly things get resolved.

- **Create daily huddles.** If you find yourself e-mailing your co-teacher obsessively throughout the day (in spite of being in the same room!) or dashing off a missive to your grade-level chair at the end of every day, consider adding a "daily huddle" to your calendar. You may find that meeting in person for a few minutes each day is all you need to discuss items that would constitute five to ten separate e-mails.

- **Shut down the e-mail chains.** You've all experienced it: the back and forth that adds another person to a largely-irrelevant e-mail chain. When you review all of the messages in full, you notice that each person involved has raised a different issue (And what about this behavior issue? And while we are at it, should this student go on the field trip? And what about this incentive system overall?), nothing is moving forward, and the only thing created is confusion. Be the person to step in and offer a concrete next step. For example, "Hey, guys, I'm so glad we have so many opinions on this important issue. I think it makes sense for us to gather for fifteen minutes tomorrow to try and resolve this. If this works, can we each bring our ideas for solving this, and can everyone be free at 4 PM? Just reply to me directly and we will meet in Ms. Anderson's room." You do not have to be the official leader of the team or grade to suggest this. Trust me, people will appreciate this necessary intervention.

This sounds great, but there is no way I can get my school on board with using e-mail like this.

This chapter can feel particularly daunting to start on your own because effective e-mail communication requires the cooperation of many people and cannot be conquered alone. If you like these ideas and think they could help your school tame e-mail (or use it more wisely), here are a few ways you could start:

- Tell your grade-level team or department what you have been reading about, what you see as a challenge with e-mail, and show them this chapter.
    - Ask them if they would be willing to try a simple set of e-mail agreements.
    - If it works, you could start slowly infiltrating your school with these techniques.
- If you have a great relationship with your principal, you could ask to start a temporary communications working group that will help save everyone time.

GET STARTED: NEXT STEPS

E-mail organization and habits are one of those things we tend to put off until a rainy day when we magically have a half-day appear so we can file the six thousand messages that have accumulated in the past few years. That day is not coming. This is one habit that I recommend you start immediately. Deal with the backlog later. Here is a checklist of how you can get started taming your in-box:

- Review the list of structural suggestions to stage the initial intervention.
- Limit your total number of e-mail accounts.
  - Unsubscribe to any junk or updates you don't bother to read.
  - Get your smartphone synchronized with your computer's in-boxes.
  - Direct your family and friends to where you want them to go.
  - Turn off the auto notifications.
  - Get friendly with the delete button.
  - Declare e-mail bankruptcy.
- Set up simple filing systems and get your e-mails filed.
  - Follow-Up
  - Projects
  - Upcoming Meetings
  - Administrative
  - Processed
- Select times of day to answer e-mails and block them into your schedule on your Weekly Worksheet.
- Use the STAR method to go through your e-mails with a clear purpose.
  - **S**can
  - **T**rash
  - **A**rchive
  - **R**espond
- Establish clear writing habits.
- Decide if e-mail is the best way to communicate the information.

*E-Mail Quiz Answer Key:

1. A daily e-mail update from your assistant principal that names the students who are *not* riding the bus: Quickly copy onto your bus list (kept in your Together Teacher System as a frequently referenced document) the names of three students who are not going on the bus. Then delete the e-mail.

2. A returned e-mail from your grade-level leader confirming she can meet with a parent on Tuesday: Reply quickly to confirm the room location and enter the information into your Comprehensive Calendar *or* send the grade-level leader an Outlook or Google meeting invitation with the room details. File the e-mail in the Meetings folder.

3. An urgent e-mail from the office staff asking if you can call a parent ASAP about a "bathroom incident": Write this down in the schedule portion of your Weekly or Daily Worksheet for the next "free time" you have and include the parent's phone number. Reply to the office staff immediately to let them know you will follow up, and delete the e-mail.

4. A lengthy e-mail from your academic coach giving feedback on your literature lesson plans: Leave the e-mail in your in-box until you revise the plans after school that day. Advanced answer: File in the Projects folder in a subfolder called Lesson Plan Feedback. Return to the feedback the next day when you have a Time Block for updating your plans. This Time Block in your schedule will trigger you to return to the information!

5. An e-mail from your after-school coordinator laying out the process for finding additional work time for students in the afternoon: File in the Projects folder in a subfolder called After School. Put a note in the Next Week section of your Weekly Worksheet and build this into your schedule the following week.

Create Stations: Arrange Your Classroom to Run Like Clockwork

CHAPTER 10

Learning Objectives

■ Identify the components of specific classroom materials stations to support classroom efficiency.

■ Set up classroom areas for student self-sufficiency and teacher ease.

■ Maintain the order through use of student jobs and regular routines.

SETTING THE SCENE

Classrooms can very easily look like tornadoes at the end of the day. I remember that in my first months of teaching I felt as if I spent at least thirty minutes just picking up remains from the day left behind by my fourth graders. A random pair of scissors was on the floor, ten library books were unshelved, and I practically broke my leg when I tripped over the electrical cord that powered my printer. As teachers, we need to have all of our supplies at our fingertips throughout the day so we can teach with maximum efficiency.

At the same time, our students, even as young as kindergarten, need to know that everything in the classroom has a specific home and that they play a role in ensuring that all the stuff gets home by the end of the day. Although this isn't a book on classroom management and procedures, given how much *stuff* is in our classrooms and how many materials we need at arm's length over the course of a teaching day, our classrooms need to be carefully set up to support great instruction, reduce fumbling, and promote student self-sufficiency.

Reflection Question:

Rate the current ease of finding "stuff" in your classroom. How quickly can you find that hole puncher? How about last year's laminated Langston Hughes poem for the introduction to your poetry unit? A = 3 seconds flat and F = What do you mean, locate stuff?! What's your rating?

AN OVERVIEW OF THE STATIONS

This chapter describes some key Teaching Stations that can be set up (no matter what your space situation), how to organize your teaching materials, and how to keep your classroom spic and span. You will see photos from other Together Teachers' classrooms and schools, and how teachers make careful use of their space and materials to support great instruction. Although each of you has different classroom space situations, materials, and budgets, all of the Teaching Stations use the same set of principles: clarity of expectations, detailed documentation, and clear labeling.

Teaching Station: *May* be your desk but is more likely a centrally located (potentially portable) place where you can put all of your teaching materials for a particular day. It should contain any materials needed for specific lessons, handouts, and general supplies needed while teaching.

As you read each section of this chapter, envision your own classroom space and materials situation and consider how you can adapt the concepts presented in that section. To get us started, Figure 10.1 illustrates a classroom with common classroom stations labeled. We will

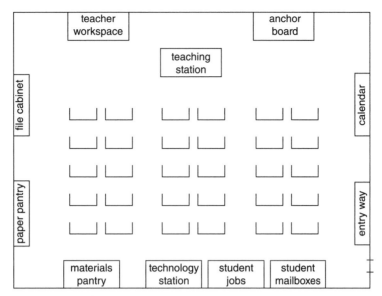

Figure 10.1 Classroom with Stations

walk through these stations, hear the *why* behind each of them, review photos, and discuss how the stations are set up and used to promote classroom efficiency.

ENTER AND EXIT CAREFULLY: CREATE YOUR CLASSROOM FOYER

Although this book is not explicitly on classroom management and efficiency procedures, it hones in on classroom entry and exiting because many of the difficulties surrounding arrival and dismissal have to do with the amount and location of *stuff* that students handle during these times. Let's walk through an organized and efficient classroom as a student would experience it. We will start with the initial entrance, look at which materials should be where, and review what expectations are set for students. Now, let's start with the *Entry Way*.

The Entry Way

Arrival and dismissal are two of the most stressful times of day for teachers and students alike. I'm convinced that the reason is we don't plan as intentionally for these times as we do for classroom lessons. Expectations for kids are unclear, and we are often caught dealing with parents, answering knocks on the door, and determining what to do with tardy students. Many Together Teachers address this challenge by being incredibly explicit in creating a very clear Entry Way, a station placed near the doorway where students check into and check out of the classroom.

Figure 10.2 Anna's Example of Entrance Expectations for First Graders

Much like your home, where you have a place to set your keys, phone, wallet, and mail, your classroom should have a similar station for students. Some teachers' Entry Ways have a place for students to turn in homework and pick up the warm-up so that when they walk to their desks they can immediately begin working. This is also a place where elementary students can trade pencils (more on that in a later section) or secondary students can pick up their homework. Let's look at a few Together Teacher examples of organized Entry Ways. Be on the lookout for the incredible levels of intentionality cultivated in these spaces.

As you can see in Figure 10.2, Anna's first-grade classroom has incredibly clear expectations for student entry, and she uses pictures to help state exactly what the students are supposed to do and in what order. If expectations were not this clear, you would quickly enter a world of piled-up jackets, scattered breakfasts, and homework shoved into backpacks.

Let's look at a few examples of secondary teachers' entrance expectations (Figures 10.3 and 10.4). Dan is a high school chemistry teacher, and Martin teaches high school math.

Figure 10.3 Dan's Classroom Entry

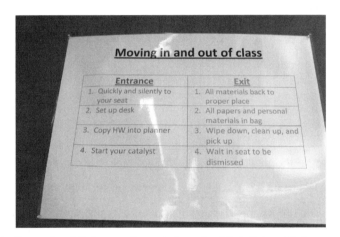

Figure 10.4 Dan's Example of Entrance Expectations for High School Science

As you can see, Dan's classroom has an Entry Way, where students may pick up their warm-up (referred to later as a "catalyst") and drop off any materials, such as permission slips or notes with questions. Once students are at their desks, Dan articulates his expectations in writing, such as "Copy HW [Homework] into planner" and "Start your catalyst." Finally, Martin shows *exactly* what an appropriate desk setup looks like for his students (Figure 10.5). This drawing remains posted on the classroom wall.

Now let's look at the elements common to Entry Ways, no matter what the grade level or space situation.

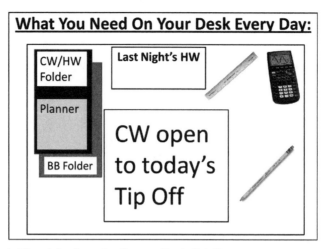

Figure 10.5 Martin's Visual Anchor of a Proper Desk Set-Up

Set Up Your Entry Way: Possible Components

- Select a location for your Entry Way. The two options listed next are the most common:
  - ○ One or two small tables or shelves located where students enter the room (being careful of traffic flow and to avoid bottle necking) OR
  - ○ Multiple locations clearly marked with the various components listed below
- After selecting a location, include the following components:

  - ○ Tray for turning in homework or assignments that won't be reviewed in class
  - ○ Tray for materials to pick up, such as the warm-up or "Do Now"
  - ○ Tray for notes for the teacher, tardy slips, or other random bits of paper
  - ○ Bin from which to pick up any other materials necessary for class that day, such as calculators
  - ○ Student Mailboxes (discussed next)

Reflection Questions:

Where can you put your Entry Way?
What materials should be placed there?
What expectations need to be stated?

Student Mailboxes

One component of an Entry Way is a set of Student Mailboxes. Most teachers have found that when they have papers to distribute to individual students, establishing some kind of

Figure 10.6 Stephanie's 3rd Grade Homeroom Mailboxes in Individualized Student Bins

individualized student mailbox system for distributing and returning papers is helpful. Together Teachers use Student Mailboxes to make paper distribution and pickup run more smoothly. This system prevents that annoying and inefficient walk up and down the aisles of your classroom to distribute and collect papers. Let's look at how a few Together classrooms, both elementary and secondary, have set up their Student Mailboxes and how they use them.

Stephanie is a third-grade teacher in her fourth year of teaching. Figure 10.6 shows how Stephanie sets up her student mailboxes so that she (or a helper) can easily distribute homework or other papers to students and they can gather them independently. You can see that the mailboxes are clearly labeled with each student's name. To make her life just a little bit easier, Stephanie printed extra sets of adhesive labels with students' names to use for labeling coat hooks, homework folders, Student Mailboxes, classroom jobs, and so on. She keeps these labels in her desk.

Student Mailboxes are not just for elementary classrooms. Middle and high school teachers make good use of mailboxes as well, particularly for returning student work as in the secondary classroom example (see Figure 10.7).

Figure 10.7 Student Mailboxes for a Secondary Classroom

Options for a Student Mailbox System

In elementary classrooms, or in any other classroom where you and the students are not moving to other classrooms throughout the day, it is helpful to have some kind of individualized cubbies or folders. As a teacher I used a cheap mail sorter and had a student helper return papers there each morning before school. This student joined me in my classroom before the rest of the class. This was also where I put homework assignments and individual notes to be picked up by students. This system is especially helpful when a student is absent. Classwork and homework can simply be distributed into that student's Mailbox. In the Recommended Resources for the Together Classroom section at the back of the book, I list a few possible supplies for purchase.

Some secondary teachers use plastic file folder crates with one hanging file per student and one crate per section. This system works well when you have multiple sections or move to different classrooms throughout the day.

Checklist: Set Up Student Mailboxes

- Determine the purpose of your Student Mailboxes.
- Decide on and purchase (or find!) whatever tool you need to create your mailboxes, such as hanging file crates or cubbies.
- Clearly label your Student Mailboxes with your students' names.
- Articulate to your students the expectations for setup and maintenance of their Mailboxes.

Reflection Questions:

Do you need a Student Mailbox system?
If so, what materials do you need?
Where can you keep the Student Mailboxes?

The Anchor Board

After your students enter the classroom, they mostly likely start a warm-up or "Do Now" and glance at what will be happening in class that day. Most Together Teachers have found that one central location, an *Anchor Board,* for posting lesson objectives, class agendas, and homework assignments works best to ensure that your students (and you!) always go to the same location to see what they will learn that day, to copy down homework assignments, and to check for any announcements. Let's look at a few examples. In each of the following photographs you will see that the teacher has recorded the lesson objectives, daily agenda, and homework assignments. Some of these teachers have their own classrooms; others share them with more than one teacher.

The teacher who created the Anchor Board in Figure 10.8 is a middle school teacher who teaches one section multiple times each day. As you can see, the Anchor Board is clearly

Figure 10.8 AF Bushwick Middle School Teacher's Anchor Board

Figure 10.9 High School Shared Classroom Multiple-Subject Anchor Board

labeled with the date, Word of the Day, Agenda, Aim, and Exit Ticket Percentage Mastery. It is neat and visually appealing to students, and it is the first place they look when they walk into the room each day. Now let's check out a high school example where a classroom is shared among three teachers.

In Figure 10.9 you can see that multiple teachers share a classroom and Anchor Board. They have designed a shared space where they can each easily record their lesson aims and agendas daily. For many teachers, filling out the Anchor Board is part of their *Opening* or *Closing Routine.*

Options for Creating Your Anchor Board

1. A dry-erase easel on wheels (more often found in elementary classrooms)

2. A cordoned-off portion of your whiteboard on which colored masking tape has been used to create sections

3. Laminated charts on which to write and rewrite each day

Whichever option you choose, you will need an appropriate writing utensil near your Anchor Board. You don't want to be the teacher who accidentally writes on your pure dry-erase board with a permanent marker! Sara, an experienced elementary school teacher, notes, "I always purchase small baskets with magnets or suction cups in the bathroom or kitchen section of home goods stores [such as Bed Bath & Beyond], and stick them to my whiteboard to hold dry-erase markers and erasers."

You will also want to ensure that your Anchor Board is essentially pristine. Messy hand-writing, dry-erase "shadows," markers that barely write, outdated information, or crooked lines are all signs to your students that the Anchor Board is not an important place. Do whatever you can to make this an incredibly organized location.

Checklist: Create Your Anchor Board

- Scout your classroom for an Anchor Board location.
- Prepare the location with section dividers (if needed), writing implements, and a big title.
- Share with your students the expectations for use of the Anchor Board.
- Determine a time to update it daily (or assign it as a student job).

Reflection Questions:

Where can you locate your Anchor Board?
What sections do you need?
How will you keep it pristine?

Now that we have laid out the components of a together Entry Way, let's turn our attention to another set of items that can easily get out of hand—our supplies!

STOCKING UP THE KITCHEN: KEEPING NECESSARY INGREDIENTS ON HAND

Without the right supplies immediately accessible, lessons can quickly disintegrate. If your math lesson is dependent on dice and you realize the day of the lesson that you are five dice short of a class set, your lesson will not be nearly as strong. For this reason, Together Teachers are vigilant in how they stock and supply the materials they need on hand each day. In this section, we will look at Teaching Stations, Distribution Centers, Pantries, and Calendars.

Establish Your Teaching Station

Let's say you are getting ready to work on a complex recipe. After reading through the instructions you realize it makes sense to prepare your ingredients completely ahead of time: garlic finely minced, soup stock made, carrots chopped. Getting ready for a day of teaching is similarly complex and you want to line up your ingredients ahead of time so that you don't waste a second of instructional time (and invite student misbehavior) by having to hunt for the copies of your test or the dice for the math game. Your Teaching Station is different from your Teacher Workspace (more on this in Chapter Twelve), in that this is where all of the

Figure 10.10 Jeff's Mobile Math Cart

materials for instruction all day long are located. Your Teaching Station *may* be your desk, but more likely you will need a centrally located (potentially portable) place where you can put all of your teaching materials for that day. Let's look at a couple of examples of both mobile and stationary Teaching Stations (Figures 10.10 and 10.11). You will notice that these two teachers chose two very different locations for their Teaching Stations, but each station contains the same elements of a highly organized, easily accessible set of instructional materials ready for the school day.

Let's start with Jeff's mobile Teaching Station. Jeff is a middle school math teacher who travels around his school all day. As you can see, he has personalized his cart with some movie paraphernalia. There will be no mistaking his cart for other ones at his middle school. On his cart Jeff always keeps carefully organized basic supplies, such as pencils, scissors, and

Figure 10.11 Anna's Easel-Based Teaching Station

tissues. If you look carefully you can see he has carefully wired a portable pencil container to the side of his cart, and his wires are in immaculate order! In addition, sorting trays are used to hold each day's papers to distribute as well as papers to collect. On top of the cart is Jeff's laptop, appropriate power cords, and a document camera.

Our next example returns us to Anna, who teaches in a stationary elementary school setting. Anna carefully describes her Teaching Station (which is baskets on the bottom of an easel):

- Basket 1: Guided reading books for the week for one guided reading group of six students

- Basket 2: Goal folders for my guided reading students and goal trackers for parents (filled out and sent home weekly)

- Basket 3: Direct Instruction (DI) workbooks, story books, mini whiteboards and dry-erase markers

- Basket 4: Props (For Firefighters: hat, shirt, badge, mug, sticky notes; for Athletes: sweat band, T-shirt, funky sunglasses, stickers)

- Shelf 1
  - Cup of colored pencils
  - Cup of pens
  - Cup of extra pencils with erasers
  - Three tiny bins filled with paper clips, safety pins, and sticky notes
  - Stickers
  - Tape
  - Staplers
  - Scissors
- Shelf 2
  - Visual anchors I've had over the years: character traits, how to make inferences, responding to a book, and so on
- Shelf 3
  - Bin of additional supplies (Velcro, extra tape, extra staples, extra pencils, extra sticky notes, and so on)
  - Treasure Chest (reward books that scholars choose from at the end of each week)

As you ponder your Teaching Station, consider your classroom's physical setup, which technology you rely on regularly, and what materials you have on hand.

Scout the Location for Your Teaching Station

Depending on the size and setup of your classroom, your Teaching Station may be

- a small space underneath your Smart Board
- a portable cart you roll around your classroom
- a shelf underneath your teaching easel

After you determine *where* you will have your Teaching Station, there is the matter of keeping it stocked with everything you need for a day of teaching.

Checklist: Create Your Teaching Station

- Determine where you will have your Teaching Station.
- Stock your Teaching Station with common contents, such as the following:
  - Markers—dry erase, overhead, permanent
  - Pens and pencils

- Baskets or folders in which to collect student work

- Tape dispenser and stapler

- Hole puncher

- Paper clips, binder clips, and thumbtacks (often best kept in a little tackle box)

- Timer

- Stickers, Scholar Dollars, or whatever extrinsic incentives you may use (if any)

- All copies needed for the day or week are placed in bins or trays in the order in which they will be used (discussed more in the next section, on Distribution Centers)

- All materials and supplies needed to support the lessons for the next day; for example, if you were teaching a lesson about comparing weights, you would want to include the Ziploc bag for each math group that already contains gram cubes, a quarter, a rock, and a paper clip

- Personal items, such as your water bottle and lunch

Although this may sound like a lot at first, it will be a relief to have one go-to location that you return to throughout the course of the teaching day. No more will you turn your back to fumble for the right marker. Everything will be clearly labeled and immediately available to you.

Reflection Questions:

Where can you use as your Teaching Station?

What materials do you need at your Teaching Station?

Distribution Centers

For some teachers, any copies or materials they distribute are picked up by students at the Entry Way or handed out at the beginning of the week. However, you need a place to store them first so that you are not running to the photocopier each day. *The Skillful Teacher*, by Jon Saphier, calls this a place to "provision" lesson materials for the day. Most teachers use some kind of hanging folders or bins with the days of the week neatly labeled on them so that when it comes time to distribute papers to the Entry Way or Student Mailboxes, the papers are neatly arranged and waiting for you. Let's look at a few examples of Distribution Centers.

In Figure 10.12 you can see that the teacher keeps all copies for the week in a student-accessible location at the front of the classroom. This practice has the added bonus that a student who was absent one day can easily pick up his or her own classwork and homework when he or she returns to class.

Figure 10.12 Copy Distribution Method for Student Self-Service

In the example shown in Figure 10.13, the teacher chooses to distribute his materials to students himself and his Distribution Center is located in his Teaching Station. There are many simple, inexpensive ways to create Distribution Centers. Tess, a middle school teacher, said, "I bought a seven-pocket file and put a day of the week on each folder. Students who were absent or had misplaced the handout had one week to get the handout. It was also easily available for me if I needed to reference the handout for a later lesson, and I could pull it out quickly to show students what I wanted to see from them. After the handouts had been in the pocket folder for a week, I would put two copies of the handouts in the correct three-ring binder and recycle any that were left over."

Figure 10.13 Copy Distribution Method for Teacher-Distributed Copies

Checklist: Create a Distribution Center

- Determine a location for your copies that is easily accessible to you while you are teaching as well as to your students.

- Find or purchase a sorted filing system that allows space for at least five days (recommendations are in the Recommended Resources for the Together Classroom at the back of this book).

- Put paper clips near the Distribution Center to keep your papers organized neatly.

Reflection Questions:

How will you distribute copies?

Do your students need a self-service model or do you need greater control?

The Pantry

Many of us find ourselves scrambling for frequently needed forms, such as weekly behavior forms, tardy slips, or reimbursement forms. Similar to how you may keep your kitchen stocked with the staples you use regularly, such as coffee or sugar or eggs, it is helpful to have a place where you or your students can go for frequently used forms or materials. The *Pantry* is where you would keep the forms, materials, and supplies you consistently rely on in your teaching day. Let's look at examples of both *Paper* and *Materials Pantries*.

The Paper Pantry

Sara, the experienced elementary school teacher we met earlier in the chapter, keeps multiple copies of each form (at least twenty) and then keeps the original in a sheet protector at the bottom of the stack. Picture this: you hand out your reading logs this week and hit the sheet protector copy. Rather than having to go to your computer, locate the file, reprint the copy, and then take it to the copier, you can take the original right out of the sheet protector and put it in your To Copy folder (discussed in Chapter Twelve) and take it to the photocopier on your next copy run.

Sue uses a method similar to Sara's (Figure 10.14). She has a Post-it on the last copy in each of her Pantry folders so her students can let her know when they hit the last one. She can then simply move the paper over to the "To Copy" folder on her desk.

Let's brainstorm what kinds of papers you may need to have accessible in your Paper Pantry. Picture those papers that you use constantly and are always running to photocopy or reproduce.

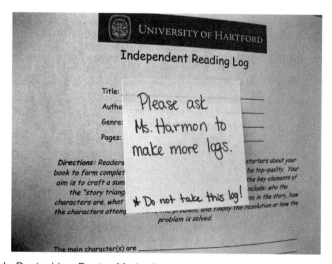

Figure 10.14 Sue's Restocking Pantry Method

Keep the Pantry Stocked: Possible Items for Your Paper Pantry

- Reading and writing logs
- Substitute-teacher activities (in case you are absent unexpectedly)
- Positive and negative consequence system forms
- Homework trackers
- Editing checklists
- Various permission slips
- Blank cards on which to write positive notes

Reflection Questions:

What papers or forms do you need to have readily available?
What papers do your students need to be easily accessible?
Where can you keep your Paper Pantry in your classroom?

The Materials Pantry

At any given point in the day, kids need *stuff* to learn. Your students will need supplies—whether pencils, calculators, or books—to accomplish their lesson objective or move ahead on an independent project. You will want to create a self-service Materials Pantry where students (or a student supply manager) can get materials. If you don't have the space or budget for an arrangement like this, you can get very creative using index cards, a Sharpie marker, and some shoeboxes. Label the boxes with titles such as Calculators or Dice. If you teach younger students, you can put photographs or magazine pictures of the materials on the front so that your students can easily retrieve what they need. Let's look at how a few teachers have set up their pantries. Be on the lookout for how intentional each teacher was in his or her setup.

Martin, a high school math teacher, carefully sets up his scientific calculators and rulers so that his students can collect and return them during each class period (Figure 10.15). Instead of just dumping them in a bin and hoping for the best, he purchased an over-the-door shoe organizer (my *favorite* inexpensive way of being organized!); labeled each calculator, ruler, and shoe pocket; and can easily *not* spend any extra time on classroom materials distribution—and keeps track of his expensive instructional materials!

Kate, the elementary teacher we met previously, and her co-teacher get all of their student materials set up in the organizer shown in Figure 10.16, with separate bins designated for each item.

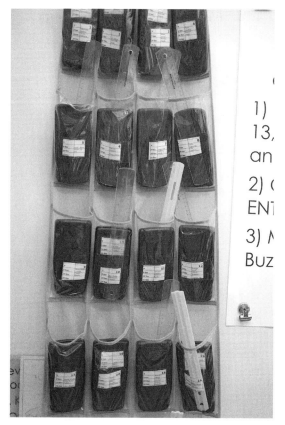

Figure 10.15 Martin's Student Supply Pantry for High School Math Materials

Now that we have reviewed a few examples, let's look at some items you may want to keep stocked in your Materials Pantry.

Keep the Pantry Stocked: Possible Items for Your Materials Panty

- Rulers
- Colored pencils
- Pencil sharpeners
- Markers
- Student-use staplers, hole punchers, tape
- Dice
- Calculators, protractors, compasses
- Scissors

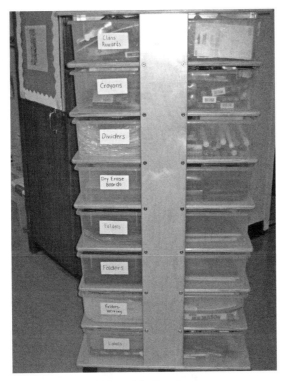

Figure 10.16 Kate's Elementary School Materials Pantry

- Index Cards
- Post-it Notes
- Glue
- Writing paper
- Printer paper
- Subject- or content-specific materials, such as graphing calculators, scales, correction fluid, and so on

The Materials Pantry should be set up in an out-of-the-way yet accessible area. The reason is twofold. First, like coffee, these are things you know you should always have on hand in your classroom. This is just run-of-the-mill, make-your-classroom-run kind of stuff. Materials Pantry items do not need to be in plain-view, prime-real-estate space. Second, your students (even as young as kindergarten) can use the Materials Pantry as a self-service center for student materials. In fact, one student's job can even be to maintain the stocking of the bins. You can keep everything right there.

Reflection Questions:

What materials do you need to have readily available?

What materials do your students need to be easily accessible?

Where can you keep the Materials Pantry in your classroom?

Classroom Calendar

All students thrive on clear expectations and knowing what is next. Even the littlest people can look at a wall calendar and at pictorial representations of class photo day or field trips. Older students can see key deadlines on the class syllabus, such as when term papers or college practice essays are due. Many Together Teachers keep a laminated *Classroom Calendar* for displaying upcoming events and deadlines for their students. This is also another great way for older students to become accustomed to working backward toward a specific deadline. Let's look at a simple example from a high school.

The high school teacher who created the calendar presented in Figure 10.17 uses a portion of his classroom's whiteboard to show important classroom events, such as Regents Testing (a mandatory New York State exam) and "Nerd Day". Figure 10.18 shows a middle school example with Interim Assessment (IA) dates and student birthdays. This shared calendar lets students see the month in its entirety and enables them to plan ahead. The trick here is to remember that this calendar is for your *students,* not for you (although your Comprehensive Calendar may contain similar items), and should be tailored to meet their academic needs.

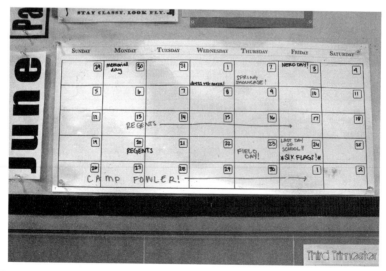

Figure 10.17 High School Classroom Calendar

Figure 10.18 Middle School Classroom Calendar

Reflection Questions:

What will you use as a Classroom Calendar?

Where can it hang?

How and when will you update it?

BATTLE OF THE BOOKS: CLASSROOM LIBRARIES AND TEXTBOOKS

Many of us are fortunate enough to have our own classroom libraries for our students. With that fortune also comes great responsibility—for us and our kids—to set up these spaces in an inviting and organized way so that students can easily access and return books. Because many outstanding professional books on reading instruction and classroom libraries are already available to refer to for ideas and support (books by Lucy Calkins, Irene Fountas and Gay Pinnell, Regie Routman, and Patricia Cunningham have been some of my staples over the years), this section on ways to organize your classroom library is limited. Sara, a teacher we met previously in this chapter, offers many of the following recommendations to her graduate literacy students.

Ways to Organize a Classroom Library

Classroom libraries need to be organized so that students can make the best possible choice of books at their level. This usually means that the book covers face outward. This arrangement requires the purchase of baskets wide enough for students to easily read the books' titles and covers. Baskets can be purchased inexpensively at most dollar or budget

Figure 10.19 Stephanie's Library Organized by Reading Level and Genre

department stores. Books can then be organized by reading level, genre, series, or author. A clear label on the front of each basket will help your students easily select books by level or interest. Teachers of pre-readers often use pictorial representations on the labels, such as a rainy cloud to represent books about weather. Many teachers add reading lamps, rugs, and beanbags to make the space inviting. Let's look at Stephanie's library organized by reading level and genre (Figure 10.19), and then at Kate and Ben's library organized by reading level (Figure 10.20) and with guided reading books (Figure 10.21).

Setting Up a Check-In and Check-Out System

Once you have set up your classroom library to be inviting and organized, there is then the business of keeping it that way! After teaching your students procedures for selecting, browsing, shelving, and transporting books, you need to create a sign-out system. Different teachers set up different systems for their classroom libraries, but the easiest system is a template with columns for name of book, name of student, date signed out, and date returned. Teachers make multiple copies of the sign-out sheet and place them in a thin binder in the classroom library.

Figure 10.20 Kate and Ben's Library Organized by Reading Level

Figure 10.21 Kate and Ben's Library Organized by Guided Reading Books

Reflection Questions:

How will you organize your classroom library?

What is the process for checking books in and out?

How will you maintain the organization of your library?

TAME THE TECHNOLOGY: GET THOSE CORDS UNDER CONTROL

At this point, most classrooms are outfitted with some or all of the following: desktop computers, laptop computers, Smart Boards, document scanners, an LCD projector, and printers. Just keeping up with all of this equipment takes a lot of work. First of all, one of your classroom jobs (more on this at the end of the chapter) should definitely be Classroom Technology Director. This student should be charged with the day-to-day maintenance of all of your classroom technology. This job was one of the most coveted in my classroom—and paid the highest weekly "salary." Even younger elementary students can accomplish a thorough cleaning armed with an easy checklist outlining such steps as "Ensure all computers are turned off, chairs are tucked in, and screens are dusted off." Tess, mentioned previously, offers this helpful tip: "I also recommend teaching two to three students how to effectively shut off, turn on, copy, and print so that they can assist you with mishaps that always seem to happen with electronics."

Figure 10.22 A Two-Desk Classroom Technology Station

Let's look at an example of an organized technology station (Figure 10.22). As you can see, there are no loose wires, all materials are set up neatly, and it is visually appealing to students.

You may need to invest time initially to get your technology tamed. Here is a checklist to get you started.

Get Your Current Technology Situation Under Control

- Make sure that ever piece of technology in your classroom works.

  - If it does not, submit a work order or try to fix it yourself.

  - If there is no hope of it ever being fixed and no one to remove it, put it away somewhere. Nothing is worse than a broken-down computer sitting in your classroom.

- Once everything works, make sure everything is neatly labeled and has all of its accompanying pieces.

- For example, if you have four desktop computers, assign each of them a number with a visible label and make sure that the accompanying accessories, such as mouse and mouse pad, are also labeled.

- Neatly tie all wires together so that there is no danger of tripping. You can buy fancy bands for this purpose or use rubber bands.

■ Gather up all installation CDs and DVDs and instructions and put each in a separate sheet protector per program or piece of hardware. Put all of these sheet protectors into one binder.

■ Gather up all of your instructional resources, games, and so on, and put them on one shelf for easy student access.

■ Post all necessary passwords on a bulletin board for easy student reference.

Reflection Question:

What are your next steps for arranging your classroom technology?

What if I don't have a classroom?

At this point a few of you may be thinking, "This all sounds fine and good, Maia, but what if I do not *have* a classroom?" Although we have addressed the challenge of mobile teachers a bit throughout this chapter, it remains a challenging role that takes an additional level of planning and organization. All of these concepts can be used on a smaller scale on a mobile cart or in tote bags. Read the next case study, about a mobile art teacher and how she stayed on top of it all.

Not surprisingly, mobile teachers need to be even more organized than classroom teachers because they're moving from place to place throughout the day! If you are a teacher who travels or teaches without a classroom, you have a special set of challenges when it comes to managing teacher and student papers and stuff. I remember I spent one semester traveling to three different fourth-grade sections of writing. I would traipse through the outdoor "hallways" that connected three temporary buildings during rainy afternoon storms with two tote bags over my shoulders. I had charts rolled up in my bags, a student SWAT team to help me with setup when I showed up in the classroom, a green "go" folder that contained the warm-up and any overhead transparencies needed (those were the days before Smart Boards!), pouches containing writing utensils, manila folders clearly labeled for each class to distribute and collect papers, and my very own mobile behavior chart—because kids love to test anyone who comes onto their turf. With all of these supplies at the ready, I guaranteed that I would not waste a minute I spent in the classroom with my kids!

MEET A MOBILE TEACHER
Paula

Paula is a first-year teacher responsible for art instruction across five grade levels in an elementary school that has students spread across two floors. Did we mention that she doesn't have her own classroom? Paula travels to almost thirty classrooms with her highly organized art cart. In order to pull this off, Paula needs to carefully plan, pack materials, and land in classrooms ready to teach excited little people engaging art lessons—with sometimes less than seven minutes during transitions. She says, "If you are not organized, your lesson will fall apart because you are not prepared and you don't have your materials ready. Without organization, being on a cart, if I forget a certain material, [the lesson] would simply not work."

So, how does she do it? Her cart is pre-packed with necessary supplies, such as paper towels, wipes, and plastic cups. Paula arrives at school by 6:30 AM daily; reviews her lesson plans, where she has outlined the materials she needs for each lesson; packs her cart with color-coded bins for each grade level and for each group per class. For a lesson in creating plaster face masks, Paula needed to ensure that each group bin had masks, tape, markers, plaster strips, and empty cups to fill up with water. Forgetting one thing would mean that the lesson could not begin.

Another challenge frequently faced by mobile teachers is carrying the right instructional materials. Paula solved this challenge in creative ways. To carry her lesson plans, she created a color-coded folder for each grade level. To ensure that she had a way to post the lesson objective and agenda, she created a laminated poster that is connected to the front of her cart. Paula pre-prints and sorts her lesson objectives by class and switches them out when entering each classroom. She has also asked teachers to ensure that their students have cleared their desks and that there is room on the Anchor Board for any visual anchors she needs to hang. This is living proof that just because you are on a cart doesn't mean you have to give up great teaching practices!

Because students frequently test teachers who enter their "home turf," Paula has creatively planned for possible disruptive student behavior. To preempt any problems, Paula took time prior to each semester to meet with each homeroom teacher, find out what behavior systems they used, then shared her own expectations with them. For example, in her art classes, students are not allowed to get out of their seats without permission because of all of the materials spread around the room. In some cases this practice differs from the classroom's regular expectations. Paula also created two mobile behavior systems to help reinforce her specific art class expectations. She created laminated seating charts for each class and carefully tracks above-and-beyond positive behavior with stars. She created an Artist of the Day award for the student with the most stars. On the flip side, she also travels with a two-minute sand timer and creates a mobile time-out for students who are off task or do not meet expectations.

Although it isn't easy to be a mobile teacher, Together Teachers like Paula, Jeff, and Nilda demonstrate that it is completely possible to maintain expectations and deliver high-quality lessons with routines and an extra dose of planning.

SPIC-AND-SPAN CLASSROOM

The suggestions in this chapter all sound fine and good, but it is really the daily use and cleanup of your classroom that will make the difference. Let's look at two ways to help this happen—regular cleaning and classroom jobs.

Deal with Cleaning Supplies

Even if you are lucky enough to have a school custodian who regularly empties your garbage and sweeps your floors, chances are your shelves and surfaces do not see much cleaning action on a regular basis. They quickly accumulate dust and grime. Although classroom cleaning can easily be a job for a student of any age, you will want extra supplies around to make sure this happens regularly and easily. One Together Teacher, Tess, explains how she efficiently keeps her middle school classroom spic-and-span with the help from her students: "At the end of every day I make sure students do a quick one-minute straighten-up of their area, and on Fridays we do a more detailed four-to-five-minute cleanup. We straighten the insides of desks, water plants, pick up the library, and sweep the carpet."

Stock Your Cleaning Supplies

- Paper towels
- Regular towels that can be laundered
- Clorox Wipes
- Broom and dustpan
- Carpet sweeper (if your school doesn't have an easily accessible vacuum cleaner)
- Dry-erase board cleaner
- Nontoxic antibacterial spray, so that keyboards, kids' desks, teachers' desks, shelves, and so on can be wiped down on a regular basis
- Hand sanitizer
- Hand soap

Reflection Questions:

What kind of cleaning supplies do you need on hand in your classroom?
Where will you store them?

Classroom Jobs

The best way to setup and maintain many of your classroom organizational stations and systems is to have your students help you. All Together Teachers have some explicit classroom expectations for the entire class *and* for individual students so that they do not spend their own time on these systems. Let's look at how a couple of Together Teachers—one a middle school teacher, the other an elementary school teacher—have set up their students to run the systems. Although they articulated the jobs in different ways, each teacher arrived at the same outcomes—clear student expectations on running the classroom.

The middle school teacher (Figure 10.23) has used a simple pocket chart and index cards to designate her student jobs, such as Messenger, Scribe, and Collector. Once per week a student helper rotates the jobs for the following week.

The elementary school teacher (Figure 10.24) has used library pockets with pictures and index cards to identify student jobs. The jobs can easily be rotated by moving the index cards each Friday.

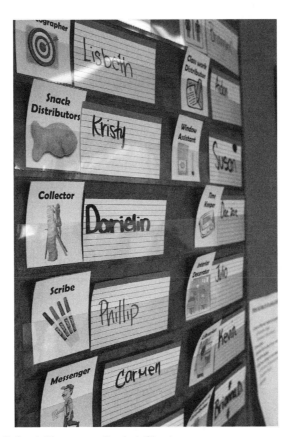

Figure 10.23 Middle School Classroom Pocket Chart

Figure 10.24 Elementary School Pictorial Representation of Classroom Jobs

Set Up Classroom Jobs

- Determine which classroom jobs are needed (your students can eventually help you).
- Share these jobs and requirements with your students.
- Either have students apply or assign jobs to students.
- Plan for periodic job rotations.
- Create a system for job loss.

Reflection Questions:

How can your students help you in the classroom?

Do you need a classroom job system?

How will you set it up?

How will you articulate expectations?

WHY DOES THIS MATTER, AGAIN?

Picture a world where you teach a science class and the study guide questions are all neatly binder-clipped per group and ready at the beginning of class. Picture a world where your capable students can help themselves to supplies they need in order to learn. It *is* possible, but it takes some pre-thinking and ongoing maintenance—and your kids can help. Classroom materials can aid your instruction, or they can quickly make your classroom an inefficient mess. Any wasted second searching for materials during the instructional day is an invitation for off-task behavior. Stephanie describes how she spends time creating an organized classroom: "In order for my kids to be successful, I have to create a space that is efficient, clean, organized, and beautiful. This way they can become self-sufficient learners who treat the classroom as their home. Although creating various stations takes some up-front planning and teaching, eventually my students end up running our classroom themselves."

Dan
A Day in the Life

Name: Dan Rouillard

Grades/subject: High school chemistry

Years teaching: 7 years

Commitments outside classroom teaching: Coach to several other high school teachers

Professional goals: Develop my teacher coaching skills and work on relationship building with parents and families

Personal commitments: Work out three to four days a week, cook at least five nights a week, keep weekends free to spend with my girlfriend, and budget one to two days a week to spend quality time with friends

Did you ever struggle with being organized? Heck, yeah!! My mother still reminds me how much a mess I was when I was in school. I told her last year that I couldn't believe how disorganized my boys were. She quickly put me in my place and told me that I was just as bad, if not worse, when I was their age.

A Day in the Life

6:15 AM: My alarm goes off and I promptly sleep walk to the shower. Freshly cleaned, I get dressed, grab my bags and my bicycle. It is about a fifteen-minute ride to work and I do it year-round, rain or shine. I like to ride to work in the morning; it clears my head and gets me ready for the day. It also saves me a bundle on public transportation costs.

7:15 AM: I arrive at school, go to my classroom, and change into my work clothes. I keep a few days' worth of pants, shirts, and ties there in my closet. When the supply is up, I transport them back home to do laundry and restock the next day. I grab a quick breakfast (which I keep at school in the refrigerator). By 7:45 AM I head downstairs to greet students with my coffee in my hand. It's interesting how something as small as a cup of coffee becomes part of your identity.

9:00 AM: This is a mixture of activities depending on which day of the week it is. It is always a combination of teaching, leadership team meetings, observations of and meetings with my coachees, and paying visits to other classrooms to check out best practices and learn from my colleagues. I also schedule about twenty to twenty-five minutes in the morning to address e-mail and small errands that can be taken care of quickly. It's amazing how, if left alone, small tasks can add up and become incredibly time-consuming. I try to knock things out as quickly as they come up so I can keep my sanity.

12:00 PM: Lunchtime! I learned very quickly to take my lunch downstairs with me for lunch duty. It's nice to be able to relax and eat in peace, but it's also nice to be able to eat, period—which I have not done at times in the past. With a schedule that includes afternoon meetings and classes, it's hard to find some downtime after lunch. So, I have learned to kill two birds with one stone. It's also nice to be able to sit and eat with the scholars. I often pull up a chair and talk about their day, my day, help them out with work from various classes. It's a good time to build relationships! There are one to two days where I do not have something to do right after lunch. On those days I will spend about thirty minutes with my colleagues in the teacher workroom decompressing, joking around, and if I haven't done so already, eating. Then I will go to my room to grade papers, make phone calls, check e-mail, or make copies for the next day's lesson.

2:30 PM: Last science class of the day and then on to freshmen advisory. By this time everyone can be tired from working all day, so I have to keep my energy and positivity very high. I make sure to find ten minutes before this home stretch to shut off the lights, put on my headphones, listen to some chill music, and drink a small cup of coffee. Doing this is key! It puts me in a good frame of mind and lets me finish the day strong.

4:00 PM: Some days I have grade-level meetings or a coaching meeting for forty-five minutes to finish my day. Regardless, I don't like leaving work without having everything in place for the next day's lesson. I take about an hour to make sure the room is straightened up, my boards are ready to go, and all lesson materials are in place. This gives me peace of mind in the morning and leaves me stress free for the evening. Before I take off I make sure to go into the gym and shoot around or throw the baseball and get a workout in. It's a great way to end the day. To be able to reflect on the moments of the day, both frustrating and positive, and work out any frustration before I leave is so important. I really value my time with my girlfriend, friends, and family and want to be in a positive mind-set to enjoy every minute with them.

6:00 PM: I cap off my day with a ride home and think of what I will make for dinner. I love to cook and will do so right when I get home! I try to accomplish all of my teacher duties at school so that this can be my personal time. There are always going to be two to three nights a week where I have some small task or tasks to complete, but I have been really good about making sure I plan my day so I am not wasting any time at work.

8:00 PM: Whatever happens here, it is not school related. I may call family or friends, hang out with some friends, or just sit and relax with my girlfriend at home. I try to read when I can, which is not as often as I would like.

10:30 PM: Before I go to bed I pack my bags for tomorrow, get my clothes ready so I can grab and go, and make sure my lunch is packed. A good night's sleep is essential to my mood, because no one wants a surly teacher.

CHAPTER 11

Subdue the Backpack Explosion: Set Expectations for Student Stuff

Learning Objectives

■ Set and support clear expectations for student lockers, backpacks, binders, and desks.

■ Organize current and past student work to support future use.

■ Support your students with the how and the why of being organized.

SETTING THE SCENE

I could easily devote this entire book to the topic of keeping kids organized and helping them deal with all of the stuff that goes along with learning. For many of us, student papers, those wonderful collections of student learning, quickly become the bane of our existence. The papers exist on teacher desks, in student desks, in teacher tote bags, in student back-packs; they litter the hallway, are shoved into lockers, and bust out of binders, seeming to multiply at every minute! Let's discuss how to get student stuff a little more under control.

Reflection Questions:

How clear are your expectations for student papers and stuff?

How well are those expectations met?

CONTAIN STUDENT PAPERS

Most teachers have an immediate reaction when I ask them about the state of their students' desks—a reaction that usually ends with a sigh. Just like adults, students need to be taught why it is important to be organized, and then exactly how to do it. In this section you will read about how to set expectations for desks, lockers, backpacks, and binders. You will also learn various ways that Together Teachers set and reinforce these expectations.

Set Clear Expectations for Desks and Lockers

When I was teaching I always started the year with a desk diagram that showed exactly how students' folders and textbooks should be arranged on their desk. For example, I had my fifth graders keep their morning materials on the left and the afternoon materials on the right. Many teachers, such as Dan (the high school science teacher mentioned in Chapter Ten), go this route and describe and diagram exactly what should be on students' desks during each lesson. Figure 11.1 shows an example of how an entire school trains its students to get organized. This is school leader Kevin's expectations for how all of the K–4 students at his school should organize their space. If you are interested in seeing an entire school's physical expectations, check out the example on the accompanying CD.

As students get older you can be less explicit about exactly where things go, but I know many high school teachers who give infamous surprise binder quizzes in which they test to see if students have kept all their lesson notes from the semester (see Figure 11.2 for a sample set of instructions).

Reflection Questions:

What are your expectations for the contents of your students' desks, both inside and on the surface?

How could you make your expectations for organizing even more clear?

Figure 11.1 Kevin's Expectations for How Students in K–4 Organize Their Desks

What You Need On Your Desk Every Day:

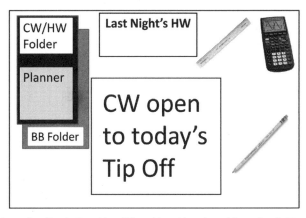

Figure 11.2 Instructions for Desk Set-Up: What You Need on Your Desk Every Day in a High School Math Classroom

Avoid the Overstuffed Binder!

Many teachers foster student organization by creating explicit directions for how they should keep their folders and binders. This section describes some of the ways Together Teachers have explicitly trained and supported their students in maintaining these particular materials.

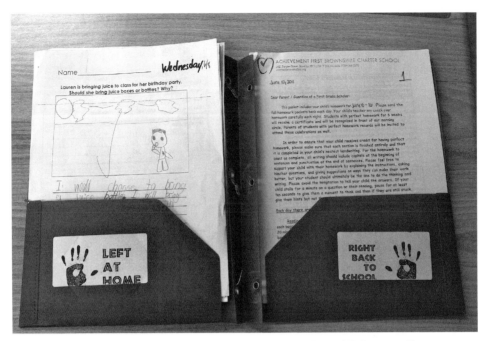

Figure 11.3 Expectations for Elementary Homework Folders from AF Brownsville

Elementary School Example of Student Organization Folders

An elementary school teacher might be specific about the layout of his students' homework folders by clearly designating the left-hand pocket for items going home and the right-hand pocket for completed items being returned to school (Figure 11.3). If you teach students to transfer papers from one side to the other and also share this system with parents, your students' folders will avoid becoming overstuffed paper traps.

Seat Sacks

Some schools or teachers purchase Seat Sacks for their students (see the Recommended Resources for the Together Classroom section for where to purchase) in which to neatly keep all of their materials so that books, papers, and supplies do not get lost in the depths of their desks or backpacks. Look at the photo of a Seat Sack in Figure 11.4 and notice how carefully they are set up within the classroom.

Of course, just setting up the Seat Sacks and giving them to students is not enough. Together Teachers carefully let students know what to put in the sack and when. Anna describes her expectations for Seat Sacks in the following list:

Expectations for Student Seat Sacks

- Only school-related materials allowed
- No food or snacks or sweaters or the like

Figure 11.4 Seat Sacks at AF Brownsville

- All notebooks, folders, and so on must be *horizontal* in the Seat Sack—if vertical, things can get knocked out
- Every couple of weeks "Deskarina" visits at night and places a treat on the desk of those scholars with *neat* and tidy seat sacks. Deskarina is a mysterious fairylike creature who floats around the school at night doing desk inspections.

Anna's method ensures that the Seat Sacks don't become dumping grounds for crumpled papers and lunch wrappers!

Secondary School Example of Student Organization
Similarly, you can set expectations for secondary students' binders by helping them create tabs for homework, classwork, lab reports, and tests. In Figure 11.5, Brent, a high school teacher with more than ten years of teaching experience, shares the expectations he gives his students at the beginning of each year. As you review his handout, note how explicit he is about what he expects and why it matters.

GET BINDERIZED

"Science is organized knowledge. Wisdom is organized life."
Immanuel Kant (18th Century Existential[1] Philosopher)

In this class I hope to not only make you better scientists, but also, more wise in ways of life. To be successful in this class, you *must* be organized. Hopefully you'll see the benefits of working hard and being organized and will implement a similar system in your other classes.

WHAT YOU NEED
- Binder—must be at least 1.5 inches (3.81 cm) and have 3 rings
- Divider Tabs—you must have 8 sections in your binder. You may purchase 8-tab dividers from Wal-Mart or you may make your (hole punch file folders, tape Stickies to colored paper etc. . .)

SETTING UP YOUR TABS
Your binder will contain all of the work that you do in this class (and *ONLY* this class) over the course of the year. It will be set up into eight basic sections:
1. General Rules / Information
2. Daily Work Organizers and TAKS Practice
3. Notes / Handouts / Homework
4. Quizzes / Tests
5. Demos / Labs / Projects
6. Readings
7. Science Fair
8. Goals / Reflections

BINDER TESTS
To test your organizational skills, we will have binder tests on every other Wednesday. They will be done on PowerPoint and each question will remain on the screen for 30 seconds. Sample questions follow below.

3. According to the lab rubric, how many points is the results section worth?	6. What was the first word on question #10 on Quiz #5?

It is *EXTREMELY* important that you keep an orderly binder for this class, as it will help your grade and will teach you invaluable organizational skills.

---

[1] A philosophy that emphasizes the uniqueness and isolation of the individual experience in a hostile or indifferent universe, regards human existence as unexplainable, and stresses freedom of choice and responsibility for the consequences of one's acts.

The above is the expectation... EXCEED IT.

NO EXCUSES!!!

Figure 11.5 Brent's High School Expectations for Student Binder Organization

That *One* Student with an Exploding Backpack

Now, at this point, you are probably thinking about *one* student—that student whose desk may be a paper explosion, who is very bright but can never find her homework, the one with the backpack that has papers from six months ago crumpled in the bottom. One of my favorite students of all time—we will call him Kenny—was a total math whiz but his grades suffered because he frequently lost homework, was late turning in essays, and forgot to bring home materials necessary to complete his homework.

To help get him on track, I worked with Kenny to develop a special checkout system: he would be the last person to leave so I could check whether his homework was copied, that he had the right materials to complete his homework, and that his homework folder was clearly arranged for his mother to check. After a few months of intensive support, we were able to dial down, and although Kenny wasn't perfect, his organization (and thus his grades!) improved dramatically.

Clearly, personal organization is an area of particular challenge for many of our kids, and I feel very strongly that teachers have a responsibility to teach it to them. I have yet to meet a student who is magically organized, so your kids will benefit from explicit expectations in this area.

Reflection Questions:

What are your expectations for how your students keep their folders and binders organized?

Are there students who would benefit from more explicit instruction in this area?

What can you do to help them?

PAST AND PRESENT STUDENT WORK

We all love displaying students' work to show what our kids are learning, and saving past work to show students' progress. The challenge is to keep these displays current rather than gathering dust, and to keep the past work from becoming a horizontal stack on your desk. This section shares a few ways to display and store student work.

Display Student Work—and Keep It Current!

Some teachers just post student work, and others go further and post the grading rubric with expectations for the assignment, or even just show the best pieces. Figures 11.6 and 11.7 show a couple of samples of how teachers and schools highlight student progress and exemplary work.

Figure 11.6 Elementary School Bulletin Board Highlighting High-Quality Student Work

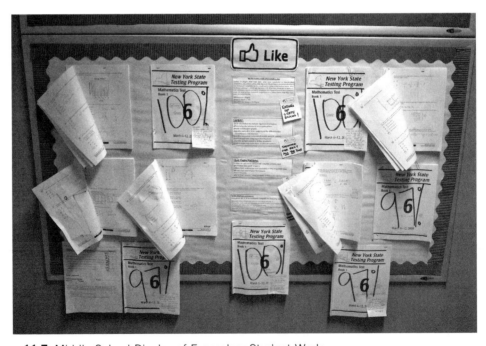

Figure 11.7 Middle School Display of Exemplary Student Work

Easy Ways to Display Outstanding Student Work

- Keep a sheet protector with each student's name (or number!) on it hung on the bulletin board or wall.

- Create a clothesline with clips strung across the classroom.

- Dedicate a bulletin board inside or outside the classroom with a fixed location for each student's work.

- Select work that reflects excellence or huge student growth and effort and blow it up to poster size or show it using a document camera as part of a lesson with students.

The point here is that you *want* to display student work because it adds to a culture of instructional excellence, not so that it can become musty and old in plain view. This goal requires regular time to switch the work on display. Many Together Teachers set a deadline on their Comprehensive Calendar to do this once every few weeks with their students, and they involve their students in the process. One teacher says, "Once per month I ask my students to select their *best* work to display. Then a student has an after-school job of shifting out the work and transferring the past work into the student past work crates."

Reflection Questions:

How and where will you display student work?
What role will your students play in the selection of this work?
How often will you or your students change the work?

Save Past Student Work

Once you have a plan for taking control of *current* student work, you need a game plan for dealing with past student work. Some of this plan depends on the policies of your school or district. Of course you do not need to display work *only* publicly. Some teaching environments have very specific instructions on which folders or portfolios to keep about specific students, others have nothing. Let's assume you do not have any guidance about keeping track of past student work. Of course you want to be judicious about what you save and about the purpose of what you save. You should *not* plan on saving everything. (Many teachers add a Take Home folder for their students to use to take home [and keep at home] work that does not need to be saved at school.) Ask yourself:

- Is the collected work intended to show student growth and celebrate success?

- Is it intended to document progress on areas of struggle?

- Is it intended for parent–teacher conferences?

- Is it intended for teacher learning and for norming on grading?

Set Up Student Files

- After reflecting on the previous questions you will likely want to keep examples of work that demonstrate how your students are progressing academically. Unless you are blessed with a number of file cabinets (and even if you are), I suggest you purchase hanging file crates and create one hanging file per student. Then arrange the hanging files alphabetically. (Efficiency tip: Instead of using students' *names,* just use their numbers, so you can easily reuse the labels year after year!)

- Keep manila folders inside the hanging file folder for each subject. For example, a high school English teacher may have four file crates—one for each section of English he teaches—and may have separate manila folders inside for essays, grammar work, and so on. An elementary school teacher may have two crates, store half of the class's work in each crate, and construct each hanging student file so that it contains manila folders for math, reading, and so on.

- Students should arrange papers chronologically inside the manila folders.

Figure 11.8 is an example of how this actually looks and how much space it takes. Martin's files for his high school math students contain a hanging folder per student and a manila folder per math unit per student.

Other teachers choose to go into even more depth and use specific student binders to maintain past student work.

- MaryAnn, a high school teacher, describes how her students maintained their work portfolios: "Every student had a three-inch binder with eleven dividers in it, one to represent each month. Every Friday, scholars got back their work from the week and they hole-punched it and filed it away in chronological order. At the end of the year, every scholar had a ready-made portfolio of how much they had grown and learned over the year."

- Kevin, an elementary school teacher and now school leader, says, "I had Platinum Data Folders for each of my kids. I would hand out tests that I'd graded, we'd review key mistakes, and they'd put the quiz in their folder and track their score on their own tracking sheet. This wasn't necessarily 'displaying' student work, but the kids were extremely proud of their folders. It was usually the first thing they would show their parents when they visited the classroom."

When I was teaching, there were not specific standards around student work, so I saved all unit assessments and long-writing samples. Additionally, I had the students select a few pieces of work for each marking period of which they were exceptionally proud and thought represented their best work.

Figure 11.8 Student Files for Martin's High School Math Classroom

Reflection Questions:

How will you organize past student work?

What materials do you need to get started?

What are your expectations for your students' role in the process?

> **Efficiency Tip for Special Educators:** Special educators often have special requirements regarding what needs to be kept and in what format for their students. Get familiar with these expectations as soon as possible. I recommend following the same system laid out in this section but making your manila folders even more specific. For example, if you need to document behavior for your students, then you would have a behavior folder in the hanging file. If you need to show spelling progress against sight words, you would create a spelling folder. As with anything, your students can learn to save and file their own work—even writing successes and growth areas when they review their own progress for you. You may also have a special folder for each student within the hanging file for Individualized Education Plan (IEP) paperwork and meeting notes.

PENCILS AND THAT OTHER "STUFF"

For whatever reason, writing implements are a source of frustration for many teachers. Perhaps it is the incessant "I can't find my pencil"; "Ms. H.-M., Joyce *took* my pencil"; "I *thought* I had a pen in my backpack." Many important classroom teaching minutes can be wasted on the pencil wars. As long as you have a clear and articulated system for how writing tools come into and out of the classroom, you can save yourself some trouble.

How Teachers Deal with the Pencil and Supply Problem

- Some teachers, particularly at the elementary level, take a communal approach by keeping two jars of pencils on hand in their classroom: one for sharpened pencils, one for pencils that need tending. A before- or after-school classroom job for a student is to sharpen all pencils.

- Some teachers create a bin for each seating group. Tess explains her system, "Group supplies were one of the toughest things for me to keep a handle on. Last year I purchased six one-dollar shower caddies, one for each group in the classroom. Into the shower caddies I put different supplies: a pair of scissors, a box of crayons, pencils, grading pens, and so on. Each group was in charge of its own supplies and would hand out and return the supplies at the end of the class. On Fridays we would refill the supply caddies. If one group had kept all of their supplies, they earned group points, and if a group was missing supplies, they lost points."

- Other teachers require that all students bring at least three respectable writing utensils to class each day.

- For more specific systems or classroom procedures, check out *The First-Year Teacher's Survival Guide* or some other resource on classroom procedures. The point here is that you *need* a system for writing implements or dealing with them will eat up precious teaching minutes.

Reflection Questions:

What is your plan for dealing with classroom writing implements?
How will you communicate this plan to your students?

AN EFFICIENT SUPPLY SYSTEM
More About Dan's High School Science Classroom

As you know, Dan is a high school science teacher with seven years of teaching experience. As a science teacher, Dan and his students must manage massive amounts of materials, including beakers, flasks, test tubes, solutions, safety supplies, goggles, meter sticks, scales, and probes. Dan has become increasingly obsessed with how his classroom functions because, as he says, "When you cannot find a paper or a student cannot find a paper, it inevitably leads to issues and to time-wasting back and forth—'Can I get a piece of paper? Where is it?'—and so on until five minutes of teaching time is lost on an exchange that could have been avoided to begin with."

Reflecting on his early years in the classroom Dan said, "When I first started teaching, I wasn't super explicit about what I wanted my students to get out of a lesson and I wasn't maniacal enough about preserving instructional time. The point of the lesson was *not* for my kids to spend ten minutes cutting up a card to play a unit-review study game. Once I realized this, I became a zealot for preparation of class materials. Now things run like clockwork. If we are using note cards to study for a unit quiz, are they neatly clipped together? Are there enough for each group? Are they in the right order?"

Dan is religious about making all of his copies the Friday before so that he is prepped for the week. He preps all lab materials (minus the perishables!) the evening before, when his energy is lowest, so he is ready to go the next morning. Small things like not having paper towels or a particular supply available can cause the loss of valuable instructional time. Dan continues to practice systems for efficiency of paper management in his classroom. For example, he will put papers on students' desks in advance and tell them, "When you come in the door you have two minutes to look at your papers and put them in this location in your binder." His students know that when they enter the classroom, they need to have their planners out or they'll get marked as unprepared for class. "As soon as I introduce homework, I check; I do a careful scan of the classroom to ensure that it is all written down and papers are placed in their binders as soon as they receive them."

As we all know, some students need extra support in the area of organization. When Dan sees kids struggling with this, he may ask them to go through their backpack while he gently offers tips on reorganizing. With those students who may really need it, he may even lay out the student's materials in the middle of the hall, where there is a lot of space, so that they really get reorganized. He also tells the parents of his less organized students that the most important thing to do with their sons and daughters is to go through their backpacks to ensure that they can find their homework and study materials. Dan noted something we have all seen: "These are pretty strong students, but the fact that they are disorganized is hurting their grades because they are late with assignments or go home without materials needed to complete the work."

WHY DOES THIS MATTER, AGAIN?

I want you to picture your students entering their first year of college. Picture them on the first day of classes receiving three or four different syllabi for the semester, plus textbooks and heavy reading packets. Remember the college professors saying, "I expect you to be in class. Your midterm paper is due in November. Good luck. Find me at office hours if you need extra help." For our students to succeed in college and beyond, organization and self-discipline are a critical foundation. By modeling clear expectations, setting up systems to support the expectations, and maintaining the systems, we are preparing our students to be successful beyond our classrooms.

Deal with *Your* Paper and Stuff: How to Find What You Need in Under Ten Seconds

Learning Objectives

- Carefully sort your incoming and outgoing papers to access materials as efficiently as possible.

- Set up your desk and instructional resources to create a focused workspace.

- Create an easily accessible method for referencing frequently used materials.

SETTING THE SCENE

I remember emptying my pockets and folders at the end of a school day and finding a note that Terrell had written to me asking to make up a math quiz, a small slip of paper the school librarian had left in my teacher mailbox informing me of a change in the library schedule, a note a parent had handed to me at dismissal asking about additional independent reading, and a confiscated Pokemon card (or three!). And that was only in my *pockets*! Never mind the permission slips collected for the upcoming class trip, the math exit tickets from the past four days, the notes from my PD session last Friday, and copies of the social studies test for next week. All of these are also sitting somewhere in the vicinity of *your* desk, which, last time you checked, was buried under paper. Let's say you teach sixth-grade math—four sections each with twenty-five kids per section. You collect exit tickets every day and send home homework every night. Your papers for math instruction alone may number over a thousand each week. In addition, you probably have notes from parents, materials from a PD session that you meant to review, and a new character-education curriculum that just landed in your mailbox. As you move from your classroom to the office to the teacher resource room throughout the day, you find that slips of paper are handed over to you "for review ASAP." This chapter is designed to help you deal with the daily paper avalanche in a systematic way by arranging a Teacher Workspace, figuring out how to transport papers between home and school, organizing your lesson plans and other teaching materials, and becoming able to locate those PD materials you "carefully" tucked away last year.

 Teacher Workspace: Most likely a desk, table, or corner that functions as a home base for you throughout your teaching day. May also be where you sit to grade, lesson plan, or enter data into your computer. Your Workspace is where you sit down and concentrate on lesson planning and other important work.

 Reflection Question:

How quickly can you locate papers and other "stuff" you need?

WHAT TO CARRY WHEN YOU ARE ON THE MOVE: YOUR TOGETHER TEACHER SYSTEM AND A TEACHER CLIPBOARD

Most teachers feel a bit lost without a clipboard. As mentioned earlier in the book, the problem is that our clipboards usually *hold* everything we need during our teaching day, including lesson plans, to-do lists, notes *on* students, notes *from* students, places to track student behavior, places to track student mastery, state standards, leveled reading books, and notes from your teacher's mailbox on the upcoming field trip. The challenge, as we well know, is that your clipboard becomes very full very quickly and transforms into a jumble of stuff—some of which requires action and some that you just need to reference occasionally.

Reflection Question:

Go get your clipboard or your equivalent (folder, notebook) and take a look at what is on it. Anything outdated? Stuff to get copied? To bring to the office?

Now that you have given your clipboard a cold, hard look, let's talk about what should be on there and how it should be arranged.

Your Together Teacher System

Your Together Teacher System is for maintaining your time, your to-dos, your thoughts, and your notes. However, to keep it *all* in one place, some teachers choose to insert their lesson plans, behavior systems, and mastery trackers right into a tab in their Together Teacher System—usually a small flexible binder with sections. That is totally fine. You just need to make sure that your Together Teacher System is easy to hold while you are teaching, recording data, or referencing questions that you inserted into your lesson plan. However, if you want to carry your instructional materials separately, which many teachers do, you can use a clipboard. Figures 12.1 and 12.2 recap these two options.

Together Teacher System
• Weekly/Daily Worksheet
• Comprehensive Calendar
• Upcoming To-Do List
• Thought Catchers
• Meeting/PD Notes
• Reference Materials
  (School Schedule, Reading)

+

Teacher Clipboard
• Lesson/Unit Plans
• Behavior/Homework
  Trackers
• Mastery Trackers

Together Teacher System
• Weekly/Daily Worksheet
• Comprehensive Calendar
• Upcoming To-Do List
• Thought Catchers
• Meeting / PD Notes
• Reference Materials
  (School Schedule,
  Reading Levels)
• Teaching Materials

Figure 12.1 Option 1: Flexy/iPhone + Clipboard

Figure 12.2 Option 2: Flexy

Your Teacher Clipboard

As teachers, we are constant collectors of data, and (at least for the time being) most of these data are on paper. I know that as a teacher I was never empty-handed. On my clipboard at all times were places to track informal instructional observations, behavior additions and deductions, participation points, and much more.

Lesson Plans

Lesson plans are usually the first things we refer to each day. Most Together Teachers like to have them on the top of their clipboard so they can refer to them while teaching. For example, if you have carefully planned higher-order thinking questions to ask while you read a history text, you will want your lesson plans easily accessible. Another option that many teachers I've worked with like is to binder-clip their lesson plans to the front or back of their Together Teacher System.

Academic Observation Charts

Academic observations are of course the backbone of our teaching practice. Now I'm going to let you know in advance that the need to properly record these observations is my obsession. As a frequent observer and evaluator of teachers, I die a little inside when I see teachers teaching *without* a handy way to capture and record valuable data to inform both their short- and long-term planning. When I was teaching, each week I would make a chart that had each of my students' names down the vertical axis and the learning objectives for the week across the horizontal axis. During each part of the lesson—the warm-up, guided practice, or independent work—I would circulate around the classroom and note who had mastered or showed partial mastery of the objective. When I observed a student struggling, I would record it on my Mastery Tracker to remind myself to return to the student during independent practice, recess, or before and after school tutoring. For example, if I noticed that Tisha and Florence consistently answered multiplication problems incorrectly on their whiteboards, I would jot that down on my clipboard and make sure I got to them first during independent practice. This method is similar to Anna's writing conference system in Chapter Four.

Behavioral Data Logs

Behavioral data are definitely other important things to track. Behavioral data include classroom participation, student positive and negative behavior, and any other student behaviors that you are monitoring and tracking. For example, to track voluntary class participation, many Together Teachers keep a sheet on their clipboard that shows the seating charts for each class each week. Many teachers say that just putting tick marks on a seating chart is much more efficient than scanning their grade book for names that are listed in alphabetical order. At the end of the week, when going through their instructional preparation routine, they count up participation points and put them in the grade book.

Homework Tracking Log

Homework tracking really depends on whether you are grading for effort, for completion, or for accuracy—or for some combination of these. At the very least you will want to know that everyone completed the homework. If you cannot grade all pieces of homework every day, you should figure out a system for at least getting to it a portion of the time.

Homework Checking Procedures: Determine How *the Homework Is Collected*

- **Physically turned in at Entry Way.** If possible, use the Entry Way so you don't waste class time collecting all of the homework. Create a form called "Missing Your Homework? Tell Me Why" that students must complete and put in the homework tray if their homework is missing.

- **Placed on desks, in a predetermined location, such as upper right-hand corner.** As students start the warm-up, the teacher does a quick circulation and notes any incomplete homework. If you teach lower elementary school, you can usually get a very quick accuracy pulse during this scan.

- **Incorporated into lesson, usually in the warm-up.** The teacher quickly circulates to ensure that it is done and then calls on specific students. You may choose to grade the answers to three to five questions. If you then go on to scan for accuracy, you may incorporate some of the homework sections in the warm-up, listen to students share with each other, and so on.

Now that we have discussed various instructional materials that Together Teachers put on their clipboards (or after a tab in their Together Teacher System), it is your turn to think about what you need to carry while teaching.

Reflection Questions:

What do you need to carry while you teach? Lesson plans? Behavior trackers? Homework logs?

Do you want to use a clipboard or a section in your Together Teacher System?

Something to Write With!

There are many classic cartoons that depict teachers in disarray, walking around in search of a pen that is tucked conveniently behind their ear! As teachers we need a variety of writing utensils on us at all times. Depending on your classroom setup, you may need dry-erase markers, permanent markers, overhead markers, and colored pens.

Ways in Which Together Teachers Have Conveniently Kept
Their Writing Implements on Them at All Times

- In their pockets
- Hooked onto a lanyard with their teacher identification card and keys
- In a fashionable apron (really, they exist) or in a fanny pack (but cooler) *or* in a repurposed overhead projector storage pocket worn as an apron!
- Clipped onto a clipboard
- In a canvas pencil pouch that can be inserted into a three-ring binder

Again, you will likely have a whole set of markers and pens in your Materials Pantry for classroom-wide use, and you will also probably have a set of writing tools at your Teacher Workspace (discussed shortly). Right now, however, we are just talking about what you need on your person during the teaching day.

Reflection Questions:

What writing utensils do you need during the teaching day?
How will you carry them around?

USE YOUR DESK FOR SOMETHING OTHER THAN STORAGE

Although as a teacher you don't have much personal space, most likely you at least have a desk, table, or corner that functions as a home base for you throughout your teaching day. This may also be where you sit to grade, lesson plan, or enter data into your computer. This space is most likely *different* from your Teaching Station (discussed in the previous chapter). Whereas your students may help you maintain your Teaching Station, your Teacher Workspace is where you sit down and concentrate on lesson planning and other important work. For some of you this may be a U-shaped table in the corner of your room, and for others it may be part of a table in a teacher workroom. The following sections outline various ways to keep your paper, projects, and materials in order in your Teacher Workspace so you can be as efficient and productive as possible. For an overview of a Teacher Workspace, start with the sketch provided in Figure 12.3.

Figure 12.3 Sketch of a Teacher's Workspace

Establish an In-Box

Many of us may already have an "action bin" or in-box but not use it smartly or systematically. In theory this is a silver basket on your desk that always looks perfectly neat, with just two or three papers to be dealt with in it. But let's be real: most people's in-boxes are full of stuff they don't know what to do with. They just sit there collecting piles of junk that you actually never refer to, except for the random rifle-through when trying to locate a piece of information—resulting in more time annoyingly wasted.

As a result, our in-boxes become a massive hodgepodge of a million different to-dos. When you glance at the stack, you cannot quickly tell what is a five-minute form to sign and what is hours of five-paragraph essays to grade. By creating more-specific categories, you may more efficiently process the massive amount of papers handed to you a daily basis. The next section describes a way to deal with your incoming and outgoing papers more intentionally. At first, all of these mailboxes seem overly complicated, but once they are set up, they empower students, who know where to put their late notes and permission slips (and therefore aren't interrupting lessons to ask nonacademic questions), and they liberate you from spending your precious prep time sorting through piles.

Teacher In-Box: A stack of sorted bins carefully divided into categories such as Grade, File, and Return. Prevents a jumbled stack of papers from accumulating on your desk.

Sort Through the In-Box

To avoid creating paper piles, you will now sort paper as it comes in. You will be forced to stop placing a stack of papers on your desk and will stop transforming your workspace into a disorganized dumping ground. We are going to be incredibly specific about where your papers go, so you can avoid digging and locate things at the drop of a hat. Although at first this may seem overly prescriptive, it is actually a preventive measure to avoid the paper pileup. On your desk or in your main teaching areas, set up stackable bins or standing files with the following labels (see Figure 12.4):

- Action (formerly known as the in-box)
- Grade
- Return
- Office
- Copy
- File

Break Up the In-Box

Now let's walk through what goes into each bin.

Action. This bin is for stuff that does not fit *any* of the following categories. You need to be careful that items do not get "stuck" in here, by sorting through it daily during your Closing Routine (discussed in Chapter Seven).

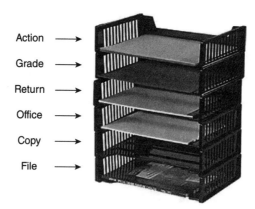

Figure 12.4 A Teacher's Sorted In-Box

Grade. This bin should get any work that you need to grade—either at school or at home. The papers that enter this bin can be graded quickly, such as homework, simple exit tickets, or classroom work. You may glance through these papers during a prep period, mark them with a check or check-plus, then record them in your grade book and return them to the "Return" bin. Or you may transport them home and then return them the next day. Of course it goes without saying that each set of papers should be paper-clipped together!

Return. This bin is for papers you have graded that need to be returned to students. You may end up emptying out your "Suitcase" (described later in the chapter) and putting your papers in there.

Office. This bin is for anything you need to take to the office or central hub of your school, such as a behavior referral form or a completed Individualized Education Plan (IEP).

Copy. This bin is for anything you need to copy (or if you are so lucky, have copied for you). After making the copies, move the papers to the bins in or near your Teaching Station, described in Chapter Ten, where you keep papers to distribute before or during class.

File. This bin is for anything that needs to be filed, such as notes from a PD session, a new insurance form you found in your mailbox, or information about an upcoming report card night. Depending on how you keep your student files, there may be pieces of student work or notes you want to keep on each student. For example, if you wanted to keep all end-of-unit math assessments for each kid, you would file them here until they got transferred (again, hopefully as a student job) into your student files.

The Mobile In-Box, aka What to Do with Papers That Come Your Way During the Day

When I was teaching, I devised a way to carefully collect the slips of paper that came my way during the day so that I could follow up on or process them. This would include papers collected out of my teacher mailbox when on a trip to the office or the resource room. As you get pieces of paper throughout the day, toss them in the "mobile" in-box in the back of your Together Teacher System. The trick here is that you can't forget about them! Each day set aside time to go through the papers and note any deadlines and so on—and then *throw them away*. This practice would be a Closing Routine, which you would list on your Weekly or Daily Worksheets.

Reflection Questions:

What can you use as your sorted in-box?

What materials do you need at your desk to make paper management as easy as possible?

What are your next steps to unbury yourself from the paper deluge?

Other Necessary Supplies

You will likely need other supplies at your desk to help deal with the deluge of incoming and outgoing paper and stuff. Some of these items also live in your Teaching Station, but I find it helpful to have duplicates for efficiency.

- Hole puncher
- Tape and masking tape
- Paper and binder clips in various sizes
- Various writing implements, such as highlighters, dry-erase markers, overhead markers, and colored pencils, sorted into either mugs on your desk or a bin in your drawer
- Empty manila folders and sticky labels, which will be helpful when you clean out your in-box on a regular basis
- Some kind of filing system, whether portable or in a desk drawer or some other location

 Reflection Question:

What kinds of supplies do you need in your Teacher Workspace to make planning and grading more efficient?

Recap of How Paper Enters Your Life

There are three ways in which paper comes to you each day:

- Through your Entry Way mailbox (discussed as a Station in Chapter Ten). This will often be notes from students, student work, permission slips, and other forms.
- Through your Teacher Workspace in-box. This is where you may collect items during the day, and where other adults may put stuff for you.
- Through your mobile in-box. This is stuff you collect along the way throughout the day.

Whew. We have just been on a paper-sorting adventure together. We have figured out how to organize a fancy teacher in-box to deal with incoming and outgoing paper, and we have outlined some other helpful materials in order to stay organized at your desk. Although it may take some initial time to sort through the stacks of paper that are currently inhabiting your desk, it will pay off when it takes just a moment to pick up the right papers to take home to grade or when you know exactly where that homework assignment is located.

Organizing Papers You Need for Projects

Most of us have some kind of ongoing project work or lesson plan creation for which we may need project folders in which to store materials near our desks. These are temporary files that contain information we may need to work on a project. For example, if you are in charge of the annual class field trip to New England colleges this spring, you may have a folder on your desk in which to keep all of the materials for the trip. The easiest way I have seen to organize these project materials is in simple manila folders in a standing file rack on your desk. An inexpensive version can easily be purchased at all major office supply stores, and a link to a tool I like is included in the Recommended Resources for the Together Classroom section of this book. This method is easier than having to spend time hole-punching papers to put into a binder, and it ensures that you have a place to put stuff that comes your way so it is right there when you determine you want to start working on it (as determined by your Comprehensive Calendar, of course!). You can view both a sample of project folders and a tool to contain those folders in Figures 12.5 and 12.6.

Reflection Question:

Where will you keep your project materials?

Rule 6: Don't Put It Away Without a Trigger!

Although you may take the ideas in this chapter and begin to go filing-wild, be careful what you put away. If there is *anything* you want to return to in the future, you should make a

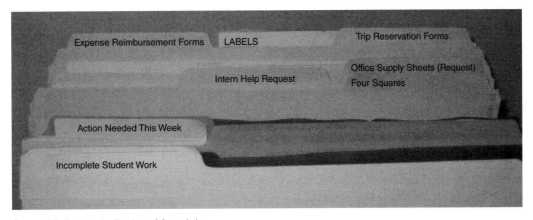

Figure 12.5 Kate's Project Materials

Figure 12.6 Kate's Wire File Rack

note about it on your Comprehensive Calendar or Upcoming To-Do List. The worst-case scenario would be that you finally unbury your desk and you carefully place a form for signing up for an upcoming summer workshop in your Action bin. However, your Action bin quickly becomes full and you miss the deadline to sign up for the workshop. *Before* you put the registration form away, be sure to give it a trigger!

Your Technology

Many teachers also keep a computer and printer in their Teacher Workspace. If you choose to do this, be sure that all cords are neatly out of the way, that it is easy to charge all of your equipment that needs to be charged, and that you have regular Internet access.

Keeping Personal Supplies at Your Desk

Many teachers like to keep personal supplies near their Teacher Workspace, in a special drawer or bin. I find it helpful to stock up on the following items at the beginning of the school year:

- Granola bars and other healthy nonperishable snacks for low blood sugar moments or so you can go to the gym right after school. Many teachers I know keep instant oatmeal, canned soups, and a few other lunch items handy for when they forget their lunch at home or need a hefty after-school snack to carry them through an evening event.

- Aspirin or Tylenol for headaches (being careful that this medication is not accessible to students).

- A few bottles of water for when you don't have time to fill yours between classes.

- A spare pair of comfortable shoes, and Band-Aids for blisters on your feet.

- Breath mints, Life Savers, or gum.

Reflection Questions:

What personal supplies do you need at your desk?
Are there any you can purchase in bulk?

The Motivation Board

Many teachers create some kind of kudos or motivational board on which to hang nice notes from students, pictures of friends and families, and key mementos from class trips. Although this certainly isn't essential, it is pleasant to take a deep breath after a long day and reread a note from a former student thanking you for the time you sent a multiplication CD to her home for her to use to get extra practice during the summer. Almost fifteen years later I still treasure that note from Joyce Green.

The Extreme Option: Going "Deskless"

Of course your other option is to go deskless. Some Together Teachers choose not to have a desk at all! Tess says, "I don't have a desk. Having a teacher desk has shown me that I will create clutter if given the extra space. So I have one small table on which I keep my essentials. I keep a stash of purple grading pens (I have designated that color to use only for grading), a desk organizer that has three compartments, and a basket for notebooks that are collected for the day. I keep the papers, exit tickets, and notebooks that have been collected to grade for the day. When I get ready to grade, they are organized by class and I'm ready to go without looking all over for papers."

CREATE A SUITCASE: TRANSPORTING WORK BETWEEN SCHOOL AND HOME

It is no secret that most teachers take work home at night and on the weekends. To do this well, you have to have a clear system for what to take home, how to transport it, and then how to get it back where it belongs the next morning. I think of this as preparing for a short trip. You likely have some things that always stay packed, such as your toiletries, and then you have some things you add for the specific time or location, such as a bathing suit if you are going to the beach. Let's think about this the same way. There are likely some things you already keep in your teaching bag, such as colored pens for grading, stickers, student phone

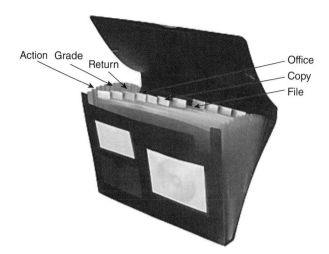

Figure 12.7 A Teacher's Suitcase to Transport Papers Between Work and Home

numbers, and so on. Then there are different things you have to pack for each trip. Let's dive in more there.

Transporting Your Materials via "Suitcase"

I recommend purchasing a five- or seven-pocket accordion file (Figure 12.7) and setting up tabs to match your teacher in-box so you can easily transfer manila folders between your Workspace and your backpack. It is helpful to have the papers in folders and an accordion file because student work can get damaged very easily when shoved into a tote bag.

- **Action.** This tab is for stuff you have to do things with, but you don't yet know what!

- **Grade.** This tab is where you would put any clipped papers to take home to grade. After you finish grading them, move them to the Return tab.

- **Return.** This tab is where you transfer already-graded work to return to your students.

- **Office.** This tab is for any papers that need to be returned to the office.

- **Copy.** If you are lesson planning or creating any materials at home, this tab is where you would put the materials you need to copy.

- **File.** You may find a paper in your tote bag about an upcoming PD session and this is where you want to file it for the future.

Each morning when you return to school you can unpack your Suitcase and put the Return Folder, for example, directly into your Teacher Workspace in-box.

Grading Materials

A lot of us need particular supplies with us while we are grading, whether the purple pen or an "incomplete sentence" stamp. It helps to put all of these materials in a zippered pouch or Ziploc bag so you can always have them with you. Doing so will save you time later when you are all settled on your couch for grading and CANNOT find that purple pen you always use.

Reflection Question:

What materials do you need in order to transport work between school and home?

YOUR TEACHING MATERIALS

As teachers we rely on many resources and books to guide our instruction. In fact, it can be overwhelming to see how quickly they accumulate when you consider the ten guides that come with any new curriculum, plus books you have borrowed and books you have purchased. Additionally, more and more materials have moved online, which makes it even harder to access them when you need them to plan that unit on the Revolutionary War. If we assume that most teachers generally teach in some sort of unit that is broken down into daily lessons, I suggest you keep as many materials as possible electronically.

Create a Professional Library

Many of us are lucky enough to have been provided with, to have borrowed, or to have purchased various books and pamphlets that support our instructional planning. The key here is actually *finding* and using them when we need them. That wonderful instructional math book you purchased does you no good just sitting on a shelf somewhere. You will want to organize these resources to be as useful as possible and to keep them where you do the bulk of your planning work. If you do most of your planning at school, it is helpful to have a bookshelf near your Teacher Workspace. If you do most of your planning at home, you may want to keep your resources in one location at home.

Most teachers choose to organize their instructional books by topic or content area. For example, if you are an elementary school teacher with responsibility for all subjects, you may designate a portion of your bookshelf for math resources and other sections for spelling, science, and so on. If you are a secondary content-area teacher, you may organize your resources by class periods or content units.

Reflection Questions:

Where are all of your professional resources currently?
Where should you situate them to be most useful?
Are there any that you are no longer using or that are available online?

Utilize Your Professional Development Materials

If you are fortunate enough to attend great professional development events, receive useful feedback on your teaching, attend helpful graduate school courses, or be part of a teacher-learning group, we want a way for you to access your learnings when you need them most. As we saw in the chapter that discusses managing your PD Notes, with a little extra time it can become easy to recall what learnings you need when you need them. Following are a few ways to do this:

- Create a binder for each subject area or unit. Then add a labeled divider inside each binder for each PD session you attend. After any workshop, graduate course, or other session, hole-punch the materials and insert them in the binder. Be sure to insert your PD Notes directly on top of any materials.

- Scan all of the materials and store them in electronic folders aligned with your lesson and unit plans. The next section models a way to name and save all of your lesson plans efficiently.

Reflection Questions:

Where do all of your workshop, PD, and graduate school materials currently exist? Are there any ways to organize them to make them more useful to you?

Organize Your Lesson Plans Electronically

Our lesson plans are the backbone of our teaching life. Given how much work we put into creating really great lessons and units, we want to be able to use them, share them, and perfect them. Doing so requires an intentional filing system. Let's follow the Revolutionary War example mentioned in the introduction to this section.

- On your computer, create a file folder for each section or class you teach. For example, if you are a secondary teacher, the folder would be called U.S. History. If you are an elementary school teacher with different subjects to teach, you may also have a Math folder and a Writing folder.

- Within each folder, include a subfolder for the unit name—in this case, Revolutionary War.

- Inside that subfolder, create further subfolders for each day of the lesson, such as Day One, Day Two, Day Three, Assessments, and Resources.

- The folder for each day would house a lesson plan, homework assignments, in-class handouts, supporting PowerPoint materials, and exit tickets.

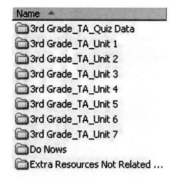

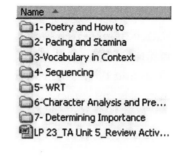

Figure 12.8 First Level: Joe's Unit Plans

Figure 12.9 Second Level: Joe's Subunit Plans

Figure 12.10 Third Level: Joe's Lesson Plans

Let's look at one Together Teacher's method for organizing his instructional materials electronically (see Figures 12.8, 12.9, and 12.10.) Joe is in his third year of teaching third grade. Take careful note of how deliberate Joe is in his arrangement of his folders and files.

Here is how Joe describes his organization system:

- To organize my lesson plans, I have a main folder for Textual Analysis.
- Within that folder, I have subfolders for each unit I have planned throughout the year, such as 3rd Grade_TA_Unit 1.
- Within each unit folder there are folders for the chronological subunits contained within each unit, such as Poetry and How to, and Pacing and Stamina.
- Finally, in each unit folder the lesson plans follow this naming pattern: LP1_TA Unit 7_Sequencing 1_Grade 3.

As you can see, Joe is incredibly thoughtful and detailed in how he stores his instructional files electronically. This system makes it easy for him to recall lessons, share resources with other teachers, and build thoughtful units. Although this intentionality takes a few extra seconds per document, it sure beats the heck out of a computer desktop with five hundred loose files on it!

Reflection Questions:

What is the current state of your electronic instructional materials?

What electronic folders, files, and document names do you need to make your life easier?

Store Lesson-Supporting Materials

Visual anchors, manipulatives, artifacts, books, Web sites, posters, and other teaching guides are incredibly helpful instructional tools. The challenge for most of us is carefully saving those materials for re-use so we can find them when we need them. The next paragraphs outline some ways to store your materials and gather them efficiently when it is time to teach a particular lesson.

Manipulatives and Artifacts

If you have teaching manipulatives or other supporting materials that accompany a unit, such as colored photographs of the Declaration of Independence, or picture books that tell the story to younger children, put them in a small, clear tub labeled Revolutionary War. Then list this tub under Resources in your Lesson Plan folder so you will remember you have these materials.

Posters and Charts

When I was a teaching, I labored over visual anchors to support my lessons. Even by the end of the first month of school, my walls were full of chart paper with specific directions on everything from "How to Select a Book" to "The Correct Way to Write a Heading." If I no longer needed the visual anchor in my classroom, and I was positive I was going to use it again in the future, I would get it laminated to make sure it would survive time in storage and all future encounters with tape.

Ways to Store Posters and Charts

Although you could spend lots of money on cool poster organizers (and I reference a few in the Recommended Resources for the Together Classroom section of this book), there are a few inexpensive ways to store posters and charts for reuse.

- **Use a chart paper box.** I kept the boxes that the chart paper came in and organized my posters in them by subject and topic. For example, I had one box titled Poetry and another titled Classroom Procedures.
- **Use coat hangers and binder clips.** Buy a few thin-wire coat hangers and use binder clips to attach multiple posters to them. These hangers can easily be hung on the wall with a nail.

If your visual anchors are smaller, such as a laminated 8.5 × 11-inch list of steps for writing a five-paragraph essay, put them in a manila folder labeled with the unit name. Otherwise, pitch *everything* else.

Summary of Instructional Materials Storage for a Sample Revolutionary War Unit

In sum, your instructional materials for a unit on the Revolutionary War would likely include the following:

- One main electronic folder called Social Studies
  - One subfolder for the Revolutionary War Unit Plan
  - Within that, each day's lesson in a separate subfolder
- One set of visual anchors—likely posters you purchased or created—in a poster box or neatly rolled up
- Potentially one clear storage bin containing some figurines of Revolutionary War heroes

Reflection Question:

How will you store your instructional materials?

Note for New Teachers

New teachers: trust me. When you go to teach the Revolutionary War unit next year, you will be so grateful to have everything in one place. The few seconds it takes to clearly name a document or put away all of the materials in a clear plastic tub will make all the difference in years to come. The reason I suggest organizing your instructional files by unit rather than by the date you previously taught the lesson is that it is easier to relocate them in the future. You may find next year that it makes sense to change the order of instruction, or you may find you want to share your instructional materials with a colleague at your school.

FINDING WHAT YOU NEED WHEN YOU NEED IT: REFERENCE INFORMATION AND FILE CABINETS

As hard as we try to be electronic and clutter-free, we still need to have certain pieces of reference information in hard-copy form at our fingertips. Depending on how frequently you refer to these pieces, you may want to keep some of them in a section of your Together Teacher System. Other pieces may be in individual manila folders in your filing cabinet or in hanging file crates so that you can find them quickly. Let's discuss both options (and remember, we already made a plan for your PD materials in Chapter Five).

Reference Information

Most teachers need to have a few key pieces of information ready at a moment's notice. Your clipboard will get cluttered if all of this information sits on it, so I recommend making a tab in your Together Teacher binder and inserting this information. In the next section,

I recommend some possible items you may need at your fingertips throughout the teaching day.

Student information. It is helpful to have frequently needed student information such as bus lists, after-school tutoring, and reading levels listed in one place to easily reference during the day.

Family contact information. Even though your students' family contact information is likely kept in a centralized database or on your own hard drive, it is helpful to have a printed version of all family phone numbers in your Together Teacher binder. You will be grateful. Plus, you are unlikely to enter eighty-something student phone numbers into your mobile phone.

Colleague list and phone numbers. Although you likely have the phone numbers of your closest colleagues in your smartphone, you likely do not have time to enter contact information for the entire staff. However, there will be times when you will want to have these phone numbers accessible—to call about a student, a snow day, or a missing homework assignment. Colleagues' and students' phone numbers may also come in handy when you are on a field trip and don't have access to your school's database.

Your File Cabinet

Most teachers find there is a set of material they need to reference regularly, but not necessarily carry around at all times. Usually these are organized in a specific binder or filing cabinet. I have found it useful to keep a stack of hanging file folders, manila file folders, file folder labels, and a Sharpie marker all near a file cabinet area. There are many schools of thought regarding best ways to organize file cabinets, but I have generally found that the more specific the file names, the better, and that grouping like-items-with-like-items will help with searching for the correct materials. Each of us has different levels of paperwork to file. Don't worry about organizing it perfectly at first. If you cannot scan the paper and file it electronically, just get in the habit of dumping papers you may need to reference in the future into a labeled file folder in your cabinet or crate. Once individual files start to accumulate and you see categories emerge, then you can take the time to organize it more clearly and group manila folders in a hanging file folder. For now, just get those papers out of your inbox! Some folders I have seen teachers create include the following:

Reading Levels

Many teachers like to have reading levels listed so they can immediately know the best books to direct their students to read.

Testing Information

Some teachers like to have information about how state test questions are formatted or specific skills their students need to master.

State and District Standards

To ensure lesson alignment with standards, teachers find it helpful to have their standards easily accessible.

Professional Development Ideas

This is where you would put flyers or other information relevant to interesting professional development ideas.

Administrative Information

This folder may contain information about benefits, retirement options, life insurance, and fingerprinting information.

Reflection Questions:

What information do you need at your fingertips during the teaching day?

What materials do you need to reference regularly?

Where should you put them so they are easily accessible (filing cabinet in labeled manila folders, hanging file crate, and so on)?

WHY DOES THIS MATTER, AGAIN?

As we mentioned at the start of this chapter, paper management is a *beast* and having the right information at your fingertips takes a lot of planning. Hopefully we have walked through almost every piece of paper you encounter as a teacher and have designated a place to put it so that you can get everything done, capture real-time data and to-dos, and have reference materials easily available. Marin Smith, a former elementary school teacher and principal, reflects back on her teaching career: "As I went into my second year of teaching, I discovered something amazing—the paper clip. No longer were student papers spread out all over my desk, the guided reading table, and student desks. No longer did I need to 'clean up' by making crisscrossing stacks of different worksheets and tests to correct. No longer was student work squashed in the bottom of my backpack with my snacks and leaky water bottle. Sounds obvious, right? It was such a simple thing, but it helped me *so* much. Not just with paper, but with my overall sense of being as a teacher. Paper clips meant more organization, which meant a cleaner classroom, which meant a calmer me, which meant calmer kids, which meant I could manage, which meant I could *teach*."

PART 5

Become a
Together Teacher

Conclusion: Become a Together Teacher

Whew. You made it. We have been on an organizing, planning, de-cluttering *adventure* together. You have created your Ideal Week Template, which shows your hard commitments and limited discretionary time. You have been introduced to multiple ways to employ each Together Teacher tool and habit. You have learned ways to create a more organized classroom through the use of specific systems, and have finally figured out a way to unbury your desk from all that paper! You have heard from other Together Teachers about how they customize tools and habits to make them work for their specific roles and lives. You now have everything you need to become a Together Teacher—to be even more effective for your students while leading a full and fulfilling life!

Of course it is *not* that easy. For many of us, the topic of organization is completely overwhelming, and your blood pressure may be permanently increased after completing this book. This is *normal*. The journey to become a Together Teacher will be hard at first. I distinctly remember sitting on the floor of my principal's office (thank-you for not firing me, Ms. Bienemy!) during my first year of teaching, crying about student behavior and how low my students' reading levels were and how-on-earth-could-I-keep-all-of-those-materials-together-to-be-a-great-teacher (said with a huge sob and sniffle). Then I had a similar meltdown with my literacy coach, Ms. Lay (but this time I had the dignity to sit in a chair and sob). There was *no way I could do this!* I was tired, my kids were acting up, and they were so far behind. But with practice I could get it together. Slowly and step-by-step, Ms. Bienemy and Ms. Lay helped me make a plan for what I needed to do first, second, third, and so on. I used my precious preparation period with my literacy coach to get help with creating better guided reading lessons. I discovered the magic of two-gallon Ziploc bags, and my students carried their independent reading books in them so that the books were not strewn about their desks and backpacks. I got my classroom library organized by reading level. And I posted a clear schedule of which reading groups met with Ms. H.-M. at which time per day. I remember the moment, several months after my meltdown, when Ms. Bienemy walked through my classroom, where soft music was playing, some students were reading independently, others were writing in their reading response logs, and the rest were working with me around a U-shaped table. My journey had started. I could *do* this.

Being a Together Teacher *is* a journey. But you can get there. Picture it. Now *you* will be the teacher with a healthy homemade lunch and the time to tutor the students who most need your help. *You* will walk into school knowing exactly what you need to accomplish and where to locate the materials and supplies you need to execute your well-planned lessons, and *you* will have the mind-space to react to the unexpected events that appear over the course of the day.

DEALING WITH DELUGE: CAN YOUR SYSTEM SURVIVE UNDER THE PRESSURE?

Now that you have assembled your Together Teacher System, there comes the incredibly challenging step of making sure that your system can hold up under the pressure of your fast-paced and important job. The test is whether *your* system—be it a paper commercial planner or an apped-out iPhone or something in between—is completely comprehensive and has no leaks for to-dos to slip out! Let's take the following quiz to test the strength of your system. If you find yourself hesitating, give it your best guess. You will likely see a few holes exposed in your organization system as you go through this process. Now is the time to make it airtight, before you bring it to school in the morning!

Test Your System

6:30 AM: You arrive at school thirty minutes early to get a little work done before everyone else arrives. What do you do with this time?

7:00 AM: You briefly check your e-mail before you go pick up your students from the cafeteria, and you receive a notice from your principal about doing more interventions in the next grading cycle that begins in the next two months. Where does this go?

8:00 AM: A member of the office staff pokes his head into your room while you are teaching and lets you know that the deadline for changing your benefits has been switched. Where do you put this information?

9:00 AM: When you are quickly getting a cup of coffee in the teachers' lounge between classes, you see a sign for a professional development session at the district office that you would like to attend. Where do you put this information?

10:00 AM: Oh, shoot! While in the middle of your preparation, you remember that your car registration is about to expire! How do you remind yourself to deal with it later?

11:00 AM: Your sixty-minute preparation period is beginning. You go to make copies for your afternoon classes and you find the copier jammed. What do you do?

12:00 PM: While on lunch duty you have a thought for your grade team about a student who needs extra support. What do you do with this information?

12:45 PM: As you walk back from lunch duty, you check your cell phone voice mail and listen to a message from a parent informing you of a student absence next week for an important family event. Where do you record this information?

1:30 PM: In the middle of teaching a lesson about dividing fractions, you have a revelation about a different way to teach it next year. Where do you put this information?

1:45 PM: You are circulating during independent work time and you notice that one of your students is having a hard time staying awake. This is the third time this week. What do you do with this information?

2:45 PM: You have a shorter, thirty-minute preparation period, so you use it to grade exit tickets. As you are grading, you realize that progress reports are due in a *week*! How do you prepare?

3:45 PM: Your students have been dismissed for the day, you are dead-dog tired, but there is still work to do. You need to leave by 5:00 PM. What do you do with this time?

5:00 PM: You leave school and head home. What do you do to relax when you arrive there?

Reflection Questions:

What is the strength of your system?

Did you have a clear answer for each of these questions?

Although there really are no exact right and wrong answers for any of these questions, they are meant to illustrate the variety and volume of stuff that flies your way each day. What I care about most is that you have designed an effective, simple, portable system that allows you to handle the big and the small, the personal and the professional, and the short- and long-term.

GET STARTED: A MONTH-BY-MONTH IMPLEMENTATION PLAN

Although school systems, educational philosophies, curriculum materials, and student needs will continue to change, the habits outlined in this book will steadily serve you well as professionals working in an unpredictable, on-your-feet, data-rich environment. Although you don't have to put every idea you've learned into place immediately, I suggest that you pick a few that resonated with you and get them up and running right away.

A Month-by-Month Implementation Plan

You do not have to take action on everything in this book all at once! Remember: if you tried to implement a new "Be Healthy" campaign, it is not likely that you would exercise seven days per week and eat not one ounce of sugar. You would take a more moderate approach by setting realistic goals of exercising five days per week and having dessert only three nights per week. Similarly, you can take a staged approach to becoming a Together Teacher. A number of teachers have said the following order has worked for them.

Month 1: Weekly or Daily Worksheets, Thought Catchers, and Weekly Round-Up Routine. This is often the easiest way to "take back" your time and to-dos, because these tools capture immediate needs and responsibilities. Most teachers have found that they breathe more easily and regain control once these tools are in place and they have established a weekly routine of looking back and looking ahead.

Month 2: Comprehensive Calendar, Upcoming To-Do List. Now that you have gotten a day and a week under control, it is easier to step back and create a Comprehensive Calendar and Upcoming To-Do List. Because these are the tools that capture ongoing tasks, they come next.

Month 3: Planning Routines and E-Mail. I recommend spending your next month really making sure your Opening, Closing, and Instructional Planning Routines are efficient and predictable. You can also slowly but surely work in the e-mail management.

Month 4: Classroom Stations. Now that you have taken back your time and to-dos, you can move to your external environment and get your classroom stations up and running for maximum efficiency.

Month 5: Your Paper and Instructional Materials. Finally, you can tackle your paper situation, your desk, and the organization of your instructional materials.

The best way to proceed is to review the notes you wrote in your Reader's Guide as you read the book. Then create a Together Teacher implementation plan for yourself using the following table (also found in the Reader's Guide). This will force you to summarize all of the ideas you had and notes you took as you went along, and it will ensure that you pace yourself.

Together Teacher Implementation Plan

Month	Next Step	Tools/Resources Needed

WHY THE WORLD NEEDS TOGETHER TEACHERS

As I mentioned in the Introduction, I have spent my entire existence surrounded by teachers. I was raised by one, married one, and have been one myself. In addition, I have spent the last decade of my professional life recruiting, selecting, training, supporting, and evaluating teachers. I am utterly convinced that there is no job more important and more complex than classroom teaching. I'm equally convinced that rigorous and intentional practices for planning, organizing, and decision making will get us better outcomes with our kids and allow us to sustain our good work for more years than we could ever imagine. Let's look at a final "Day in the Life" of Sue Harmon, an amazing Together Teacher with more than fifteen years of experience and a record of great results. Sue juggles her job with a rich home life and many outside interests.

Now, I'm *not* advocating that you all start getting up at 4:20 AM a few days per week. That just happens to work for Sue at this point in her teaching and personal life. The greatest takeaway from Sue's "Day in the Life" is how clearly she has figured out how to be a really good teacher and have the life she wants. A big part of the way she achieved those goals was to be really disciplined in how she used her most important resource—time.

I know from my own years in the classroom that tight planning and organization makes your day with your students more enjoyable. Forget fumbling for copies, losing track of which kids are tardy or absent or without their homework, spending prep periods procrastinating by checking your favorite Web sites or hanging in the teachers' lounge—only to end up taking all those parent phone calls home. Being a great teacher *and* having a life is completely possible. It takes a little bit of time, a medium amount of discipline, and a wholehearted belief that it *is* possible. Ms. Bienemy and Ms. Lay were kind enough to help me create a step-by-step plan for meeting my students' needs when I found out that my first year of teaching was in a high-stakes testing year. Hopefully this book has helped you to create a plan for making your own teaching a little stronger and your life a little easier.

Teaching *is* different from many other professions, but it is not so unique that we have to give in to the occasionally chaotic and sometimes unexpected parts of our work. Students figure out in an instant if you will be the type of teacher who returns the graded midterm on the day you committed to and if you follow-through on the Scholar of the Month outing. Similarly, in a profession that is easily all-consuming and never-ending, intentionality about planning, work time, and nonwork time helps us have more balance—which is good for *everyone* in our lives. Although being organized is certainly not the ultimate goal in teaching, being "together" plays a huge role in ensuring that we can impact kids' lives for a long, long time while doing work we all love.

Sue
A Day in the Life

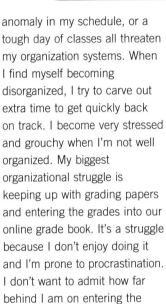

Name: Sue Harmon

Subject/grade: Middle school English

Years teaching: 15

Professional goals: Become a National Board certified teacher

Personal commitments: Go to the gym three days a week, make a healthy dinner every night, and keep weekends mostly work-free in order to spend time with my family.

Proudest student moment: I had a really tough scholar during my second year teaching at Amistad Middle School—Keith. We didn't hit it off. In fact, Keith despised me so much that he went home and spun yarns to his family about how evil I was. His grandmother went so far as to fly to Connecticut from her home in Florida to see what was up with this awful teacher. Unannounced, she parked herself in the back of my fifth-grade classroom. Keith straightened up in his seat and began to beam excitedly. He was confident that I was done for. But Grandma was a former educator and thought my class was well run. She couldn't figure out who this horrible teacher was and wanted me to help track her down.

Thus began my long relationship with Keith. Keith was retained in fifth grade and

retained again in seventh grade. This meant that Keith spent six years at Amistad Middle School, and I taught him for three of those years. When I didn't have him as a student, Keith spent countless hours in my office while I was academic dean.

I adore Keith. He was disorganized, hard-headed, academically low-skilled, unmotivated, and moody. When Keith graduated from eighth grade I was ecstatic and supported his parents' decision to send him to a New Haven public school. I've kept in touch with his mother and I love hearing updates about Keith and his two younger brothers.

Last week, a tall young man showed up at my classroom door looking for help with his trigonometry. He told me that this, his senior year of high school, is his year to shine. It isn't enough anymore to make the honor roll. He wants high honors. It was Keith. He hopes to be a physical education teacher and told me all about his college plans.

How she is working to become even more together: I always struggle with being organized! Even though I run a well-oiled machine, it doesn't take much to knock it off balance. A power outage, an

anomaly in my schedule, or a tough day of classes all threaten my organization systems. When I find myself becoming disorganized, I try to carve out extra time to get quickly back on track. I become very stressed and grouchy when I'm not well organized. My biggest organizational struggle is keeping up with grading papers and entering the grades into our online grade book. It's a struggle because I don't enjoy doing it and I'm prone to procrastination. I don't want to admit how far behind I am on entering the data right now!

A Day in the Life

4:20 AM: Wake up—I'm going to preface this with, "No, I am not crazy." Three days a week I wake up at 4:20 AM. This allows me to leave the house at 4:50 AM and be at the gym for a 5:30 to 6:30 AM workout. Our new school doesn't have a shower, so I anticipate that I'll arrive to school at about 7:00 AM fully showered and dressed and ready to go. I feel it's important to note that I'm not a morning person. I've simply found that going to the gym before school is vital to sustaining my energy through the day. On the days that I don't go to the gym, I wake up at 5:50 AM and leave the house at 6:20 AM.

7:00 AM: I always begin my school morning with a quick visual scan of the classroom. Everything needs to be in its place. I make sure the rows of desks are straight, nothing is on the floor, my desk is relatively clean, and all of my supplies are on the overhead cart. Most years I also "employ" one or two scholar morning helpers. The scholars arrive to my classroom with their breakfast as soon as they get off the bus. Typical morning helper tasks are taking down chairs, cleaning the board, writing the aim and agenda on the board, passing back papers and handouts, filing papers, doing simple grading tasks, maintaining the classroom library, and running errands. Morning helpers are a delight and allow me to do other tasks such as check e-mail for any morning notices or late-arriving e-mails from parents, review my schedule for the day in my Together Teacher System, check in with colleagues about the day ahead, eat my breakfast, and of course drink a cup of coffee.

9:00 AM: Teaching.

12:00 PM: Lunchtime! I will take twenty to thirty minutes just to eat and relax as long as I have one full preparation block at another time in the day. Some days I really need this lunch time to mentally regroup and recharge for the latter half of the day. If I don't have the luxury of this time, I multitask. I make sure to eat, check and sort e-mail (I'll return quick ones now), check my paper mailbox in the office, make or return parent phone calls from the morning, check off to-dos on my Weekly Worksheet (or more likely add more to-dos), and check over lesson plans for the afternoon. Even on hectic days, I still try to take five minutes to just sit and reflect and relax before I pick the scholars up from lunch.

2:30 PM: Teaching.

4:00 PM: Two days per week I stay at school until about 5:00 PM and do more heavy-duty lesson planning, make copies for the weeks ahead, and return longer or more detailed e-mails. On the other days, I pick my son up from school and bring him to after-school activities. While my son is in karate, I pick one or two of the following activities as needed: make parent phone calls, grade papers, plan lessons, read professional journals and books, read for enjoyment. This hour has become really productive time for me. Once we get home I supervise my son's homework.

6:00 PM: I am at home making dinner for the family and my cell phone is turned off. I also make and pack everyone's lunch boxes for the next day at this time. I'll check for any messages at about 8:00 PM and then turn my phone off for the night.

8:00 PM: I put my son to bed. At this point I'll take a half-hour to review to-dos and calendar in my Together Teacher System, clean up lesson plans, grade essential papers, or answer e-mails. I do this on an as-needed basis and try to limit my after-8 PM school work to about two or three days per week.

Bedtime: You remember that I was up at 4:20 AM, right? Some nights I go to bed as early as 8:30 PM, but usually it's no later than 9:30 PM, and never after 10:00 PM. Before I go to sleep I shower, pack my school bags, and on nights before workout days I prepare my gym bag with professional clothes for the next day. I lay out my gym clothes right down to socks and hair fasteners. My partner sets the coffee pot to go off in the morning for me. Basically, anything that needs to be done in the morning gets done the night before. I always read before going to sleep, even if it's just five minutes, but on a good night I read for twenty!

Recommended Resources
for the Together Classroom

Throughout *The Together Teacher*, I reference various tools that teachers can use to organize themselves and their classrooms. Although you could easily spend a small fortune purchasing the beautiful tools listed here, I would encourage you to get very friendly with a local Dollar Store or Walmart. In my experience, it is usually possible to create a makeshift item that gets you most of the way there without breaking the bank. Please note that the links are accurate at the time of publication, but they may change. For each tool, I have included the name of the store or a Web site, as well as the product, so you can easily do a search for a particular item. I do not receive any commercial sponsorship from any of these vendors. These recommendations are based solely on my own experience teaching, training, and observing in classrooms.

FOR YOUR TOGETHER TEACHER SYSTEM (BINDERS)

- Flexible binder, Wilson Jones Report Cover with Five View Tab Dividers; this is the tool I often distribute at Together Teacher workshops and is affectionately known as the Flexy Friend to many teachers across the country

- Any other 8.5 × 11 binder that is less than one-inch deep

- Paper planner (more info on which ones I like is provided later)

CLASSROOM MATERIALS

General

- Clipboards
- Plastic tubs and baskets
- File crates
- Hanging file folders and manila folders
- Tape—Scotch, masking, duct
- Paper clips and binder clips
- Ziploc bags in every possible size
- Markers—permanent, dry erase, overhead
- Labels—printable adhesive, file folder
- Sheet protectors
- Staplers and staples
- Colored paper
- Library card pockets
- Index cards
- Post-it Notes
- Timer
- Hole puncher
- Small desktop paper scanner (Fijitsu models are my favorite)

Shared Classroom Materials

- *For Student Mailboxes:* Hanging file crates, over-the-door shoe racks, mail sorters
- *For Distribution Centers:* Hanging wall folders
- *For Student Jobs Board:* Commercial board created with student jobs already populated or a piece of poster board with adhesive pockets with class jobs listed
- *For Student Calendar:* Dry-erase rewritable monthly calendar or hanging yearly calendar

Teacher Materials

- *For Teacher Workspace:* Accordion file racks, stacking plastic file drawers
- *For Teacher File Cabinet:* Hanging file folders, manila folders, file labels
- *For Teacher Suitcase:* Expandable accordion file

GREAT SOURCES FOR TOGETHER TEACHER MATERIALS

Paper Planners

Franklin Covey (http://store.franklinplanner.com). I like the Build Your Own versions:

- Start with the Metropolitan Ring Bound Weekly Planner (which functions as a Weekly Worksheet).
- Add the Metropolitan Two-Page Monthly Calendar (which functions as your Comprehensive Calendar).
- Add the Classic Metropolitan Three-Pack Notes Booklet (for PD and Meeting Notes).
  - Modify a portion of the Notes Booklet for your Thought Catchers.
- Add Classic Tabbed Divider Pockets.

Uncalendar (http://www.uncalendar.com). I like the Uncalendar Lifestyle Fullsize version.

Levenger (http://www.levenger.com). The Circa systems are very good. The only challenge is you have to purchase their paper and hole punchers.

Staples (http://www.staples.com). The M by Staples Arc System allows you to customize a notebook and costs less than Levenger products, but less variety is available.

Moleskine planners (http://www.moleskineus.com). These are my favorite paper planners. I prefer the 18-Month Extra Large Soft Cover Planners with weekly and monthly options.

Really Good Stuff (http://www.reallygoodstuff.com):

- Store More Deluxe Chair Pockets
- Multifunction Timer
- Store More Book Pouches (for transporting books to and from school)
- Store More Portfolio Storage Boxes (for storing visual anchors, posters, and so on)
- Large Stackable Storage Tubs with Locking Lids (Debbie Diller Designs)
- Our Job Jar Pocket Chart (for classroom jobs)
- Store More Binder Nook (for if you have your students leave their binders in your classroom)
- Really Good Classroom Mail Center (for Student Mailboxes)
- Really Good Storage Pail (a great option for the Materials Pantry)
- Early Learning Station (for elementary school Teaching Station)

- Store More Wire Works Desk Secretary (good starting point for Teacher Workspace)
- Pencil boxes

Barclay's School Supplies (http://www.barclayschoolsupplies.com):

- 24 Paper Tray Cubbie with colored paper trays (good for Student Mailboxes or Paper Pantry)
- 32 Cubbie Tower with Colored Tubs (good for Materials Pantry)

Resources: Books, Blogs, Applications, and More!

As mentioned in the Introduction, there is no shortage of great resources on time and task management out there. Here are some of my favorites at the time of publication.

BOOKS

General Productivity

Getting Things Done by David Allen

The 7 Habits of Highly Effective People by Stephen Covey

Total Workday Control Using Microsoft Outlook: The Eight Best Practices of Task and Email Management by Michael Linenberger

Never Check E-Mail in the Morning and *Time Management from the Inside Out* by Julie Morgenstern

The Power of Full Engagement by Tony Schwartz

168 Hours: You Have More Time Than You Think by Laura Vanderkam

Classroom Setup and Great Instruction

Driven by Data by Paul Bambrick-Santoyo

Spaces & Places: Designing Classrooms for Literacy by Debbie Diller

Teach Like a Champion: 49 Techniques That Put Students on the Path to College by Doug Lemov

The Skillful Teacher by Jon Saphier

The First Year Teacher's Survival Guide: Ready-To-Use Strategies, Tools & Activities for Meeting the Challenges of Each School Day by Julia Thompson

The First Days of School: How to Be an Effective Teacher by Harry Wong and Rosemary Wong

BLOGS

www.Zenhabits.net

www.ProductiveFlourishing.com

www.43folders.com

www.Lifehacker.com

APPLICATIONS AND TOOLS

Applications and Web Sites

www.Boomeranggmail.com

www.RememberTheMilk.com

www.Toodledo.com

http://teuxdeux.com

Electronic Tools

Evernote: http://www.evernote.com

Microsoft OneNote

Meet the Together Teachers

Let's meet the teachers who have elected to allow you into their professional and personal lives, who have put themselves out there, and who are willing to share that it *is* possible to be a great teacher *and* have a life. A few of these teachers are in their first few years as educators and juggle graduate school with their full-time teaching responsibilities. Some of them are closing in on a decade or more as classroom instructors and have leadership responsibilities such as coaching other teachers, serving as department heads, or overseeing schoolwide attendance programs. Others have significant out-of-school commitments, such as children of their own, or intense hobbies like running marathons. The teachers vary in their use of paper or Web-based tools, each of their schools has a unique way of operating, and each is constantly refining his or her systems to become increasingly efficient and organized. No one featured teacher is perfectly *together* all the time, but each has particular strengths and systems that they are willing to share with you.

Morgan Barth is the principal of Achievement First (AF) Bridgeport Elementary School. He has been teaching for a decade and is committed to "running the highest performing school in the state." His essential Together Teacher tool is a black leather binder where he stores his daily schedule, Weekly Worksheet, Thought Catchers, and classroom observation templates. His systems have enabled him to attain remarkable student achievement results. Before moving to Bridgeport, Morgan served as the principal of Elm City College Prep, which ranked number one in African American student achievement for three years in a row during his tenure.

Gilbert Cardenas is a third-year teacher in California. He balances teaching with church commitments and activities and personal time with his fiancée. He intersperses his pre-K schedule with quick Weekly Worksheet checks to ensure that he stays on task, and with occasional visits to ESPN's Web site to ensure that he is up on the latest sports happenings. Organizing paperwork remains an organizational challenge for Gilbert, but one he's determined to stay on top of in order to achieve his goal of becoming an educational leader within his school.

Jenny Cortez has six years of teaching experience and currently works as a kindergarten teacher at AF Crown Heights Elementary School. Jenny enjoys "looking back at the end of the year and reflecting on how much my scholars have learned." Her students progress because of her airtight organization system that allows her "to be totally present and with [her] scholars during school, instead of worrying about the copies [she] forgot to make." More of a paper than an electronic organizer, Jenny's favorite tool is the Weekly Worksheet— the use of which gives her an added sense of accomplishment when she crosses off completed tasks.

Sara Cotner has nine years of experience teaching first through sixth grade and is currently starting a national network of high-performing, authentic Montessori charter schools, called Montessori For All. She has worked on the national staff of Teach For America and for AmeriCorps, and began her own education consulting business. After spending her first semester of teaching "drowning in sticky notes," Sara realized that her college organization system would not survive in the teaching world. Now Sara defines organization as "the vehicle that I use to take me where I want to go in life. It is never the destination itself."

Brendan Csaposs is a ninth-grade ELA and math mentor with City Year Baton Rouge. He is currently in his third year of teaching, a career he began right out of college. He admits that he was "super disorganized until he started using the Together Teacher System! The couple of times I've lost my system it was like the world was coming to an end." Being organized has helped Brendan become laser-focused on what his students need rather than what he must accomplish. It also enables him to participate in fulfilling activities outside the classroom such as performing in his church choir.

A fourth-year teacher, **Stephanie Frost** teaches third-grade math and reading skills and serves as a grade-level leader at AF Brownsville Elementary School. She adopted her current Together Teacher skills halfway through her first year of teaching when she realized how crucial they were to "balancing [her] professional and personal life." These skills have led her to become a stronger instructor intent on building relationships with her students and "[helping] them succeed academically and in life."

Jacqueline Futrell is in her first year of teaching sixth- and seventh-grade ELA at Baltimore IT Academy. She currently balances teaching with school—she's earning her master's in education at Johns Hopkins University—as well as with her personal commitment to marathon training. Jacqueline cannot live without her calendar and needs both paper and electronic tools to keep it all together. "I like electronic because you cannot lose it," she says, "and you can access it from almost anywhere; on the other hand, I like paper because I enjoy the action of crossing tasks off my calendar or schedule. This allows me to feel a sense that something was accomplished."

Julie Gronquist-Blodgett serves as a manager for Teacher Leadership Development at Teach For America. Julie taught for four years before assuming her current position and says she first honed her organization skills as president of the student body during her junior year of college. That role "forced [her] to be incredibly focused on the intended outcomes for each week and to ensure that [her] actions were aligned to those outcomes." Julie could not do without her Outlook calendar, which captures both her personal and professional commitments—she even uses it to plan nightly meals with her husband. The dinner appointment most nights includes a link to a recipe as well as a list of who's in charge of cooking!

The co-director of the College Office at AF Amistad High School, **MaryAnn Holland** has five years of teaching experience. "My scholars know how everything works in my room," she says. "They feel a sense of comfort and security in our systems and consistency." During high school, MaryAnn worked as a reporter at the *Miami Herald*. Working at the paper and going to school full-time pushed MaryAnn to get organized. Now she "needs electronics to keep track of all my roles and responsibilities," but she states, "nothing will ever top the satisfaction you get from physically crossing something off a list."

Tess Hamons teaches sixth grade at Mastery Charter School in Philadelphia. Five years into teaching, Tess is committed to "help all students on the path of becoming lifelong readers." Not only have Tess's strong organizational habits enabled her to guide 88 percent of her scholars up 1.5 grade reading levels in a single year, but they have also allowed her to be "a more precise planner, a more communicative teacher, and in general a happier person." Whether they propel her to fulfill her personal goal to "quit drinking soda" is yet to be seen.

With fifteen years of experience under her belt, **Sue Harmon** teaches English at Amistad Academy Middle School. Her strong organization skills allow her to uphold a regular gym habit (which requires a 4:20 AM wake-up call!), cook healthy dinners nightly, and keep her weekends as work free as possible. Despite her commitment to her Together Teacher System, Sue is the first to admit that it is not easy to maintain; even the slightest scheduling change can throw her day out of whack! When that happens, Sue carves out additional time to get back on track so that she remains at the top of her game and the best teacher possible for her students.

After six years of teaching special education in a public middle school in the Bronx, **Kerri Kannengieser** is special services coordinator at AF East New York Elementary School. A paper-based organizer, Kerri uses her Together Teacher System to prevent her from being a "hot organizational mess." When teaching, Kerri lives for "that moment on a child's face when they finally understand something!" She aims to remain an advocate for students with special needs, to become increasingly effective in her role, and (perhaps one day) to transition into education policy.

A fourth-year teacher, **Martin Kleinbard** teaches high school math at AF Brooklyn High School. Along with another teacher, Martin founded TeachingXChange, which aims to become a nationally recognized teacher resource exchange aligned with the Common Core State Standards. After receiving a wake-up call during his first year of teaching, Martin established an airtight organization system that enables him to achieve his favorite aspect of teaching: "the emotional high of being engaged in an interesting lesson and seeing an hour go by in what feels like five minutes."

Kevin Lohela is the K–4 academic dean at AF Crown Heights Elementary School and has six years of teaching experience. Outlook is his must-have organization tool—"I have so many buckets, projects, and so on that I simply could not manage myself without it." As a Together Teacher, Kevin can focus on supporting the development and growth of his fellow teachers, as well as on his personal commitments—which include soccer, reading, cooking, and spending time with his fiancée.

Brent Maddin serves as provost of Relay Graduate School of Education, where he oversees all of the program's instructional and curricular endeavors. Since 2001, Brent has mentored and trained new teachers through the Teach For America Summer Institute and the New Teacher Project, as well as regional science learning teams. A principally electronic organizer, Brent uses his systems to achieve his personal commitment to "[live] each day in such a way that I wouldn't mind repeating it ad infinitum."

A second-year teacher, **Kate McCabe** teaches third grade at AF Brownsville Elementary School. In addition to her role as a teacher, she is the field trip coordinator for her grade and is currently enrolled in graduate school. Kate relies on her Together Teacher skills to keep up with her personal commitments, such as running, staying current with the live music scene in Brooklyn, and being a good big sister. Kate holds her weekly meeting time sacred to ensure that she can be relaxed and maximally productive in school, and have fun when she leaves.

Alice Meyer graduated from the University of North Carolina at Chapel Hill, then went to work for Joshua Butler Elementary School through Teach For America, where she was a first-grade teacher and reading interventionist. In 2006, Alice moved to New York City and became a program director for Teach For America. A year later she began teaching first grade and kindergarten at Edward Brooke Charter School in Massachusetts. She moved to New Orleans in 2009 as an Incubation School Leader at Samuel Green Charter School before becoming Primary School Principal at John Dibert Community School.

Susan Oba currently serves as associate director of math achievement at AF. Prior to that position, Susan taught middle school math for four years, one of which she spent as an academic dean. Teaching was Susan's first job and she admits that "I was a mess before my Together Teacher System." In fact, in her first year, some of her students took pity on her and offered to organize the papers on her desk—"at least I think it was pity," she writes. "My students may have been acting to prevent the thousands of papers piled on my desk from crashing down and injuring someone."

Ami Patel teaches fourth-grade literacy at AF Brownsville Elementary School. Her Together Teacher System is a combination of paper and electronic (she describes herself as a "a wannabee electronic who cannot nullify the immense comfort of paper") and her must-have organization tool is the Outlook calendar. Ami's ability to capture her tasks and priorities free her to be really "in the moment" with her kids, without any outside worries or thoughts infiltrating her instruction. It also enables her to achieve outstanding results with her students and actively guide them towards those critical aha moments.

Joe Pirro currently works for United Talent Agency in NYC. Previously, he taught third grade for three years at AF Crown Heights Elementary School. Although he is no longer in the classroom, Joe remains committed to "[closing] the achievement gap forever, no matter the field in which I'm working." When he was at his Together Teacher best, "there was *no* time wasted in my classroom." "I knew exactly what my students should be doing at all moments of the day," he says, "and I was never fumbling for materials or what needed to happen next."

Dan Rouillard teaches high school chemistry at AF Brooklyn High School. Despite struggles with organization early in life (ask his mom for stories!), Dan currently balances his teacher load with regular workouts, homemade dinners, and quality time with friends. He plans so well ahead for each week that he is able to ride his bike to school each morning and then changes into work attire on site. His trick? He carts freshly cleaned shirts, pants, and ties into his classroom closet so that he has a work wardrobe ready to go when he arrives!

Robby Rutkoff is currently the manager of special projects at Relay Graduate School of Education. Previously Robby taught second and third grade for three years at AF Brownsville Elementary School. Principally an electronics person, Robby's favorite organizational tool is his iPhone. Not one to take it easy, he uses his Together Teacher skills not only to drive ahead his pursuit of improved teacher quality in low-income K–12 communities, but also to assist him in his goals to stay politically active and complete the New York City Marathon annually.

Emily Scheines works as a private tutor at Revolution Prep, an SAT prep company. She has five years of teaching experience and previously taught high school social studies. Emily "loves the moments when kids show you a part of their personality you never expected, the excellent joke, the act of kindness, the hidden talent, or even the first homework assignment that doesn't look like it was left in a rainstorm." A believer in the idea that "you can't beat

[Outlook's] automatic reminders," Emily uses her organization skills to make time for what she cares about outside of class as well—exercise, the great outdoors, or just a great book.

Kaya Schmandt is in her first year of teaching at KIPP Academy Lynn, where she teaches seventh-grade science. Kaya began honing her organization skills in college when she worked as a biologist in one of her university's labs. "Managing important datasheets filled with irreplaceable field notes forced me to learn to keep my papers neat and organized." As a teacher, she cannot live without her Weekly Worksheet and has found that her students benefit from her Together Teacher skills because they enable her to "spend more time giving feedback on my students' work, seeking them out for one-on-one help, and connecting with families."

Marin Smith has worked as an elementary school teacher and principal of AF Crown Heights Elementary School and served as an adjunct professor for the Relay Graduate School of Education. After discovering paper clips, she also found the stapler, the three-hole puncher, and, eventually, Microsoft Outlook. Being organized has helped Marin keep a steady focus on one task or person at a time. It also helps her plan for important upcoming events, both big and small. She is currently working toward her master's degree in clinical social work at Bryn Mawr College.

Anna Tattan taught kindergarten and first grade at AF Brownsville Elementary School, where she also monitored student attendance systems and served as a teacher coach. She recently transitioned into a dean of students role. An avid marathon runner, Anna's tight organization skills allow her to accommodate her training schedule and pursue other extra-curricular interests such as learning German.

A second-year educator, **Paula Torres** teaches fifth-grade visual arts at KIPP Austin Academy of Arts and Letters in Texas. Paula began honing her organization skills in middle school and explains that she's a "visual person and need[s] to be able to *see* that everything is organized." An art teacher through and through, Paula prefers a paper-based Together Teacher System because she is "also a tactile person who needs to be able to hold and manipulate materials." Her system also sets up her students for success and enables them to "understand that art is a vital part of learning and life."

A father of three and a twelfth-year teacher, **Jeff Vasquez** teaches sixth-grade math at AF Bushwick Middle School. He is both a paper and electronic organizer and moves between those two worlds depending on "what is appropriate for the task at hand." His students benefit from his organization in that they "always know I'm ready for them." As one of his students put it, "Mr. Vasquez is always prepared, but you know he has a Plan B if Plan A doesn't work."

Nilda Velez is an English language arts teacher at AF Bushwick Middle School. With nine years of experience under her belt, Nilda currently coaches two other teachers and serves as a grade-level chair in addition to carrying her own workload. Nilda intends to use these

Together Teacher skills to achieve other professional goals such as getting work published in a scholarly periodical and continuing on her journey to teaching mastery.

Jennifer Wynn works at AF East New York Middle School, where she taught fifth-grade English language arts for two years. She recently transitioned into a dean of students role. Jennifer was a management consultant before she became a teacher and first honed her organization skills while at McKinsey & Company. Now she "cannot live without having my Outlook calendar synched to my iPhone," and she has used those Together Teacher skills to do what she enjoys most—"empowering students to learn from one another through class discussion."

Join Us Online ~ Share Your Story

One of the most satisfying parts of writing this book was hearing the stories of teachers whose lives were completely changed as a result of taking control and getting more organized.

These stories inspire others, including me, to want to get even better and because I think the stories from this community are so powerful, I want to continue gathering them.

Are you a Together Teacher? Do you have your own story to tell?

Please join our growing community at www.thetogetherteacher.com.

Not only can you tell your own story by sharing pictures, telling us about your favorite tool and, most importantly, describing how you are impacting lives in the classroom, but you can also access and share the free Reader's Guide, connect with other Together Teachers, and learn more about Together Teacher workshops and events.

Other ways to connect:

f www.facebook.com/thetogetherteacher

www.twitter.com/togetherteacher

www.pinterest.com/togetherteacher

Appendixes

Glossary of Terms

Comprehensive Calendar: A monthly calendar that lays out all of your time commitments and deadlines in one easy-to-access location.

Daily Worksheet: A very intentional and narrow view of your work for a particular period. A tool for helping you look at a single point in time and balance your time against your to-dos.

Deadline, Hard: A must-do-at-all-costs-other-people-are-counting-on-you deadline.

Deadline, Soft: A to-do that you would like to accomplish at some point, but it does not have a specific due date.

Individual Development Notes: A way to capture the feedback you may receive as a result of lesson plan review, classroom observations, or any other kind of performance review.

Instructional Planning Routine: The ritualized ways in which you use your preparation periods over the course of a week to complete high-impact instructional planning and grading work.

Lead Time: The amount of time you need to get something done in advance, often through the use of Time Blocks.

Meeting and Professional Development (Meeting/PD) Notes: Methods for organizing your professional learnings so they can be useful in both the short and the long term.

Project Plans: A simple list of to-dos that are grouped together chronologically and assigned to various people involved with the project. Project Plans may come in handy when you are in charge of something that has multiple to-dos. Good rule of thumb: Any project with more than ten steps is worthy of a plan.

Routine, Closing: A ritualized set of to-dos that you complete each and every afternoon before departing from school. It may be short or long, but it matters that the routine is planned into your day.

Routine, Opening: A ritualized set of to-dos that you complete each and every morning upon arrival at school. It may be short or long, but it matters that the routine is planned into your day.

Schedule: An hour-by-hour view of how you intend to use your time. Whereas the Comprehensive Calendar is most often just the big picture of deadlines and reminders, the Schedule spells out exactly what you want to do hour-by-hour each week.

Teacher In-Box: A stack of sorted bins carefully divided into categories such as Grade, File, and Return. Prevents a jumbled stack of papers from accumulating on your desk.

Teacher Workspace: Most likely a desk, table, or corner that functions as a home base for you throughout your teaching day. May also be where you sit to grade, lesson plan, or enter data into your computer. Your Workspace is where you sit down and concentrate on lesson planning and other important work.

Teaching Station: *May* be your desk but is more likely a centrally located (potentially portable) place where you can put all of your teaching materials for a particular day. It should contain any materials needed for specific lessons, handouts, and general supplies needed while teaching.

Thought Catchers: Provide you with a space to track nonurgent ideas that you can refer to whenever you have sufficient time to talk them through or take action. You can also have Thought Catchers for things you need to write regularly, such as parent updates, team updates, or a student newsletter.

Time Block: An appointment with yourself at a time specified on your Comprehensive Calendar or Weekly Daily Worksheet. It is meant to preserve professional or personal time for working on what matters most, rather than just trying to squeeze it in around the edges of your teaching duties.

Upcoming To-Do List: A long-term sorted list of your to-dos that will drive the creation of a Weekly or Daily Worksheet. The Upcoming To-Do List is a combination of deadlines, interim steps, and would-like-to-dos.

Weekly or Daily Worksheet: The tool to help you look at a single point in time and balance your time against your to-dos. It is prepared in advance of the week it illustrates, and it is the sheet of paper you look at as you move around your school all day. It maps out an hour-by-hour view of how you intend to use your time.

Weekly Round-Up: The time to take stock of the week that just happened and plan ahead for the upcoming week. I sometimes think of it as the convergence of your time and your to-dos. This activity doesn't require tons of brainpower, but it must be systematic in order to be effective.

The Weekly Round-up: Your Agenda

As we discussed in the main text of the book, the process of your Weekly Round-Up matters more than your product. Teachers have therefore found that having a sample agenda beside them as they complete their Weekly Round-Up is a helpful starting point. As you get more comfortable with the process, you will undoubtedly customize this agenda to make it your own.

WHAT TO HAVE AT YOUR WEEKLY ROUND-UP

- Computer (laptop or desktop)
- Recycle bin
- Together Teacher System, including your
  - Comprehensive Calendar
  - Upcoming To-Do List
  - Thought Catchers
  - Meeting/PD Notes
- Any data you need to review regularly (objective mastery, attendance, homework completion, and so on)
- Any loose papers that may have come in that week from any direction
- Clipboard, notebooks, your binder or whatever contains your Together Teacher Tools
- Printer
- Unit and lesson plans

YOUR AGENDA

- Name your priorities (you may want to review your Ideal Week Template from Chapter One).

  - What is *most* important, personally and professionally, this week?

    - If one of your personal priorities is "Train for marathon," you will want to block time to run in your schedule.

    - If one of your professional priorities is "Get guided reading groups on track," you will want to find time to speak with your literacy coach during the week. By naming a priority, you are reminded to add Time Blocks for achieving this priority to your schedule.

  - Review any classroom data you have. Are there any important areas on which to focus this week?

- Create your schedule: review your Comprehensive Calendar.

  - Enter time that is already "spoken for".

    - When are you teaching?

    - When do you have meetings?

  - Make time to meet important deadlines.

    - What deadlines do you have this week?

    - Check your Comprehensive Calendar. Do you need a Time Block in your schedule to accomplish any of the deadlines?

    - What deadlines do you have in the next three weeks? Do you need Time Blocks in your schedule to work toward these deadlines?

  - Sketch out your instructional planning routines.

    - What will happen during your Opening Routine, Closing Routine, and preparation periods? Spell them out in detail in your schedule. (After doing this once, you can just leave them typed into the template or leave space to write what you will do in your preparation periods each day.)

  - Block time for routine work (at low-energy times).

    - When will you enter grades, make or return parent phone calls, make copies, and answer e-mail?

  - Block time for rest and rejuvenation.

    - When are you *not* working?

- You do not *have* to plan what you do with this time. Simply leave it blank. However, if you have specific priorities, such as "keep in touch with friends," scheduling a meal with them in advance makes sense.
  - Leave some wiggle room for the inevitable changes that can happen in a school. That unexpected yet mandatory evacuation training exercise can certainly throw off our best intentions!
  - Fill in your basic physical needs and necessities:
    - When are you eating? Sleeping? Showering?
    - When are you commuting?
- Define your To-Dos.
  - Review your Upcoming To-Do List for soft commitments and deadlines for the current month.
  - Are there any events or deadlines that require Time Blocks to prepare?
  - What else do you *want* to do this week, if time allows?
- Review your Thought Catchers.
  - Is there anything recorded that needs to be typed into a Microsoft Word document?
  - Is there anything that cannot wait until a meeting with someone this week?
- Review your Meeting/PD Notes.
  - Do you need to type up or transfer any PD Notes into documents on your computer? Do you need to scan in any materials from PD?
  - Did you take any Meeting Notes this week that need to be transferred to your Comprehensive Calendar or Upcoming To-Do List? Once you have transferred them, throw the Meeting Notes away.
- Review any loose scraps of paper you have gathered this week.
  - Are there any calendars or notices in your teacher mailbox that you need to transfer to your Comprehensive Calendar?
  - Are there any student data you have gathered on your clipboard that you need to add a Time Block to deal with?
- Review any communications that will take time to respond to.
  - Are there any phone calls to return? At what time in your schedule will you do this?
  - Are there any e-mails that need longer replies? What time in your schedule will you answer them?

Project Plans for Teachers

Too often, grade-level teams, departments, or groups scramble to complete and communicate larger plans but get their lines crossed and messages mixed up in the process. They quickly forget what they are trying to accomplish and end up hounding colleagues with last-minute requests, forgetting important steps, and completing huge volumes of work at the last minute! These large-scale projects often need a long-term plan, often called a *Project Plan* or *work plan*.

Occasionally teachers ask about to-dos or projects that have multiple steps over a long period and that rest outside their regular classroom instructional duties. Examples of these types of projects include field-trip planning, test coordination, or planning an evening parent workshop. However, as teachers become organizational masters, they typically find the need for a more complex level of planning to match their more complicated projects.

WHEN WOULD I CREATE A PROJECT PLAN?

Project Plans: A simple list of to-dos that are grouped together chronologically and assigned to various people involved with the project. Project Plans may come in handy when you are in charge of something that has multiple to-dos. Good rule of thumb: Any project with more than ten steps is worthy of a plan.

HOW DO I CREATE A PROJECT PLAN?

Although many complex pieces of software are available for project planning, I have found that the easiest way to create a Project Plan is to sit down with a blank sheet of paper or in front of Microsoft Word and simply list all of the steps that need to happen, making them as small as possible so that it is easy to complete them.

Creating Your Project Plan

- Get clear on roles and responsibilities and identify key players.

- Identify dates, key deadlines, and anything that has to be created, such as a document.

- Figure out how and what you are going to communicate.

- Make the list, transfer it to Microsoft Excel or Word.

Let's look at how Kate, a teacher we met in the main text of the book, did this when she was in charge of a third-grade field trip to Columbia University. As you review a portion of her plan (Figure A3.1), be aware of the following issues:

- How small are the to-dos?

- How many people are in charge of various steps?

- What is the timeline of the project?

	A	B	C	D
6	WHO	Action or deadline	DATE	NOTES
7	Kate	send template for permission slip to team member	4/5/	
8	Kate	Finalize day-of schedule	4/5/	
9	Kate	ask team for volunteer to stay behind with friends	4/5/	
10	Kate	give team overview of the day	4/5/	
11	Kate	Find out exactly where buses will pick us up and where they will drop us off	4/5/	
12	Robby	make permission slips and distribute to team	4/7/	
13	Kate	find directions to columbia university	4/8/	
14	Kate	print directions to columbia and map of surrounding area	4/8/	
15	Homeroom Teachers	send permission slips home	4/11	
16	Parents	permission slips due	4/13	
17	Ami	make slide with overview of columbia university & volume/behavior expectations	4/13/	
18	Ami	send columbia slide to team	4/13/	
19	Kate	send day-of schedule to team & circulate hard copy with contact	4/14/	
20		determine room for all students who aren't going on the trip	4/14/	
21	omeroom Teache	call parent chaperones to ask them to come	4/14/	
22	omeroom Teache	call parents of anyone who is eligible but did not return slip	4/14/	
	Homeroom			

Project Plan / Schedule / Rain Schedule / Address and Other Info

Figure A3.1 A Portion of the Project Plan for Kate's Third-Grade Trip to Columbia University

As you can see, Kate used Microsoft Excel to carefully list all of the steps it would take to have a successful third-grade trip, and she coordinated her grade-level team to help her pull it off. An Excel template that can be used for Project Plans is available on the accompanying CD. The benefit of Excel is that you can easily sort and categorize, although you can create a Project Plan using any tool you wish.

Get Some Help! Get Clear on Roles and Responsibilities

Picture a grade-level meeting in which it is incredibly clear who is responsible for what and when each step will be completed. So much time would be saved. Although Kate carried the bulk of the planning work in the preceding example, she had the homeroom teachers play various roles—asking another team member to make permission slips, and so on. Let's look at what she did:

- Homeroom teachers were asked to call parents and ask for chaperones.
- Robby was asked to make permission slips.
- Ami made slides of an overview of Columbia University for all teachers to share with their students.

It is important to note that Kate didn't just assign people work in an Excel spreadsheet and tell them to do it. She presented her plan at a grade-level meeting, explained each person's work, and got agreement from the whole group before setting the plan in stone.

Why Wouldn't I Just Use an Upcoming To-Do List?

Great question. In some cases, this may make sense. However, for most Project Plans, our brains need to think through all of the to-dos as a cluster of steps that should be considered as a whole. Eventually you may want to take all of the dates and put them in your Comprehensive Calendar (if they are true deadlines); but to do the good thinking that is needed, it helps to create a Project Plan when you are initially trying to figure out what needs to be done.

AVOID PUTTING THE PROJECT PLAN ON THE SHELF

As I mention throughout the book, plans are only as good as the use they get! Your Project Plan should become a temporary tab in your Together Teacher System for the duration of the project. Let's look at how to make this happen.

Using the Project Plan Yourself

The easiest way I have found to keep Project Plans alive is to review them once per week during your Weekly Round-Up. During this time you would pull out the to-dos for that week from the Project Plan and add them to your Weekly or Daily Worksheet, then tuck the Project Plan away until the following week.

Using a Project Plan with a Group

If your project involves multiple people, you can easily keep it alive by bringing it to any regular meeting you have about the project and/or sending out an e-mail update to the project group about what happened the previous week and what is coming up the following week. If you do not have a regular meeting with the people involved in the project, it may be worth establishing a time to get together regularly in order to move the project ahead efficiently. In the field-trip case, Kate brought copies of the Project Plan to her regular grade-level meeting and designated a small portion of the agenda to reviewing the progress the team had made in the prior week. Just think of the satisfaction this third-grade team felt after coordinating an educational and fun field trip for their students!

What If Something Changes on the Project Plan?

The purpose of good plans is that they allow us to be *more* flexible and responsive to a changing environment. Let's say a homeroom teacher forgets to send home the permission slips one day. As the person responsible for the project, Kate can decide if it makes sense to extend the deadline for that classroom's parents by a day or if that will have a negative impact on the field trip. Another example might be if Kate and the team have a hard time securing parent chaperones for the trip. They may need to extend the deadline to call more parents. The important thing is not that all of the steps in the plan are completed exactly on time but rather that all of the steps of the project are in one place so that anything that comes up is easy to evaluate against the larger goals. Ami Patel, a member of the third-grade team working on this project, said, "The level of specificity in our project plans for field trips ensured total team accountability for safe, seamless, and highly-rewarding trips. Accounting for all logistics so thoroughly and far in advance of our trips allowed us and our kids to reap all of the possible benefits of the trips themselves!"

USE 'EM ONLY WHEN YOU NEED 'EM

It is important to remember not to go overboard with your Project Plans. You certainly don't need them all the time and for everything that requires multiple steps. However, when you have something large to execute that will involve multiple people, that extends over time, and that has a lot of to-dos, it may make sense to group your to-dos into a Project Plan.

Sample School Communication Agreement

Why? Part of strengthening our team and family relationships, increasing our efficiency, and improving communication is deciding when to use what form of communication.

Goals

- We don't feel glued to our gadgets (laptops, iPhones, BlackBerries).

- We know what method of communication is best for every situation.

- We keep communication over e-mail, text, and calls concise and organized so that we can put most of our energy into "face-time" with each other and our scholars.

PART ONE: E-MAIL VERSUS TEXT VERSUS CALL?

E-Mail

- We love e-mail at AF Brown. It is best for issues that are (1) noncontroversial and (2) nonurgent.

- Our norm is to reply to each other's e-mails within twenty-four hours of receipt. So, we want to use e-mail for items that have at least twenty-four hours of lead time.

Note: This document was created by Achievement First Brownsville Elementary School.

- Great times to use e-mail:
  - Questions
  - Reminders
  - Meeting notes
  - Meeting setup
  - Recurring structures (giving or responding to lesson plan feedback, logistics for a field trip, and so on)

Text

- Texting is awesome. The leadership team all carry our phones. So if you need something quickly but it's not a safety concern, texting works.
- Great times to use a text:
  - You'd like help with a child but the child is *not in any danger.*
  - You'd like help for you but you are *not in any danger.*

Call

- Thank goodness for cell phones. I live on mine. When to use at school: something urgent that will affect you or the children immediately has happened or might happen.
- Examples of when to call:
  - You are not sure where a child is for any reason (God forbid).
  - A child is in danger (including serious illness) or causing danger or destruction.
  - You are extremely ill and will be out or are extremely ill and need to leave.
  - You have a personal emergency and need help. My BlackBerry is always on for you!

PART TWO: THE GREAT E-MAIL, TEXT, CALL!

Why? Part of strengthening our team and family is increasing the personal/professional life balance by increasing our efficiency.

E-Mail

- Everyone in the AF Brown Team and Family checks e-mail and replies to requests at least once every twenty-four hours.
- We try to avoid "discussions" over e-mail. If something could cause great difference of opinion, is a big change, is complex, or requires significant rationale to understand, let's

not put it in an e-mail. E-mail "tone" is easily misunderstood, so let's stick to neutral subjects, reminders, and FYIs when using it.

- In the subject line, put the topic in detail, and the "reply requested" date in brackets.
  - *Sample:* Reading A-Z Renewal Decision <reply requested by 9/5>
  - OR <FYI only; no action needed>
  - OR <30-second reply requested>
- Greetings/salutations: clearly address *one* person (not an administrative team) and include an explicit cc: to others, so that it is clear who should answer, for example, Hi Michelle (FYI Tina).
- If an e-mail *is* to multiple people and one of the addressees has the answer, rather than replying to "all" with the answer or conversation, reply "all" to say "On it!" and then reply privately to the person with the question.
- Put questions in bold so that you get all your questions answered and don't have to play e-mail tag.
  - *Sample:* **Do you want to meet at 2 or 3 PM on Thursday?**
- Ensure that questions are not buried in paragraphs. Use bullets for all questions.
- Pose solutions to issues rather than end e-mails with blanket statements like "Reactions?"
- Highlight action steps that the recipient needs to take *or* list them at the end of the e-mail.
  - *Sample:* Let Michelle or Tina know if you want help with F&P testing by 8/12/2010 at 5 PM.

or

  - *Sample:* Action steps:
    - Let Michelle or Tina know if you want help with F&P testing by 8/12/2010 at 5 PM.

Habits of Great E-Mails

- As a sender: Use *task or meeting* requests for anything dated; this way, recipients don't have to worry about remembering a date in an e-mail.
- If you find yourself e-mailing the same person more than two times per day, consider setting up a ten-minute meeting that you can always cancel.
- As a recipient: Drag the e-mail into your calendar for a few days before the due date. An inbox is not a to-do list.

- Don't use e-mail for controversial things unless you have to; use it for easy wins and logistics, and use *conversations* for things that require more back and forth *or* that could be solved in a five-minute discussion rather than a five-e-mail exchange.

- For e-mails between or to teachers, do not send after 7 PM. Befriend the "Delay Delivery" button.

- Hit the "work offline" button when you need to work on a project using your e-mail or calendar but *don't* want to see or hear new e-mails popping up!

Texts

- *Great text examples:* You'd like help with a child but the child is *not in any danger.*

  - "Sammie, Daveon is under a desk and I'd like help getting him to time out."

  - "Pascale, a bus just came in late and there are five kids who didn't have breakfast—Nutri-Grain Bars available?"

  - "Michelle, Kerniel just wrote the BEST STORY!!! Can you come give him some praise???"

- *Great text examples:* You'd like help for you but you are *not in any danger.*

  - "Gina, I've been feeling sick today. . . . I think I can get through the day, but in an hour can someone transition my kids down and up from lunch so I can rest for a few minutes?"

  - "Inslee, the busses are late for the field trip. . . . Is there any way one of the interns can make some copies of a math sheet for us so the kids have something meaningful to do while we wait?"

Calls

- We are always here for you! If you need immediate help, err on the side of *calling.*

- Don't hesitate to call more than one person. You called Sammie because a child in her portfolio ran out of the room, but she didn't answer? *Call someone else!* Immediately! (Or if your co-teacher is in the room, call and go find the child.) There are dead zones in our school, like the cafeteria, and if you call Anna while she's on lunch, she might not get the message for an hour. This seems like common sense but it's worth saying because I know how considerate you all are and that you don't want to "bother" people, but when your safety or a child's safety is in question, *call.*

Classroom Efficiency: Quick and Dirty Tips

Assign each student a number. I've found it's easiest to go alphabetically. Starting from Day One, have them write this number on every book, assignment, pencil, and so on. Have them line up in this order *always*. It will make your life much easier when your papers are already alphabetized as you grade them—no toggling up and down the grade book. This system also makes it easy to divide the class quickly, "Odds on this side. Evens over here." Student numbers also help when you create visual aids in your classroom. For example, on a classroom jobs chart, write student numbers instead of names. It might sound impersonal but you'll be grateful you have the time to focus on instruction!

Make a durable folder for each day of the week. Make each folder a different color and laminate them for durability. Keep them on your desk. That way, when a stack of papers comes from the office to be "Sent home Friday" you can just pop them into the Friday folder and you won't have to think about it again. As you photocopy assignments, stick them in the appropriate folder (as in the Distribution Center discussed in Chapter Ten of the book). This will avoid major desk pileups. It is also handy when you have a substitute teacher.

Make a hard-copy binder or electronic folder for each month of the school year. It might sound tedious but think of how happy you'll be during your second year of teaching when you open up the February binder and find materials on Valentine's Day, Black History Month, and Presidents' Day all ready for you. Of course this requires diligent collection of materials throughout the year, but remember, we're talking sustainability! So, if you see a fellow teacher copying stuff for Thanksgiving, ask for a copy, and just pop it into the November folder. Done.

Make at least forty copies of your class list on lined paper or formatted in a table. You'll be amazed how many times the office will buzz your room asking for a list of students. This list is also useful to keep track of money collected, books checked out, turns in the Author's Chair, and so on. Keep them in your file cabinet.

Send all notices home on the same brightly colored paper. I liked to use purple. Buy a huge batch of it at the beginning of the school year. Let parents know to always look for this color.

Label all small objects in groups. For instance, if you have a puzzle (and you want to keep it beyond your first year of teaching), number all of the pieces with the number three. This will help when pieces are missing or mixed up.

Keep all parent communication in one central location. I used a binder with the students' numbers on tabs. Each time I spoke with a family member, I wrote notes on that student's page. I hole-punched and filed any tardy slips and doctor's notes and filed them in the binder. I also inserted parent conference forms in the binder. This made parent conferences much easier, because my data was in one place. You can also easily refer to anecdotal records and previous conversations you may have had with parents. I took mine home every night just in case I spoke with parents so I could document the discussion.

File student work chronologically and by subject. Invest in two crates that can hold hanging files. Again: assign each hanging file a student number (think: this can be reused!). Within each file place six to seven manila folders, one for each subject. File every piece of work you grade in the appropriate place (or have the students file—we called it Friday file time). This system allows you and the students to access student work at any time. At the end of each semester or quarter, have students rubber band all work and file it in a box or take it home.

Collect all student supplies that come in on the first day of school. I know this sounds strict and some parents may not be happy. However, explain that you keep all supplies in a central location so that you can distribute them as needed. You will have students who will come with a lot of stuff and some who will come with none. This method allows you to redistribute materials quietly to those students who need it. If a student brings something big and fancy, give them two choices—take it home or store it in a shoe box on the shelf for special occasions. This whole system levels the playing field a bit and allows *you* to control how and when glue is used.

Print one to two sheets of adhesive mailing labels per student. After doing the initial formatting, you can use the labels all year long. It becomes easy to label coat hooks, homework folders, student mailboxes, class jobs, and anecdotal records when you can easily get these labels out of your desk.

Have parents thoroughly state their preferred modes of communication. When you collect parent contact info at the beginning of the year, create a form that asks what they want you to call them and whether they prefer phone calling, texting, or e-mailing, and in what order (this tip is courtesy of Robbie Rukoff). This information will save you time when contacting parents.

Create materials that *last*. Whenever possible, think about creating materials that can last the entire year—or more. For example, don't make a paper bathroom pass that can easily be torn or lost. Laminate as much as possible, or get creative. My students used Mardi Gras beads with a brightly laminated bathroom sign strung onto the beads as their bathroom pass. There was *no way* these were getting lost. Cover your bulletin boards with inexpensive fabric instead of butcher paper. You can wash it over the summer and use it again the next year.

Boldly number or name anything you can. If you have four computers, give them each a number or a name and then create a big label to stick near the monitor. If you have cupboards or file cabinets, clearly number each one. It becomes so much easier to give directions, "Kate, can you please return that puzzle to cupboard 1?"

Name your documents clearly. The *last* thing you want to spend your time doing is searching for that great unit plan or really super math assessment. Save yourself time now by clearly making electronic files by content area or subject, then unit plan, then lesson plan and *all* accompanying materials—for example, PowerPoint lesson, exit ticket. Pick a naming convention that you can stick with, and be consistent when you are labeling. This will make later years of teaching so much more efficient.

Acknowledgments

The journey to create *The Together Teacher* has been shaped by many, many people I have known and had the honor of working with for more than a decade. These are the people who taught me to teach, the students I taught, other organizational ninjas, early advocates of my work, path-clearing champions, wholehearted supporters, and committed educators.

I do not claim to have a monopoly on "being organized." These days, no one does or could. At the end of the day, when you boil it down, all productivity experts tell you to pause, plan, and then do. While all of us have variations on that theme, the gist remains the same. My personal twist on helping teachers get organized has been shaped by the incredible communities I have been a part of during my career in education, namely Delmont Elementary School, Children's Charter School, Teach For America, and Achievement First. I am fortunate to be a product of these remarkable environments. During my time teaching fourth and fifth grades, I was lucky to be involved in several adult learning communities, most notably the National Writing Project and a teacher-led inquiry group, that influenced the structure of my Together Teacher workshops. At Teach For America, many people relied on a "Weekly Action Plan," which greatly influenced the "Weekly Worksheet" and several other tools featured in this book. At Achievement First, I witnessed many of my team members utilize Microsoft Outlook to the fullest and built on their examples to develop some of my electronic and Web-based calendar recommendations. Additionally, countless clients have shared their best practices with me and allowed me to share them with others. Thank you to my friends, colleagues, and partners at the organizations mentioned above who have significantly shaped my approach.

There are also many experts who have done amazing work in the area of time management and productivity. When I started teaching and was searching desperately to keep my head above water, I read the works of David Allen, Steven Covey, Tony Schwartz, Julie Morgenstern, and Harry Wong. More recently I have relied on books by Laura Vanderkam and Michael

Linenberger. Thank you for inspiring me. I hope my adaptation of some of your concepts increases the effectiveness of the people working hard in schools to change the lives of students.

First and foremost, I want to thank my original education role models—Antoinette Bienemy, Lynne Lay, Quentina Timoll, Liz Frishertz, Jim Geiser, Deborah Russell, Mary West, and Toni Teepell—who taught me everything I know about teaching. You are some of the best educators I have *ever* met, and your dedication to the profession is unparalleled. Thanks for investing your time and patience in a twenty-something girl from Maine. I hope I have done you proud!

Three colleagues of mine while I worked at Teach For America stand out as complete and total organizational ninjas. I am fortunate that we founded a team that relied on many organizational practices that I have continued to use in my daily work. Michael Ambriz, you are a gifted executor and have a flawless attention to detail. Rebecca Helmer, you remain the most efficient human I have ever met. I still have *no* idea how you do it, but I'm not going to mess with your systems. Shannon Simmons, you are the best project and long-term planner on this entire planet. I live in awe of you three, and I think about our years together every day of my professional life. I also feel similarly fortunate to have regularly benefitted from the thought-partnership of Kelly Harris Perrin and Emily Barton.

When I began giving workshops around the country on how to become a Together Teacher, there was an early group of believers who encouraged me along the way. Norman Atkins, founder of Uncommon Schools and Relay Graduate School of Education, believed that this topic was an essential component of teacher preparation and has worked tirelessly to make organization part of the revolutionary teacher preparation approach of Relay Graduate School of Education. Without Norman, this book would not exist. Brent Maddin, Mayme Hostetter, and Yutaka Tamura, also at Relay, fine-tuned the original Together Teacher workshop to get it ready for prime time. Ever since, they have remained superb sources of expertise about great adult learning. Evan Rudall of Uncommon Schools; Jay Altman of FirstLine Schools; Mike Goldstein and Orin Gutlerner of MATCH Charter Schools; Matt Kramer, Aimee Eubanks Davis, Jeff Wetzler, and Elisa Villanueva Beard at Teach For America; Kate Mehr of Citizen Schools; and Jerry Hauser at The Management Center all championed my work and often opened up their organizations as test runs for many iterations of my Together Teacher training. For all of this I am deeply grateful.

I am indebted to my beloved colleagues at Achievement First (AF) for their support, kindness, and patience throughout this process. Many, many staff, school leaders, and teachers at AF have shaped this book and I am forever grateful for your honesty and openness, and for letting me roam around your school buildings. The following schools were particularly generous and opened their doors to me over the course of several years: AF Brownsville Elementary, AF Crown Heights Elementary, AF Amistad-Elm City High, AF Brooklyn High, AF Bridgeport Middle, AF Bushwick Middle, and our flagship school, Amistad Academy Middle School. AF's co-CEOs, Dacia Toll and Doug McCurry, gave me amazing opportunities within the network to make a difference in the lives of teachers and students. Doug and Dacia are living, breathing models of truly great leaders—excellence-focused optimists who operate with urgency and joy. I am grateful to work alongside them as we strive to do great work in the world. After five years of partnership with them I continue to learn from them like crazy!

To my wonderful AF team, you are not only amazing colleagues, but also good friends: Sarah Coon, Becca Howlett, Sara Keenan, Mel Ochoa, Jon Schwartz, Mila Singh, and Erica Williamson. Thank you for your unfailing patience during my summer sabbatical to finish this book. Pam Bookbinder, Liz Mitha, and Genna Weinstein served as partners-in-crime, teaching assistants, and emergency conference call partners, available whenever I was struggling to articulate a concept. Max Polaner deserves a special shout-out for being an endless supplier of iced coffee and a tireless cheerleader whenever I showed up to work bleary-eyed after an early morning of writing.

Although countless teachers invited me into their worlds and daily teaching lives and are featured throughout the text, I want to thank a few by name here. (You can read more about them in the book!) Anna Tattan, Nilda Velez, Dan Rouillard, Sue Harmon, Gilbert Cardenas, Jenny Cortez, Kate McCabe, and Jeff Vasquez endured endless conversations, e-mail requests, and other general peskiness from me. Thanks for putting your lives out there for all teachers to learn from. You guys are astounding examples of the fact that it is possible to be great teachers and live full lives.

I am appreciative of Kate Gagnon, Lesley Iura, Tracy Gallagher, Pamela Berkman, Alice Morrow Rowan, Susan Geraghty, and Diane Turso at Jossey-Bass for consistently finding better ways to organize my materials, relay information to our teacher audience, and grapple with a book that is very complicated to produce. Thanks for encouraging a first-time author who is really just a lady with a whole bunch of ideas, and for synthesizing the ideas that bubbled ceaselessly from my brain. You helped tame, refine, and impose order on a whole bunch of stuff I just said at workshops.

While I have been building my startup organization to support *The Together Teacher*, a small group of people has served as an invaluable source of expertise and wisdom. I would like to thank Josh Lowitz for his overall wise and constant counsel, Natalie Sulimani for her sound legal advice, Lisa Sandbank and Brotherlab Collective for their incredible design skills, Rusty Shelton and Shelton Interactive for helping me understand the purpose of Twitter (and other such things!), Nuri Adler for his PowerPoint prowess, and Carla Licavoli for her photography work. Throughout the writing process I have benefitted from the amazing writing and revision skills of two fantastic educators, Sara Cotner and Marin Smith. You ladies are good with the red pen! Thanks for making this book infinitely more readable. Doug Lemov and Paul Bambrick-Santoyo generously took time out from their busy schedules to offer writing advice to a new author. Thanks also to the crew at Court Street Grocers in Brooklyn who provided me with a home away from home. Eric and Matt, the co-owners, never blinked an eye when I set up my "office" on Mondays and Fridays.

Anne Lac, Karn Engelsgjerd, Amy McInnis, and Hilary Gipson are some of the best friends a woman could ask for and I feel honored to have been joined at the hip with each of you for over a decade. Thank you for the e-mail pick-me-ups, words of support, little treats, and for being wonderful women. You guys are the constant reminder of why I want to have a life to begin with! And I know you really secretly are glad when I take the lead on cookie baking extravaganzas and beach vacations. And to my WoMoWiBiJo (Working Moms with Big Jobs) group, our monthly breakfasts and frequent communication have kept me inspired and motivated along the way.

My parents, Helga Heyck and Morris Merlin, were my original role models in organization and systems. Collectively they juggled raising kids, overnight shift work, full-time jobs, and resuming their own college educations. Thanks for teaching Sonja (my sister) and me to be hard-working and resourceful, and that social justice is our responsibility in the world. Those chore charts, dinner rotations, and cleaning responsibilities were essential models for how to run an efficient household!

There are three women who are the unsung heroes of this book and who have worked unerringly behind the scenes on every possible aspect of it. Emily Koh and Kate McCabe, my constant companions throughout this process, have served as cheerleaders, breakfast brainstormers, proofreaders, meltdown-preventers, bad cops, photocopiers, and thought-partners, and they are the *best* team imaginable. I am beyond fortunate to have hired each of you as my executive assistants some years ago when you were in your early twenties and I have been wonderfully pleased to watch your careers develop. I love you ladies like little sisters, and I deeply respect your remarkable levels of tenacity, personal responsibility, and attention to detail. This book would not exist had you not committed to it as a "side job." To our family's wonderfully kind and conscientious babysitter, Glenda Henry—without your flexibility and commitment, this book would not have been written. Our daughter adores you and so do we!

Finally, and most important, I want to wholeheartedly acknowledge my little Brooklyn family. To my husband, Jack, an English teacher and guinea pig for all of my ideas—thanks for fueling me with Diet Coke and Skittles and for giving me time on a balcony in Florida to talk about how your lesson plans are stored on your laptop instead of deservingly drinking a beer and watching the Final Four. *That* is true love. I'm still sorry for the time I questioned whether your taking out one piece of recycling at a time was really the most efficient way to use your time. This book wouldn't exist without your enduring support for my workshops and travel, your cooking skills, and your quiet patience while I interviewed teachers by phone in our bedroom every evening for months. I could not have completed this book without you, and I am forever appreciative. Last, to my daughter, Ada: *The Together Teacher* really emerged while I was home on maternity leave staring at your chubby cheeks. Thank you for being a source of unending joy and a good sleeper to boot. Our little family is *the* reason I'm obsessed with getting more free time. Because that is what it is all about. Being organized is simply a means to the end of living a rich and rewarding life.

About the Author

Maia Heyck-Merlin is the founder of Brass Tacks, the consulting practice that is behind The Together Teacher. She spends the majority of her time designing and delivering training for busy teachers and school leaders around the country. Prior to this she was chief talent officer for Achievement First, a high-performing charter school management organization. Maia was a fourth- and fifth-grade teacher and she spent five years on the staff of Teach For America in a number of leadership roles. Please join Maia and the growing Together Teacher community at www.thetogetherteacher.com.

Prior to joining AF, Maia worked at Teach For America, in a variety of capacities. She began as a corps member in South Louisiana, where she taught fourth grade for two years at Delmont Elementary School and was selected as Delmont's Teacher of the Year. During this time she was also selected as a Fulbright Memorial Scholar Fund participant and joined Louisiana State University's Summer Writer's Project, where she served as editor of the course anthology. After completing her teaching commitment with Teach For America, she went on to teach fifth grade at Children's Charter School and directed Teach Baton Rouge's first summer training institute through The New Teacher Project. In 2002 she returned to Teach For America as executive director in South Louisiana, overseeing development and programmatic efforts for a teaching corps that had recently doubled in size. She then served for three years as director of the Teach For America Houston Institute, leading the training and development efforts for the incoming corps. In her last role at Teach For America, she founded and led the National Institute Operations team, which managed the national operations for all five summer training institutes.

Maia grew up in a town of six hundred people in rural Maine and is a proud graduate of the Maine public school system. She holds a bachelor of arts degree in child development from Tufts University. She lives in Brooklyn, New York, with her husband, Jack, their daughter, Ada, and three playful cats, and when she is not trying to organize the world, she enjoys swimming slowly, trying to keep up with her farm-share deliveries, and reading magazines while eating Oreos. Learn more about her passion by visiting www.thetogetherteacher.com.

Index

unsolicited feedback, 197; unsubscribing to junk e-mail, 179–180; and Upcoming To-Do List, 186; use vs. abuse of, 196–199; and Web-based or electronic Comprehensive Calendar, 181; when to answer, 188–189; when to check, 188

E-mail folders: Administrative folder, 183; Follow-Up folder, 181–182, 185–186; Meetings folder, 182; Processed Mail folder, 183; Projects folder, 182; School Readiness folder, 183

Efficiency, 4–6; tips for the classroom, 313–314

Efficient supply system, 249

Electronic folders, 313–314

Electronic Thought Catchers, 93–94

Emergency buffer, and Ideal Week Template, 24

Emily, 293–294; Comprehensive Calendar, 41–43; Weekly Worksheet, 169–170

End-of-day checklist, 156

Energy levels, managing, 17, 24–26

Entry Way, 203–206; components of, 206; examples of, 204–206

Events, inserting in Comprehensive Calendar, 49

Evernote, 112

Execution, 6; Together Teacher, 4

F

File cabinet, 270–271

Filing: creating simple folders for, 181–5; professional development ideas, 271; reading levels, 270; state and district standards, 271; student work, 314; testing information, 270

First-Year Teacher's Survival Guide, The, Thompson, 248

Focusing, and e-mail, 188

Folders: Administrative folder, for e-mail, 183; e-mail, 184–185; electronic, 313–314; Follow-Up folder, for e-mail, 181–182; Meetings folder, for e-mail, 182; Processed Mail folder, for e-mail, 183; Projects folder, for e-mail, 182; School Readiness folder, for e-mail, 183; student organization, 240; and student organization, 240; Take Home folder, 245

Follow-Up folder, for e-mail, 181–182, 185–186

Fountas, I., 223

Franklin Covey planner, 14, 45, 285

Free time, designating, 51

Frost, S., *See* Stephanie

Futrell, J., *See* Jacqueline

G

Getting Things Done (Allen), 16

Gilbert, 290; Comprehensive Calendar, 39–41; *Day in the Life, A,* 98–99; Weekly Worksheet, 125–127

Google Calendar, 33, 46, 135

Google Tasks, and Upcoming To-Do List, 73

Grade-level meeting, follow-up notes from (table), 115

Grading materials, transporting, 265

Gronquist-Blodgett, J., *See* Julie

Group Meeting Notes template, 113–114

Guiding Readers and Writers (Fountas/ Pinnell), 64

H

Habits, developing to be "together," 6

Hammons, T., *See* Tess

Hard-copy binder, 313–314

Hard deadlines, 48

Harmon, S., *See* Sue

How to Use the CD

SYSTEM REQUIREMENTS

PC with Microsoft Windows 2003 or later
Mac with Apple OS version 10.1 or later

USING THE CD WITH WINDOWS

To view the items located on the CD, follow these steps:

1. Insert the CD into your computer's CD-ROM drive.

2. A window appears showing the End User License Agreement. Accept this agreement to continue.

3. A window appears with the following options displayed as tabs:

   Contents: Allows you to view the files included on the CD.

   Links: Displays a hyperlinked page of websites.

   Software: Allows you to install useful software from the CD.

   About the Author: Displays a page with information about the author.

   Contact Us: Displays a page with information on contacting the publisher or author.

   Exit: Closes the interface window.

If you do not have autorun enabled, or if the autorun window does not appear, follow these steps to access the CD:

1. Click Start → Run.

2. In the dialog box that appears, type d:\start.exe, where d is the letter of your CD-ROM drive. This brings up the autorun window described in the preceding set of steps.

3. Choose the desired option from the menu. (See Step 3 in the preceding list for a description of these options.)

To save CD documents to your computer, click on the document, choose Save and navigate to the place on your hard drive where you wish to save it. You can also choose Open to open the document, choose Save As, and navigate to the place on your hard drive where you wish to save it. You cannot save a modified document to the CD itself.

IN CASE OF TROUBLE

If you experience difficulty using the CD, please follow these steps:

1. Make sure your hardware and systems configurations conform to the systems requirements noted under System Requirements above.

2. Review the installation procedure for your type of hardware and operating system.

To speak with someone in Product Technical Support, call 800-762-2974 or 317-572-3994 Monday through Friday from 8:30 a.m. to 5:00 p.m. EST. You can also contact Product Technical Support and get support information through our website at www.wiley.com/techsupport.

Before calling or writing, please have the following information available:

- Type of computer and operating system.
- Any error messages displayed.
- Complete description of the problem.

It is best if you are sitting at your computer when making the call.